Karl Marx

A CONTRIBUTION
TO THE CRITIQUE
OF POLITICAL ECONOMY

KARL MARX

With an Introduction by
MAURICE DOBB

INTERNATIONAL PUBLISHERS

New York

Translated from the German by S. W. Rya-
zanskaya, edited by Maurice Dobb. Published
in Moscow by Progress Publishers, in London
by Lawrence & Wishart, and in New York
by International Publishers, Inc.

Library of Congress Catalog Card Number: 69-20357
SBN (cloth) 7178-0042-3; (paperback) 7178-0041-5

Printed in the Union of Soviet Socialist Republics

PUBLISHERS' NOTE

This translation has been made from Marx/Engels, *Werke*, Band 13, Dietz Verlag, Berlin, 1964. The aim has been to make the translation as close as possible to the original. When for the sake of clarity it has been found necessary to insert a few words these are enclosed in square brackets. Italicised passages and words indicate emphasis by Marx; but following the English custom titles of publications and foreign words are also italicised. Footnotes and marginal notes by Marx are indicated by asterisks, the editor's footnotes by index letters, and reference notes by superior numbers.

CONTENTS

INTRODUCTION

Marx's *Critique* was first published (in German as the *Kritik*) in 1859, eight years before the first volume of *Das Kapital*. As such it played the rôle of curtain-raiser to the main work—or perhaps a more worthy simile would be an overture. (Marx himself refers to it as "the first small book" of his economic studies, and the Preface to the first edition of Volume I of *Capital* speaks of the latter as "the continuation" of the *Critique* of 1859.) By contrast, the shorter manuscript known as *Introduction to a Critique*, which was written at the same time as the voluminous manuscripts of 1857-58 known as the *Grundrisse der Kritik der Politischen Oekonomie (Rohentwurf)*, was never published in Marx's lifetime. Discarded by Marx himself as an "anticipation of results that are still not proven", and not intended as part of the published *Critique*, it was found (as "a fragmentary sketch" dated August 23, 1857) among his manuscripts after his death, and was deciphered and published by Karl Kautsky in the magazine *Neue Zeit* in March 1903. Its first appearance in English was, along with the *Critique*, in an edition by N. I. Stone in Chicago in 1904.

If the *Critique* can rightly be compared to an overture, it was the opening bars of *Das Kapital* rather than the central *motifs* of that *opus* which it anticipated. The *Critique* was itself, apparently, a condensation of certain parts of the *Grundrisse* of 1857-58. Some of these themes had already been opened up in the *Economic and Philosophical Manuscripts of 1844*. In a sense the focus of attention of the *Critique* is methodological. To say this is not to detract from its interest and importance, both in itself and as an introduction to Marx's main work. In the progress of science one finds revolution in theory associated with revolution in methodology. By its stress on the primacy of production, and especially on the social relations of production (including appropriation or ownership of the means of production), the essentially *historical* angle of approach distinguishing his work is brought clearly into view in the *Critique* (where we find his theory of value, and more specifically theory of money, first adumbrated). The historical perspective from which he surveyed the emergent "bourgeois" (or capitalist) society of his day at once sets the distinctive focus and emphasis of his economic theory as well as its boundaries (both focus and boundaries which differentiate it sharply from the increasingly narrowed theories of "market equilibria" that were to characterise accepted academic theory at the end of the century and in the present century). The progress and maturing of Marx's thought, indeed, lay in the direction of deepening it in a sense quite opposite to the development of "bourgeois economics" with its increasing formalisation of purely quantitative market relations and linkages. Marx started, indeed, from concepts such as supply and demand, competition and the market. This is most in evidence in the manuscripts of 1844, the economic sections of which consist largely of notes and commentaries on the writings of Sir James Steuart, Adam Smith and Ricardo and the like. But it is apparent also in the present work, the *Critique* of fifteen years later. (*Capital*, however, deals with the market 'level' towards its close, towards the end of Vol. III.)* In the course of criticising and explaining these concepts—of revealing the *essence* behind the phenomenal *appearance* of market relations, as he frequently put it—he was led progressively into the examination of production and of production relations (division of labour in general terms initially, and then to the specific forms assumed by division of labour under capitalism) and of the social and class roots of a society dominated by exploitation and the pursuit of surplus value.

If Marx's economic analysis was distinguished by its historical setting, his historical interpretation had deep philosophical roots—roots originating in the Hegelian philosophy that was the preoccupation of his early student years (first at the University of Bonn and then at the University

---

* *Cf.* Marx's letter to Engels of April 30, 1868: "At last we have arrived at the *forms of appearance* which serve as the *starting point* in the vulgar conception."

of Berlin). It is sometimes said that, whereas for Hegel the dialectic as a principle and structural pattern of development started from abstract Being as Mind or "Spirit", for Marx the dialectic of development started from Nature, and from Man as initially an integral part of Nature. But while part of Nature and subject to the determinism of its laws, Man as a conscious being was at the same time capable of struggling with and against Nature—of subordinating it and ultimately transforming it for his own purposes. This he did by consciously devised productive and creative activity. This human activity that differentiated Man from Nature and from most other animate creatures was productive labour. Human history accordingly began from this dialectic of Man's struggle with Nature, and essentially consisted in the various forms and stages assumed by productive labour in its development and progress. A principal feature of this dialectic of Man v. Nature was, of course, the invention and use of productive instruments (tools and mechanisms) which were simultaneously durable embodiments of labour and aids to productive labour—instruments "which the labourer interposes between himself and the subject of his labour, and which serve as the conductor of his activity". It is these more than anything else which make of productive labour a collective or *social* process (he speaks of "the appropriation of nature by the individual within and through a definite form of society"); and on the development of these inanimate 'forces of production' the progressive increase in the productive powers of labour in the course of human history crucially depended. "In production men not only act on nature but also on one another. They produce only by co-operating in a certain way and mutually exchanging their activities." Hence the division of labour, which starts as a division between various crafts and callings, under capitalism was to become the intricate division into separate productive operations in a mechanised collective process within a factory.

With division of labour is connected exchange ("the social metabolic process") and hence the growth of commodity production: *i.e.*, production of objects for exchange on the market ("the world of commodities implies the existence of a highly developed division of labour"); and it is here that the recently much-discussed notion of 'estrangement' or 'alienation' of labour first comes in. I think there can be little doubt that in his earliest writings (such as those of 1844), when Marx, following his first detailed study of the classical economists, was dealing with economic questions at the level of exchange, his emphasis is on commodity production as the condition and basis for this alienation; and that he interprets the latter as the alienation of the producer or labourer from the *product* of his activity, since this is produced not for his own use and appropriation but for exchange and hence as a use-value for others. Here exchange and hence money as the social medium of exchange intervenes between production and consumption. It takes the form of the separation or 'objectivisation' of labour from its product in a society based on private property and exchange; this in turn implying alienation of man as a producer from *other men*, or from mankind in general. He speaks in the Manuscripts of 1844 of the fact that "the object which labour produces—labour's product—confronts it as *something alien*, as a *power independent* of the producer", and that "the alienation of the worker in his product means not only that his labour becomes an object, an *external* existence, but that it exists *outside him*, independently, as something alien to him, and that it becomes a power on its own confronting him". To this he adds the remark: "political economy conceals the estrangement inherent in the nature of labour by not considering the direct relationship between the worker and production".

Even here, however, it is stressed that what private property in conjunction with commodity production yields is the specific type of alienation that is embodied in the relationship of labour to the capitalist ("or whatever one chooses to call the master of labour"). Thus, while private property is treated as "the product, the result, the necessary consequence of alienated labour" (the latter being inherent or potential in commodity production), at the same time it becomes "the realisation of this alienation", and "the relationship [between alienation and private property] becomes reciprocal". In other words, the treatment of alienation is double-sided, and it is a mere question of emphasis as to whether commodity production *per se* or appropriation of the product by the capitalist is regarded as the crux of the matter. Later the emphasis is undoubtedly shifted to the latter, following Marx's more detailed analysis of exploitation and production of surplus value, with its accent on the distinction between labour and labour-power and on capitalism as being characteristically a *form* of commodity production in which "labour-power itself becomes a commodity".

This shift of emphasis is fully apparent by the time of the *Critique*. In *Capital*, it may be noted, Marx is quite explicit about the historical distinction between "commodity" (or commodity-producing society) and "capital", the former being a wider category than the latter: "the appearance of products as commodities," he writes, "presupposes such a development of the social division of labour that the separation of use-value from exchange-value, a separation which first begins with barter, must already have been completed. But such a degree of development is common to many forms of society, which in other respects present the most varying historical features." On the other hand, it is "otherwise with capital. The historical conditions of its existence are by no means given with the mere circulation of money and commodities. It can spring into life, only when the owner of the means of production and subsistence meets in the market with the free labourer selling his labour-power. And this one historical condition comprises a world's history. Capital therefore announces from its first appearance a new epoch in the process of social production."*

Despite this shift of emphasis, the *Critique* starts from the question of commodities and commodity production, and linked therewith the question of money as a universal measure of value and medium of exchange—a similar preoccupation to that of the early chapters of Volume I of *Capital*.** But interest is now centred on explaining exchange *in terms of production* and depicting relations of exchange, including monetary relations, as essentially relations between men as producers, or between *human labours*. (Ricardo is incidentally praised in the *Grundrisse* of a year or two earlier—and by implication contrasted with Smith as well as with the economists who came after him—as "the economist *par excellence* of production".) This, indeed, is Marx's distinctive emphasis, without which his approach in *Capital* and the rôle he cast for the theory of value cannot be properly understood. Exchange relations or market 'appearances' could

---

* *Capital*, Vol. I (trans. Moore and Aveling, London, 1886), pp. 148-49.
** To quote again the Preface to the latter: "the substance of that early work is summarised in the first three chapters of this volume", the opening sentences of the two being indeed the same.

only be understood, and the 'fetishes' or 'mystifications' to which these had been subject could only be removed, if they were seen as the expression of these more fundamental relations at the basis of society—of labour as the social activity *par excellence* and of the social division of labour. Thus labour as basis of exchange-value and price "is characterised by the fact that even the social relations of men appear in the inverse form of a social relation of things", and "a relation of commodities as exchange-values is nothing but a mutual relation between persons in their productive activity ... exchange-value of commodities is in fact nothing but a mutual relation of the labours of individuals" (to which the comment is added that "as soon as the modern economists, who sneer at the illusions of the Monetary System, deal with more complex economic categories, such as capital, they display the same illusions"). I believe incidentally that it is in this context, indeed in this sense, that we have to take his references to labour as the "substance of value"—a phrase that has puzzled many modern readers unfamiliar with this context.

The same idea about relations of exchange and relations of production is echoed in the opening chapter of *Capital* in the well-known reference to the so-called Fetishism of Commodities: "the relation of the producers to the sum total of their own labour is presented to them as a social relation, existing not between themselves but between the products of their labour.... It is a definite social relation between men that assumes in their eyes the fantastic form of a relation between things." This very distinction between "real relations of production" and market "appearances" formed the crux of his distinction between "classical political economy" ("that economy which, since the time of W. Petty, has investigated the real relations of production in bourgeois society") and "vulgar economy", in particular the *epigoni* and theoretical apologists who were prominent in the reaction against Ricardo ("which deals with appearances only"). Even "the best representatives" of the former, because they did not analyse the full nature of the relationship between "value" and "exchange-value", failed to see the "special historical character" and roots of contemporary society, and were apt to treat the bourgeois mode of production as "one eternally fixed by nature".

One could, indeed, say that Marx's theory of value was

something *more* than a theory of value as generally conceived: it had the function not only of explaining exchange-value or prices in a quantitative sense, but of exhibiting the historico-social basis in the labour-process of an exchange- or commodity-society with labour-power itself become a commodity. In which connection one may note the reference in the *Introduction to the Critique* to Rousseau's "individuals [who] ... have mutual intercourse by contract" as being "the anticipation of 'bourgeois society' ", in which "society of free competition the individual appears free from the bonds of nature, etc., which in former epochs of history made him part of a definite, limited, human conglomeration".

In view of the place occupied in his thought by this concept of labour and the labour-process as the key to human history, the crucial place occupied by the labour theory of value in his system of economic analysis is easily appreciated. This happened to be the accepted theory of the classical school which he inherited; but for him it was much more than this, and carried a larger meaning in his system than it had in theirs. As representing the determining rôle of "social relations of production", and as a category distinct from "exchange-value", "value" was defined *sui generis* and in its own right. But from the standpoint of economic explanation—*explaining* exchange-values—it would have remained an 'arbitrary' definition unless some quantitative relation could be demonstrated between the two; enabling one to speak of exchange-values as in some way 'governed' by, determined by, or 'derived' from values. Marx certainly had no illusions about the two being identical (as some have supposed), or even about the relation between the two categories being direct or simple (*vide* his reference early in Volume I of *Capital* to prices diverging from values, in which case "we must first of all reduce the former to the latter, in other words treat the difference as accidental in order that the phenomena may be observed in their purity, and our observations not interfered with by disturbing circumstances that have nothing to do with the process in question"*). Parts I and II of Volume III, as we know, were occupied with demonstrating how and why "prices of production" diverge from values—diverging in a systematic and demonstrable way. Although this demonstration as he

---

* *Ibid.*, p. 144.

left it was incomplete, we now know as a result of subsequent discussion and analysis of the so-called 'Transformation Problem' that, when the essential relations are expressed as a system of simultaneous equations, these 'prices of production' can be derived from values and from the essential conditions of production in the 'value situation' (given, i.e., the rate of exploitation or of surplus value). Since his interpretation was primarily concerned with what would be called today the 'macroscopic' configuration of a commodity-producing society, at least the more essential relationships could be depicted in terms of value relations, or of labour expenditures, without rendering the resulting 'approximation' too remote from the world of microscopic 'appearances'.

It is in the same context that we must understand the importance which Marx attached to his distinction between "labour" and "labour-power": an importance essential for the context of exploitation as a key to understanding the bourgeois (or capitalist) mode of production. The rôle of the labour theory of value in relation to the theory of surplus value is frequently misunderstood. Often this is interpreted as embodying a Lockean 'natural right' principle, to the effect that the product of a man's labour belongs 'of right' to the labourer; whence it is held to follow that the appropriation of part of this product by the capitalist is 'unnatural' and unethical. Hence exploitation is interpreted as a quasi-legal or ethical concept rather than a realistic economic description. If what we have said about labour and the labour process has been appreciated, it should be clear that this is an incorrect interpretation. What could be said, of course, is that the notion of labour as productive *activity* implicitly afforded the definition of exploitation as an appropriation of the fruits of activity by *others*—appropriation of these fruits by those who provided no productive activity of their own. But far from being an arbitrary or unusual definition of 'productive' and 'unproductive', this would, surely, meet with general agreement as normal usage of these words. The problem for Marx was not to prove the existence of surplus value and exploitation by *means* of a theory of value: it was, indeed, to *reconcile* the existence of surplus value with the reign of market competition and of exchange of value equivalents. As he himself expressed it: "To explain the *general nature of profits,* you must

12

start from the theorem that, on an average, commodities are *sold at their real values*, and that *profits are derived from selling them at their values....* If you cannot explain profit upon this supposition, you cannot explain it at all."[*]

The point of this can the better be appreciated if it is remembered that the school of writers to whom the name of the Ricardian Socialists has been given (such as Thomas Hodgskin, William Thompson and John Bray), who can be said to have held a 'primitive' theory of exploitation, explained profit on capital as the product of superior bargaining power, lack of competition and "unequal exchanges between Capital and Labour" (this bearing analogy with Eugen Dühring's 'force theory' which was castigated by Engels). This was the kind of explanation that Marx was avoiding rather than seeking. It did *not* make exploitation *consistent* with the law of value and with market competition, but explained it by departures from, or imperfections in, the latter. To it there was an easy answer from the liberal economists and free traders: namely, "join with us in demanding *really* free trade and then there can be no 'unequal exchanges' and exploitation".

It is not always easy for the modern mind, in this monopoly-age of the second half of the twentieth century, to realise the appeal and the hold which the theory of competition had over men's minds at its inception (except for the fact that traces of this still linger in economists' theories today, especially in those of the 'neo-classical' persuasion). Accordingly it may seem strange that Marx should spend so much time in the *Critique* expatiating upon and probing the nature of commodity-exchange and of money as the "universal equivalent". Especially when contrasted with preceding economic forms, *e.g.*, with feudalism, the notion of the beneficent 'automaticity' of competition was very persuasive. In the *Grundrisse* Marx made the comment that "in simple forms of the money-relation all the immanent contradictions of bourgeois society appear extinguished, which is the reason why bourgeois democrats take refuge within them.... So long as a commodity or labour is seen only as an exchange-value, and the relations between them only as exchange relations ... the subjects between whom this process takes place are merely partners in exchange: there

---

[*] *Value, Price and Profit*, ed. Eleanor Marx Aveling (London, 1898), pp. 53-54 (italics in the original).

is no formal difference between them."* (This comment has, indeed, quite a modern ring, since it is above all true of modern theories of income-distribution in terms of abstract 'factors of production'.) Economic relationships appear as those of equality; contracts are those entered into of the free will of the parties concerned; and exchange is necessarily exchange of equivalents, in which exploitation can have no meaning, almost by definition—"a very Eden of the innate rights of man" where "alone rule Freedom, Equality, Property and Bentham".**

The importance which Marx attached to the distinction between labour and labour-power lay precisely in its enabling him to show how there could be inequality and non-equivalence in "equivalent exchange"—or exploitation and appropriation of what was created by the producers *consistently* with the theory of value (*i.e.*, demonstrating how "profits are derived by selling them at their values"). Labour-power, converted into a commodity by the historical process whereby a proletariat was created and from thenceforth freely bought and sold on the market, acquired a value like other commodities in terms of the amount of labour that its production (or reproduction) cost. In *Capital* Marx defines labour-power as "energy transferred to a human organism by means of nourishing matter", as "a capacity or power of the living individual" and as "the aggregate of those mental and physical capabilities existing in a human being". ("Creation of value" is also spoken of as "transformation of labour-power into labour": something that "becomes a reality only by its exercise" and "thereby a definite quantity of human muscle, nerve, brain, etc., is wasted, and these require to be restored".***) It follows that the value of labour-power is determined by the amount of labour normally required to produce the subsistence of the labourer. The capitalist, having purchased labour-power on the market, makes use of it in the labour-process which he commands to turn out a product (for which very reason, Marx says in the *Grundrisse*, "the exchange between labour and capital is already formally different from ordinary exchange, they are two different processes"). In conditions of modern industry the value of that product exceeds the

---

* *Cit.* Martin Nicolaus, *New Left Review*, No. 48, p. 50.
** *Capital*, Vol. I (trans. Moore and Aveling, London, 1886), p. 155.
*** *Ibid.*, pp. 149, 198.

value of the labour-power in question: this it is which makes labour-power "unique" among commodities: its capacity for yielding a surplus value when put to use. Inverting the statement, one can say that only *part* of the labour of a day (or of a week or a year) is needed to replace the labour-power used up in that working period. On a global scale this can be expressed by saying that the crucial exploitation-ratio (or rate of surplus value) depends upon the proportion of the total labour-force that is needed to produce subsistence for that labour-force. On this crucial proportion (or the exploitation-ratio expressed as the ratio of the reciprocal of this proportion to this proportion itself) the whole configuration of income-distribution crucially depended as well as the structure of relative prices (*i.e.*, the 'prices of production', depending as these do on the postulating of a general and uniform rate of profit). In the mature development of Marx's thought it is evidently not just commodities and money, but capital and labour-power as a commodity that is the crux of human estrangement, just as it is of class struggle, through the vehicle of which solution and emancipation will eventually come.

More than half of the *Critique* deals with money—money as a measure of value or unit of account and as a medium of exchange; much of this dealing in some detail with the theories of eighteenth- and early nineteenth-century economists, which were still of moment to his contemporaries and had influence over men's minds. Adam Smith had but recently attacked the myths of what he called the Mercantile School surrounding gold and silver as objects of national policy towards foreign trade. The decade when Marx was writing witnessed the results of the Californian and Australian gold discoveries which seemed (in the words of the Preface) to be introducing "a new stage of development" for bourgeois society. To the reader of today such theories will have less interest; but both they and Marx's treatment of them retain enduring interest for the critical history of economic thought. It is in the course of examining the "two distinct cycles" of which "the process of circulation" consists that we have his answer to what has come to be called 'Say's Law': a concept by means of which the possibility of general overproduction was denied, and one that has come to the forefront of economic discussion and controversy over the past three decades once more. In this connection we meet his emphasis on the use of money for 'hoarding', or as a store of value, and the potentially disruptive influence of this upon the circulation of commodities, and hence upon production—a notion which again has quite a modern ring. Here it is that Ricardo and his school come under criticism as sponsors of the Quantity Theory of Money: a truism that was destined to reign for more than a century in the guise of a causal theory. In which form it will be noted that criticism is here directed against it. In the light of revived criticism (indeed, in anticipation of it) Marx's statement can be underlined to the effect that "Ricardo's theory of money was exceedingly convenient, because it lends a tautology the semblance of a statement of causal connection".

Most widely known, doubtless, in connection with this work is the passage in the 1859 Preface in which is given a summary (no more than one long paragraph) of his general doctrine to which, "as a leading thread in [his] studies", the name of historical materialism was to be given. This is the passage, which by many must be known almost by heart, beginning: "in the social production of their existence, men inevitably enter into definite relations, which are independent of their will". There follow those much-thumbed references to "existing relations of production" "at a certain stage of their development" turning "from forms of development of the productive forces ... into their fetters", thus ushering in "the era of social revolution". The passage ends with the famous remark that "the bourgeois mode of production is the last antagonistic form of the social process of production"; and since the productive forces already create "the material conditions for a solution of this antagonism", "the prehistory of human society ... closes with this social formation". At the time when this appeared (in advance of most of the mature work of Marx and Engels) one can imagine the deep and arresting impact this passage must have had upon the minds of those first reading it—an impact which, indeed, it continues to have upon a very greatly extended scale of readership today, including those who have sensed his words embodied in the recent history of their own countries.

MAURICE DOBB

Cambridge, January 1969

Karl Marx

A CONTRIBUTION
TO THE CRITIQUE
OF POLITICAL ECONOMY

PREFACE[1]

I examine the system of bourgeois economy in the following order: *capital, landed property, wage-labour; the State, foreign trade, world market*. The economic conditions of existence of the three great classes into which modern bourgeois society is divided are analysed under the first three headings; the interconnection of the other three headings is self-evident. The first part of the first book, dealing with Capital, comprises the following chapters: 1. The commodity; 2. Money or simple circulation; 3. Capital in general. The present part consists of the first two chapters. The entire material lies before me in the form of monographs, which were written not for publication but for self-clarification at widely separated periods; their remoulding into an integrated whole according to the plan I have indicated will depend upon circumstances.

A general introduction,[2] which I had drafted, is omitted, since on further consideration it seems to me confusing to anticipate results which still have to be substantiated, and the reader who really wishes to follow me will have to decide to advance from the particular to the general. A few brief remarks regarding the course of my study of political economy may, however, be appropriate here.

Although I studied jurisprudence, I pursued it as a subject subordinated to philosophy and history. In the year 1842-43, as editor of the *Rheinische Zeitung*,[3] I first found myself in the embarrassing position of having to discuss what is known as material interests. The deliberations of the Rhenish Landtag on forest thefts and the division of landed property; the official polemic started by Herr von Schaper, then Oberpräsident of the Rhine Province, against the *Rheinische Zeitung* about the condition of the Moselle peasantry, and finally the debates on free trade and protective tariffs caused me in the first instance to turn my attention to economic questions. On the other hand, at that time when good intentions "to push forward" often took the place of factual knowledge, an echo of French socialism and communism, slightly tinged by philosophy, was noticeable in the *Rheinische Zeitung*. I objected to this dilettantism, but at the same time frankly admitted in a controversy with the *Allgemeine Augsburger Zeitung*[4] that my previous studies did not allow me to express any opinion on the content of the French theories. When the publishers of the *Rheinische Zeitung* conceived the illusion that by a more compliant policy on the part of the paper it might be possible to secure the abrogation of the death sentence passed upon it, I eagerly grasped the opportunity to withdraw from the public stage to my study.

The first work which I undertook to dispel the doubts assailing me was a critical re-examination of the Hegelian philosophy of law; the introduction to this work being published in the *Deutsch-Französische Jahrbücher*[5] issued in Paris in 1844. My inquiry led me to the conclusion that neither legal relations nor political forms could be comprehended whether by themselves or on the basis of a so-called general development of the human mind, but that on the contrary they originate in the material conditions of life, the totality of which Hegel, following the example of English and French thinkers of the eighteenth century, embraces within the term "civil society"; that the anatomy of this civil society, however, has to be sought in political economy. The study of this, which I began in Paris, I continued in Brussels, where I moved owing to an expulsion order issued by M. Guizot. The general conclusion at which I arrived and which, once reached, became the guiding principle of my studies can be summarised as follows. In the social production of their existence, men inevitably enter into definite relations, which are independent of their will, namely relations of production appropriate to a given stage in the development of their material forces of production. The totality of these relations of production constitutes the economic structure of society, the real foundation, on which arises a legal and political superstructure and to which correspond definite forms of social consciousness. The mode of production of material life conditions the general process of social, political and intellectual life. It is not the consciousness of men that determines their existence, but their social existence that determines their consciousness. At a certain stage of development, the material productive forces of society come into conflict with the existing relations of production or—this merely expresses the same thing in legal terms—with the property relations within the framework of which they have operated hitherto. From forms of development of the productive forces these relations turn into their fetters. Then begins an era of social revolution. The changes in the economic foundation lead sooner or later to the transformation of the whole immense superstructure. In studying such transformations it is always necessary to distinguish between the material transformation of the economic conditions of production, which can be determined with the precision of natural science, and the legal, political, religious, artistic or philosophic—in short, ideological forms in which men become conscious of this conflict and fight it out. Just as one does not judge an individual by what he thinks about himself, so one cannot judge such a period of transformation by its consciousness, but, on the contrary, this consciousness must be explained from the contradictions of material life, from the conflict existing between the social forces of production and the relations of production. No social order is ever destroyed before all the productive forces for which it is sufficient have been developed, and new superior relations of production never replace older ones before the material conditions for their existence have matured within the framework of the old society. Mankind thus inevitably sets itself only such tasks as it is able to solve, since closer examination will always show that the problem itself arises only when the material conditions for its solution are already present or at least in the course of formation. In broad outline, the Asiatic, ancient, feudal and modern bourgeois modes of production may be designated as epochs marking progress in the economic development of society. The bourgeois mode of production is the last antagonistic form of the social process of production—antagonistic not in the sense of individual antagonism but of an antagonism that emanates from the individuals' social conditions of existence—but the productive forces developing within bourgeois society create also the material conditions for a solution of this antagonism.

The prehistory of human society accordingly closes with this social formation.

Frederick Engels, with whom I maintained a constant exchange of ideas by correspondence since the publication of his brilliant essay on the critique of economic categories[6] (printed in the *Deutsch-Französische Jahrbücher*), arrived by another road (compare his *Lage der arbeitenden Klasse in England*[a]) at the same result as I, and when in the spring of 1845 he too came to live in Brussels, we decided to set forth together our conception as opposed to the ideological one of German philosophy, in fact to settle accounts with our former philosophical conscience. The intention was carried out in the form of a critique of post-Hegelian philosophy.[7] The manuscript, two large octavo volumes, had long ago reached the publishers in Westphalia when we were informed that owing to changed circumstances it could not be printed. We abandoned the manuscript to the gnawing criticism of the mice all the more willingly since we had achieved our main purpose—self-clarification. Of the scattered works in which at that time we presented one or another aspect of our views to the public, I shall mention only the *Manifesto of the Communist Party*, jointly written by Engels and myself, and a *Discours sur le libre échange*, which I myself published. The salient points of our conception were first outlined in an academic, although polemical, form in my *Misère de la philosophie...*,[b] this book which was aimed at Proudhon appeared in 1847. The publication of an essay on *Wage-Labour*[8] written in German in which I combined the lectures I had held on this subject at the German Workers' Association in Brussels,[9] was interrupted by the February Revolution and my forcible removal from Belgium in consequence.

The publication of the *Neue Rheinische Zeitung*[10] in 1848 and 1849 and subsequent events cut short my economic studies, which I could only resume in London in 1850. The enormous amount of material relating to the history of political economy assembled in the British Museum, the fact that London is a convenient vantage point for the observation of bourgeois society, and finally the new stage of develop-

---

[a] See Frederick Engels, "The Condition of the Working Class in England", *On Britain*, Moscow, 1962, pp. 3-338.—*Ed.*

[b] See K. Marx, *The Poverty of Philosophy*, Moscow, 1962.—*Ed.*

ment which this society seemed to have entered with the discovery of gold in California and Australia, induced me to start again from the very beginning and to work carefully through the new material. These studies led partly of their own accord to apparently quite remote subjects on which I had to spend a certain amount of time. But it was in particular the imperative necessity of earning my living which reduced the time at my disposal. My collaboration, continued now for eight years, with the *New York Tribune*,[11] the leading Anglo-American newspaper, necessitated an excessive fragmentation of my studies, for I wrote only exceptionally newspaper correspondence in the strict sense. Since a considerable part of my contributions consisted of articles dealing with important economic events in Britain and on the Continent, I was compelled to become conversant with practical detail which, strictly speaking, lie outside the sphere of political economy.

This sketch of the course of my studies in the domain of political economy is intended merely to show that my views—no matter how they may be judged and how little they conform to the interested prejudices of the ruling classes—are the outcome of conscientious research carried on over many years. At the entrance to science, as at the entrance to hell, the demand must be made:

> *Qui si convien lasciare ogni sospetto*
> *Ogni viltà convien che qui sia morta.*[a]

Karl Marx

London, January 1859

---

[a] Dante, *Divina Commedia*.
　　　　Here must all distrust be left;
　　　　All cowardice must here be dead.
　　　(The English translation is taken from Dante, *The Divine Comedy*, Illustrated Modern Library, Inc., 1944, p. 22.)—*Ed.*

Book One

ON CAPITAL

Part One

CAPITAL IN GENERAL

CHAPTER ONE

THE COMMODITY

The wealth of bourgeois society, at first sight, presents itself as an immense accumulation of commodities, its unit being a single commodity. Every commodity, however, has a twofold aspect—*use-value* and *exchange-value*.*

To begin with, a commodity, in the language of the English economists, is "any thing necessary, useful or pleasant in life", an object of human wants, a means of existence in the widest sense of the term. Use-value as an aspect of the commodity coincides with the physical palpable existence of the commodity. Wheat, for example, is a distinct use-value differing from the use-values of cotton, glass, paper, etc. A use-value has value only in use, and is realised only in the process of consumption. One and the same use-value can be used in various ways. But the extent of its possible applications is limited by its existence as an object with distinct properties. It is, moreover, determined not only qualitatively but also quantitatively. Different use-values have different measures appropriate to their physical characteristics; for example, a bushel of wheat, a quire of paper, a yard of linen.

Whatever its social form may be, wealth always consists of use-values, which in the first instance are not affected by

---

* Aristoteles, *De Republica*, L. I, C. 9 (edit. I. Bekkeri, Oxonii, 1837): "Of everything which we possess there are two uses: ...one is the proper, and the other the improper or secondary use of it. For example, a shoe is used for wear, and is used for exchange; both are uses of the shoe. He who gives a shoe in exchange for money or food to him who wants one, does indeed use the shoe as a shoe, but this is not its proper or primary purpose, for a shoe is not made to be an object of barter. The same may be said of all possessions...." [The English translation is taken from Aristotle, *Politica*, by Benjamin Jowett, revised edition, Oxford, 1966, 1257a.]

27

this form. From the taste of wheat it is not possible to tell who produced it, a Russian serf, a French peasant or an English capitalist. Although use-values serve social needs and therefore exist within the social framework, they do not express the social relations of production. For instance, let us take as a use-value a commodity such as a diamond. We cannot tell by looking at it that the diamond is a commodity. Where it serves as an aesthetic or mechanical use-value, on the neck of a courtesan or in the hand of a glass-cutter, it is a diamond and not a commodity. To be a use-value is evidently a necessary prerequisite of the commodity, but it is immaterial to the use-value whether it is a commodity. Use-value as such, since it is independent of the determinate economic form, lies outside the sphere of investigation of political economy.* It belongs in this sphere only when it is itself a determinate form. Use-value is the immediate physical entity in which a definite economic relationship—*exchange-value*—is expressed.

Exchange-value seems at first to be a *quantitative relation*, the proportion in which use-values are exchanged for one another. In this relation they constitute equal exchangeable magnitudes. Thus one volume of Propertius and eight ounces of snuff may have the same exchange-value, despite the dissimilar use-values of snuff and elegies. Considered as exchange-value, one use-value is worth just as much as another, provided the two are available in the appropriate proportion. The exchange-value of a palace can be expressed in a definite number of tins of boot polish. London manufacturers of boot polish, on the other hand, have expressed the exchange-value of their numerous tins of polish in terms of palaces. Quite irrespective, therefore, of their natural form of existence, and without regard to the specific character of the needs they satisfy as use-values, commodities in definite quantities are congruent, they take one another's place in the exchange process, are regarded as equivalents, and despite their motley appearance have a common denominator.

Use-values serve directly as means of existence. But, on the other hand, these means of existence are themselves the

---

* That is why German compilers write *con amore* about use-values, calling them "goods". See for example the section on "goods" in L. Stein, *System der Staatswissenschaft*, Bd. I. Useful information on "goods" may be found in "manuals dealing with merchandise".

products of social activity, the result of expended human energy, *materialised labour.* As objectification of social labour, all commodities are crystallisations of the same substance. The specific character of this substance, i.e., of labour which is embodied in exchange-value, has now to be examined.

Let us suppose that one ounce of gold, one ton of iron, one quarter of wheat and twenty yards of silk are exchange-values of equal magnitude. As exchange-values in which the qualitative difference between their use-values is eliminated, they represent equal amounts of the same kind of labour. The labour which is uniformly materialised in them must be uniform, homogeneous, simple labour; it matters as little whether this is embodied in gold, iron, wheat or silk, as it matters to oxygen whether it is found in rusty iron, in the atmosphere, in the juice of grapes or in human blood. But digging gold, mining iron, cultivating wheat and weaving silk are qualitatively different kinds of labour. In fact, what appears objectively as diversity of the use-values, appears, when looked at dynamically, as diversity of the activities which produce those use-values. Since the particular material of which the use-values consist is irrelevant to the labour that creates exchange-value, the particular form of this labour is equally irrelevant. Different use-values are, moreover, products of the activity of different individuals and therefore the result of individually different kinds of labour. But as exchange-values they represent the same homogeneous labour, i.e., labour in which the individual characteristics of the workers are obliterated. Labour which creates exchange-value is thus *abstract general* labour.

If one ounce of gold, one ton of iron, one quarter of wheat and twenty yards of silk are exchange-values of equal magnitude or equivalents, then one ounce of gold, half a ton of iron, three bushels of wheat and five yards of silk are exchange-values which have very different magnitudes, and this quantitative difference is the only difference of which as exchange-values they are at all capable. As exchange-values of different magnitudes they represent larger or smaller portions, larger or smaller amounts of simple, homogeneous, abstract general labour, which is the substance of exchange-value. The question now arises, how can these amounts be measured? Or rather the question arises, what is the quantitative form of existence of this labour, since the quantitative differences of the commodities as exchange-values are merely the quantitative differences of the labour embodied in them. Just as motion is measured by time, so is labour by *labour-time*. Variations in the duration of labour are the only possible difference that can occur if the quality of labour is assumed to be given. Labour-time is measured in terms of the natural units of time, *i.e.*, hours, days, weeks, etc. Labour-time is the living state of existence of labour, irrespective of its form, its content and its individual features; it is the quantitative aspect of labour as well as its inherent measure. The labour-time materialised in the use-values of commodities is both the substance that turns them into exchange-values and therefore into commodities, and the standard by which the precise magnitude of their value is measured. The corresponding quantities of different use-values containing the same amount of labour-time are equivalents; that is, all use-values are equivalents when taken in proportions which contain the same amount of expended, materialised labour-time. Regarded as exchange-values all commodities are merely definite quantities of *congealed labour-time*.

The following basic propositions are essential for an understanding of the determination of exchange-value by labour-time. Labour is reduced to simple labour, labour, so to speak, without any qualitative attributes; labour which creates exchange-value, and therefore commodities, is specifically *social labour*; finally, labour in so far as its results are use-values is distinct from labour in so far as its results are exchange-values.

To measure the exchange-value of commodities by the labour-time they contain, the different kinds of labour have to be reduced to uniform, homogeneous, simple labour, in short to labour of uniform quality, whose only difference, therefore, is quantity.

This reduction appears to be an abstraction, but it is an abstraction which is made every day in the social process of production. The conversion of all commodities into labour-time is no greater an abstraction, and is no less real, than the resolution of all organic bodies into air. Labour, thus measured by time, does not seem, indeed, to be the labour of different persons, but on the contrary the different working individuals seem to be mere organs of this labour. In other words the labour embodied in exchange-values could be called *human* labour *in general*. This abstraction, human labour in general, *exists* in the form of average labour which, in a given society, the average person can perform, productive expenditure of a certain amount of human muscles, nerves, brain, etc. It is *simple* labour* which any average individual can be trained to do and which in one way or another he has to perform. The characteristics of this average labour are different in different countries and different historical epochs, but in any particular society it appears as something given. The greater part of the labour performed in bourgeois society is simple labour as statistical data show. Whether A works 6 hours producing iron and 6 hours producing linen, and B likewise works 6 hours producing iron and 6 hours producing linen, or A works 12 hours producing iron and B 12 hours producing linen is quite evidently merely a different application of the *same* labour-time. But what is the position with regard to more complicated labour which, being labour of greater intensity and greater specific gravity, rises above the general level? This kind of labour resolves itself into simple labour; it is simple labour raised to a higher power, so that for example one day of skilled labour may equal three days of simple labour. The laws governing this reduction do not concern us here. It is, however, clear that the reduction is made, for, as exchange-value, the product of highly skilled labour is equivalent, in definite proportions, to the product of simple average labour; thus being equated to a certain amount of this simple labour.

The determination of exchange-value by labour-time, moreover, presupposes that the *same amount* of labour is materialised in a particular commodity, say a ton of iron, irrespective of whether it is the work of A or of B, that is to say, different individuals expend equal amounts of labour-time to produce use-values which are qualitatively and quantitatively equal. In other words, it is assumed that the labour-time contained in a commodity is the labour-time *necessary* for its production, namely the labour-time required, under the generally prevailing conditions of production, to produce another unit of the same commodity.

From the analysis of exchange-value it follows that the conditions of labour which creates exchange-value are *social categories* of labour or categories of *social labour*, social however not in the general sense but in the particular

---

* English economists call it "unskilled labour".

sense, denoting a specific type of society. Uniform simple labour implies first of all that the labour of different individuals is *equal* and that their labour is treated as equal by being in fact reduced to homogeneous labour. The labour of every individual in so far as it manifests itself in exchange-values possesses this social character of equality, and it manifests itself in exchange-value only in so far as it is equated with the labour of all other individuals.

Furthermore, in exchange-value the labour-time of a particular individual is directly represented as *labour-time in general*, and this *general character* of individual labour appears as the *social character* of this labour. The labour-time expressed in exchange-value is the labour-time of an individual, but of an individual in no way differing from the next individual and from all other individuals in so far as they perform equal labour; the labour-time, therefore, which one person requires for the production of a given commodity is the *necessary* labour-time which any other person would require to produce the same commodity. It is the labour-time of an individual, *his* labour-time, but only as labour-time common to all; consequently it is quite immaterial *whose* individual labour-time this is. This universal labour-time finds its expression in a universal product, a *universal equivalent*, a definite amount of materialised labour-time, for which the distinct form of the use-value in which it is manifested as the direct product of one person is a matter of complete indifference, and it can be converted at will into any other form of use-value, in which it appears as the product of any other person. Only as such a *universal* magnitude does it represent a *social* magnitude. The labour of an individual can produce exchange-value only if it produces *universal equivalents*, that is to say, if the individual's labour-time represents universal labour-time or if universal labour-time represents individual labour-time. The effect is the same as if the different individuals had amalgamated their labour-time and allocated different portions of the labour-time at their joint disposal to the various use-values. The labour-time of the individual is thus, in fact, the labour-time required by society to produce a particular use-value, that is to satisfy a particular want. But what matters here is only the specific manner in which the social character of labour is established. A certain amount of a spinner's labour-time is materialised, say, in 100 lbs. of linen yarn. The same amount of labour-time is assumed to be represented in 100 yards of linen, the product of a weaver. Since these two products represent equal amounts of universal labour-time, and are therefore equivalents of *any* use-value which contains the same amount of labour-time, they are equal to each other. Only because the labour-time of the spinner and the labour-time of the weaver represent universal labour-time, and their products are thus universal equivalents, is the social aspect of the labour of the two individuals represented for each of them by the labour of the other, that is to say, the labour of the weaver represents it for the spinner, and the labour of the spinner represents it for the weaver. On the other hand, under the rural patriarchal system of production, when spinner and weaver lived under the same roof—the women of the family spinning and the men weaving, say for the requirements of the family—yarn and linen were *social* products, and spinning and weaving *social* labour within the framework of the family. But their social character did not appear in the form of yarn becoming a universal equivalent exchanged for linen as a universal equivalent, *i.e.*, of the two products exchanging for each other as equal and equally valid expressions of the same universal labour-time. On the contrary, the product of labour bore the specific social imprint of the family relationship with its naturally evolved division of labour. Or let us take the services and dues in kind of the Middle Ages. It was the distinct labour of the individual in its original form, the particular features of his labour and not its universal aspect that formed the social ties at that time. Or finally let us take communal labour in its spontaneously evolved form as we find it among all civilised nations at the dawn of their history.* In this case the social character of labour is evidently not effected by the labour of the

---

* At present an absurdly biased view is widely held, namely that *primitive* communal property is a specifically Slavonic, or even an exclusively Russian, phenomenon. It is an early form which can be found among Romans, Teutons and Celts, and of which a whole collection of diverse patterns (though sometimes only remnants survive) is still in existence in India. A careful study of Asiatic, particularly Indian, forms of communal property would indicate that the disintegration of different forms of primitive communal ownership gives rise to diverse forms of property. For instance, various prototypes of Roman and Germanic private property can be traced back to certain forms of Indian communal property.

individual assuming the abstract form of universal labour or his product assuming the form of a universal equivalent. The communal system on which this mode of production is based prevents the labour of an individual from becoming private labour and his product the private product of a separate individual; it causes individual labour to appear rather as the direct function of a member of the social organisation. Labour which manifests itself in exchange-value appears to be the labour of an isolated individual. It becomes social labour by assuming the form of its direct opposite, of abstract universal labour.

Lastly, it is a characteristic feature of labour which posits exchange-value that it causes the social relations of individuals to appear in the perverted form of a social relation between things. The labour of different persons is equated and treated as universal labour only by bringing one use-value into relation with another one in the guise of exchange-value. Although it is thus correct to say that exchange-value is a relation between persons,* it is however necessary to add that it is a relation hidden by a material veil. Just as a pound of iron and a pound of gold have the *same* weight despite their different physical and chemical properties, so two commodities which have different use-values but contain the same amount of labour-time have the *same exchange-value*. Exchange-value thus appears to be a social determination of use-values, a determination which is proper to them as things and in consequence of which they are able in definite proportions to take one another's place in the exchange process, *i.e.*, they are equivalents, just as simple chemical elements combined in certain proportions form chemical equivalents. Only the conventions of our everyday life make it appear commonplace and ordinary that social relations of production should assume the shape of things, so that the relations into which people enter in the course of their work appear as the relations of things to one another and of things to people. This mystification is still a very simple one in the case of a commodity. Everybody understands more or less clearly that the relations of commodities as exchange-values are really the relations of

---

* "La ricchezza è una ragione tra due persone." Galiani, *Della Moneta*, p. 221. In Volume III of Custodi's collection of *Scrittori classici Italiani di Economia Politica. Parte Moderna*, Milano, 1803.

people to the productive activities of one another. The semblance of simplicity disappears in more advanced relations of production. All the illusions of the Monetary System arise from the failure to perceive that money, though a physical object with distinct properties, represents a social relation of production. As soon as the modern economists, who sneer at the illusions of the Monetary System, deal with the more complex economic categories, such as capital, they display the same illusions. This emerges clearly in their confession of naïve astonishment when the phenomenon that they have just ponderously described as a thing reappears as a social relation and, a moment later, having been defined as a social relation, teases them once more as a thing.

Since the exchange-value of commodities is indeed nothing but a mutual relation between various kinds of labour of individuals regarded as equal and universal labour, *i.e.*, nothing but a material expression of a specific social form of labour, it is a tautology to say that labour is the *only* source of exchange-value and accordingly of wealth in so far as this consists of exchange-value. It is equally a tautology to say that material in its natural state does not have exchange-value* since it contains no labour, and that exchange-value as such includes no material in a natural state. It is true that William Petty calls "labour the father and earth the mother of wealth",[12] Bishop Berkeley asks

"whether the four elements, and man's labour therein, be not the true source of wealth",**

and the American Thomas Cooper explains in popular form:

"Take away from a piece of bread the labour bestowed by the baker on the flour, by the miller on the grain brought to him, by the farmer in ploughing, sowing, tending, gathering, threshing, cleaning and transporting the seed, and what will remain? A few grains of grass, growing wild in the woods, and unfit for any human purpose."***

---

* "In its natural state, matter ... is always destitute of value." McCulloch, *A Discourse on the Rise, Progress, Peculiar Objects, and Importance of Political Economy*, Second Edition, Edinburgh, 1825, p. 48. This shows how high even a McCulloch stands above the fetishism of German "thinkers" who assert that "material" and half a dozen similar irrelevancies are elements of value. See, *inter alia*, L. Stein, *op. cit.*, Bd. I, p. 170.

** Berkeley, *The Querist*, London, 1750.

*** Thomas Cooper, *Lectures on the Elements of Political Economy*, London, 1831 (Columbia, 1826), p. 99.

But all these observations are concerned not with abstract labour, which is the source of exchange-value, but with concrete labour as the source of material wealth, in short with labour in so far as it produces use-values. Since the use-value of the commodity is postulated, the specific utility and the definite usefulness of the labour expended on it is also postulated; but this is the only aspect of labour as useful labour which is relevant to the study of commodities. In considering bread as a use-value, we are concerned with its properties as an article of food and by no means with the labour of the farmer, miller, baker, etc. Even if the labour required were reduced by 95 per cent as a result of some invention, the usefulness of a loaf of bread would remain quite unaffected. It would lose not a single particle of its use-value even if it dropped ready-made from the sky. Whereas labour positing exchange-value manifests itself in the equality of commodities as universal equivalents, labour as useful productive activity manifests itself in the infinite variety of use-values. Whereas labour positing exchange-value is *abstract universal* and *uniform* labour, labour positing use-value is concrete and distinctive labour, comprising infinitely varying kinds of labour as regards its form and the material to which it is applied.

It would be wrong to say that labour which produces use-values is the *only* source of the wealth produced by it, that is of material wealth. Since labour is an activity which adapts material for some purpose or other, it needs material as a prerequisite. Different use-values contain very different proportions of labour and natural products, but use-value always comprises a natural element. As useful activity directed to the appropriation of natural factors in one form or another, labour is a natural condition of human existence, a condition of material interchange between man and nature, quite independent of the form of society. On the other hand, the labour which posits exchange-value is a specific social form of labour. For example, tailoring if one considers its physical aspect as a distinct productive activity produces a coat, but not the exchange-value of the coat. The exchange-value is produced by it not as tailoring as such but as abstract universal labour, and this belongs to a social framework not devised by the tailor. Women in ancient domestic industry, for instance, produced coats without producing the exchange-value of coats. Labour as a source of material wealth was well known both to Moses, the law-giver, and to Adam Smith, the customs official.*

Let us now examine a few propositions which follow from the reduction of exchange-value to labour-time.

A commodity as a use-value has an eminently material function. Wheat for example is used as food. A machine replaces a certain amount of labour. This function, by virtue of which a commodity is a use-value, an article of consumption, may be called its service, the service it renders as a use-value. But the commodity as an exchange-value is always considered solely from the standpoint of the result. What matters is not the service it renders, but the service** rendered to it in the course of its production. Thus the exchange-value of a machine, for instance, is determined not by the amount of labour-time which it can replace, but by the amount of labour-time expended in its production and therefore required for the production of a new machine of the same type.

Thus, if the amount of labour required for the production of commodities remained constant, their exchange-value would also remain unchanged. But the facility or difficulty of production varies continually. If the productivity of labour grows, the same use-value will be produced in less time. If the productivity of labour declines, more time will be needed to produce the same use-value. The amount of labour-time contained in a commodity, and therefore its exchange-value, is consequently a variable quantity, rising or falling in inverse proportion to the rise or fall of the productivity of labour. The level of the productivity of labour, which is predetermined in manufacturing industry, depends in agriculture and extractive industry also upon unpredictable natural conditions. The *same* quantity of labour will result in a larger or smaller output of various metals—depending on the relative abundance of the deposits

---

* Friedrich List has never been able to grasp the difference between labour as a producer of something useful, a use-value, and labour as a producer of exchange-value, a specific social form of wealth (since his mind being occupied with practical matters was not concerned with understanding); he therefore regarded the modern English economists as mere plagiarists of Moses of Egypt.

** It can easily be seen what "service" the category "service" must render to economists such as J. B. Say and F. Bastiat, whose sagacity, as Malthus has aptly remarked, always abstracts from the specific form of economic conditions.

of these metals in the earth's crust. The *same* amount of labour may yield two bushels of wheat in a favourable season, and perhaps only one bushel in an unfavourable season. Scarcity or abundance brought about by natural circumstances seems in this case to determine the exchange-value of commodities, because it determines the productivity of the specific concrete labour which is bound up with the natural conditions.

Equal amounts of labour-time, or equal amounts of exchange-value, are contained in unequal volumes of different use-values. The smaller the volume of a use-value which contains a given amount of labour-time as compared with other use-values of commodities, the greater is the *specific exchange-value* of that commodity. If we find that in different epochs of civilisation separated by long periods of time, various use-values—for example gold, silver, copper and iron, or wheat, rye, barley and oats—form a series of specific exchange-values which on the whole retain their relative order in relation to one another, though not their exact numerical proportions, it follows that the progressive development of the social productive forces has exerted a uniform or nearly uniform effect on the labour-time required for the production of these commodities.

The exchange-value of a commodity is not expressed in its own use-value. But as materialisation of universal social labour-time, the use-value of one commodity is brought into relation with the use-values of other commodities. The exchange-value of one commodity thus manifests itself in the use-values of other commodities. In fact the exchange-value of one commodity expressed in the use-value of another commodity represents equivalence. If one says, for instance, one yard of linen is worth two pounds of coffee, then the exchange-value of linen is expressed in the use-value of coffee, and it is moreover expressed in a definite quantity of this use-value. Once the proportion is given, the value of any quantity of linen can be expressed in terms of coffee. It is evident that the exchange-value of a commodity, *e.g.*, linen, is not exhaustively expressed by the proportion in which a particular commodity, *e.g.*, coffee, forms its equivalent. The quantity of universal labour-time represented by a yard of linen exists simultaneously in infinitely varied amounts of the use-values of all other commodities. The use-value of any other commodity taken in the proportion which represents the same quantity of labour-time constitutes an equivalent for the yard of linen. The exchange-value of *this particular commodity* can therefore be exhaustively expressed only by the infinite number of equations in which the use-values of all other commodities form its equivalent. The only exhaustive expression for a *universal equivalent* is the sum of these equations or the totality of the different proportions in which a commodity can be exchanged for any other commodity. For example the series of equations—

1 yard of linen $= \frac{1}{2}$ lb. of tea
1 yard of linen $= 2$ lbs. of coffee
1 yard of linen $= 8$ lbs. of bread
1 yard of linen $= 6$ yards of calico

may be put in the following form—

1 yard of linen $= \frac{1}{8}$ lb. of tea $+ \frac{1}{2}$ lb. of coffee $+ 2$ lbs. of bread $+ 1\frac{1}{2}$ yards of calico.

Thus if we had all the equations in which the value of a yard of linen is exhaustively expressed, we could denote its exchange-value in the form of a series. This is in fact an infinite series, for the range of commodities can never be finally circumscribed but expands continuously. Since the exchange-value of one commodity is measured by the use-values of all other commodities, the exchange-values of all other commodities are on the contrary measured in terms of the use-value of the one commodity measured by them.* If the exchange-value of one yard of linen is expressed in $\frac{1}{2}$ lb. of tea, or 2 lbs. of coffee, or 6 yards of calico, or 8 lbs. of bread, etc., it follows that coffee, tea, calico, bread, etc., must be equal to one another in the proportion in which they are equal to linen, a third magnitude, linen thus serves as a common measure of their exchange-value. The exchange-value of any commodity considered as materialised universal labour-time, *i.e.*, as a definite quantity of universal labour-time, is measured successively in terms of definite quantities of the use-values of all other commodities; and on the other hand the exchange-values of all other commodities are measured in the use-value of this one exclusive commodity. But any commodity considered as

---

* "It is another peculiarity of measures to enter into such a relation with the thing measured, that in a certain way the thing measured becomes the measure of the measuring unit." Montanari, *Della Moneta,* p. 41 in Custodi's collection, Vol. III, *Parte Antica.*

exchange-value is both the exclusive commodity which serves as the common measure of the exchange-values of all other commodities and on the other hand it is merely one commodity of the many commodities in the series in which the exchange-value of any other commodity is directly expressed.

The existing number of different types of commodities does not affect the *value* of a commodity. But whether the series of equations in which its exchange-value can be realised is longer or shorter depends on the greater or smaller variety of different commodities. The series of equations which express, say, the value of coffee shows the range of its exchangeability, the limits within which it functions as an exchange-value. The exchange-value of a commodity as the objective expression of universal social labour-time finds its appropriate expression of equivalence in the infinite variety of use-values.

We have seen that the exchange-value of a commodity varies with the quantity of labour-time directly contained in it. Its realised exchange-value, that is its exchange-value expressed in the use-values of other commodities, must also depend on the degree to which the labour-time expended on the production of all other commodities varies. For example, if the labour-time necessary for the production of a bushel of wheat remained unchanged, while the labour-time needed for the production of all other commodities doubled, the exchange-value of a bushel of wheat in terms of its equivalents would have been halved. The result would actually be the same as if the labour-time required to produce a bushel of wheat had been halved and the labour-time required to produce all other commodities had remained unchanged. The value of commodities is determined by the amount of them which can be produced in a given labour-time. In order to examine what changes are liable to affect this proportion, let us take two commodities, A and B. *First*. The labour-time required for the production of B is assumed to remain unchanged. In this case the exchange-value of A expressed in terms of B falls or rises in direct proportion to the decrease or increase in the labour-time necessary for the production of A. *Secondly*. The labour-time necessary for the production of commodity A is assumed to remain unchanged. The exchange-value of commodity A in terms of B falls or rises in inverse proportion to the decrease or increase in the labour-time required to produce B. *Thirdly*. The labour-time required for the production of A and of B is assumed to decrease or increase at the same rate. The equation expressing the value of commodity A in terms of B remains unchanged in this case. If some factor were to cause the productivity of all types of labour to fall in equal degree, thus requiring the same proportion of additional labour for the production of all commodities, then the value of *all* commodities would rise, the actual expression of their exchange-value remaining unchanged, and the real wealth of society would decrease, since the production of the same quantity of use-values would require a larger amount of labour-time. *Fourthly*. The labour-time required for the production of both A and B is assumed to increase or decrease but in unequal degree, or else the labour-time required for the production of A is assumed to increase while that required for B decreases, or *vice versa*. All these cases can be simply reduced to the position where the labour-time required for the production of one commodity remains unchanged, while that required for the production of the other either increases or decreases.

The exchange-value of any commodity is expressed in terms of the use-value of any other commodity, either in whole units or in fractions of that use-value. Every commodity as exchange-value can be just as easily divided as the labour-time contained in it. The equivalence of commodities is just as independent of the physical divisibility of their use-values as the summation of the exchange-values of commodities is unaffected by the changes which the use-values of the commodities may undergo in the course of their transformation into a *single* new commodity.

So far two aspects of the commodity—use-value and exchange-value—have been examined, but each one separately. The commodity, however, is the direct *unity* of use-value and exchange-value, and at the same time it is a commodity only in relation to other commodities. The *exchange process* of commodities is the *real* relation that exists between them. This is a social process which is carried on by individuals independently of one another, but they take part in it only as commodity-owners; they exist for one another only in so far as their commodities exist, they thus appear to be in fact the conscious representatives of the exchange process.

The commodity *is* a use-value, wheat, linen, a diamond, machinery, etc., but as a commodity it is simultaneously *not* a use-value. It would not be a commodity, if it were a use-value for its owner, that is a direct means for the satisfaction of his own needs. For its owner it is on the contrary a *non-use-value*, that is merely the physical depository of exchange-value, or simply a *means of exchange*. Use-value as an active carrier of exchange-value becomes a means of exchange. The commodity is a use-value for its owner only so far as it is an exchange-value.* The commodity therefore *has* still *to become* a use-value, in the first place a use-value for others. Since it is not a use-value to its owner, it must be a use-value to owners of other commodities. If this is not the case, then the labour expended on it was useless labour and the result accordingly is not a commodity. The commodity must, on the other hand, become a use-value *for its owner*, since his means of existence exist outside it, in the use-values of other people's commodities. To *become* a use-value, the commodity must encounter the particular need which it can satisfy. Thus the use-values of commodities *become* use-values by a mutual exchange of places: they pass from the hands of those for whom they were means of exchange into the hands of those for whom they serve as consumer goods. Only as a result of this universal *alienation* of commodities does the labour contained in them become useful labour. Commodities do not acquire a new economic form *in the course* of their mutual relations as use-values. On the contrary, the specific form which distinguished them as commodities disappears. Bread, for instance, in passing from the baker to the consumer does not change its character as bread. It is rather that the consumer treats it as a use-value, as a particular foodstuff, whereas so long as it was in the hands of the baker it was simply representative of an economic relation, a concrete and at the same time an abstract thing. The only transformation therefore that commodities experience in the course of becoming use-values is the cessation of their formal existence in which they were non-use-values for their owner, and use-values for their non-owner. To become use-values commodities must be altogether alienated; they must enter into the exchange

---

* It is in this sense that Aristotle speaks of exchange-value (see the passage quoted at the beginning of this chapter).

process; exchange however is concerned merely with their aspect as exchange-values. Hence, only by being realised as exchange-values can they be realised as use-values.

The individual commodity as a use-value was originally regarded as something independent, while as an exchange-value it was from the outset regarded in its relation to all other commodities. But this was merely a theoretical, hypothetical, relation. It realises itself only in the process of exchange. On the other hand, a commodity is an exchange-value in so far as a definite amount of labour-time has been expended on its production and it accordingly represents *materialised labour-time*. Yet the commodity as it comes into being is only materialised individual labour-time of a specific kind, and not *universal* labour-time. The commodity is thus *not* immediately exchange-value, but has still to *become* exchange-value. To begin with, it can be materialisation of universal labour-time only when it represents a particular useful application of labour-time, that is a use-value. This is the material condition under which alone the labour-time contained in commodities is regarded as universal, social labour-time. A commodity can only therefore become a use-value if it is realised as an exchange-value, while it can only be realised as an exchange-value if it is alienated and functions as a use-value. The alienation of a commodity as a use-value is only possible to the person for whom it is a use-value, *i.e.*, an object satisfying particular needs. On the other hand, it can only be alienated in exchange for another commodity, or if we regard the matter from the standpoint of the owner of the other commodity, he too can only alienate, *i.e.*, realise, his commodity by bringing it into contact with the particular need of which it is the object. During the universal alienation of commodities as *use-values* they are brought into relation with one another as discrete things which are physically different and because of their specific properties satisfy particular needs. But as mere use-values they exist independently of one another or rather without any connection. They can be exchanged as use-values only in connection with particular needs. They are, however, exchangeable only as equivalents, and they are equivalents only as equal quantities of materialised labour-time, when their physical properties as use-values, and hence the relations of these commodities to specific needs, are entirely disregarded. A commodity functions as an exchange-value if it can freely take the place of a definite quantity of any other commodity, irrespective of whether or not it constitutes a use-value for the owner of the other commodity. But for the owner of the other commodity it becomes a commodity only in so far as it constitutes a use-value for him, and for the owner in whose hands it is it becomes an exchange-value only in so far as it is a commodity for the other owner. One and the same relation must therefore be simultaneously a relation of essentially equal commodities which differ only in magnitude, *i.e.*, a relation which expresses their equality as materialisations of universal labour-time, and at the same time it must be their relation as qualitatively different things, as distinct use-values for distinct needs, in short a relation which differentiates them as actual use-values. But equality and inequality thus posited are mutually exclusive. The result is not simply a vicious circle of problems, where the solution of one problem presupposes the solution of the other, but a whole complex of contradictory premises, since the fulfilment of one condition depends directly upon the fulfilment of its opposite.

The exchange process must comprise both the evolution and the solution of these contradictions, which cannot however be demonstrated in the process in this simple form. We have merely observed how the commodities themselves are related to one another as use-values, *i.e.*, how commodities as use-values function *within* the exchange process. On the other hand, exchange-value as we have considered it till now has merely existed as our abstraction, or, if one prefers, as the abstraction of the individual commodity-owner, who keeps the commodity as use-value in the warehouse, and has it on his conscience as exchange-value. In the exchange process, however, the commodities must exist for one another not only as use-values but also as exchange-values, and this aspect of their existence must appear as their own mutual relation. The difficulty which confronted us in the first place was that the commodity as a use-value has to be alienated, disposed of, before it can function as an exchange-value, as materialised labour, while on the contrary its alienation as a use-value presupposes its existence as exchange-value. But let us suppose that this difficulty has been overcome, that the commodity has shed its particular use-value and has thereby fulfilled the material condition of being socially useful labour, instead of the particular labour of an individual by himself. In the exchange process, the commodity as exchange-value must then become a universal equivalent, materialised general labour-time for all other commodities; it has thus no longer the limited function of a particular use-value, but is capable of being directly represented in all use-values as its equivalents. Every commodity however is *the* commodity which, as a result of the alienation of its particular use-value, must appear as the direct materialisation of universal labour-time. But on the other hand, only particular commodities, particular use-values embodying the labour of private individuals, confront one another in the exchange process. Universal labour-time itself is an abstraction which, as such, does not exist for commodities.

Let us consider the series of equations in which the exchange-value of a commodity is expressed in concrete terms, for example—

$$1 \text{ yard of linen} = 2 \text{ lbs. of coffee}$$
$$1 \text{ yard of linen} = 1/2 \text{ lb. of tea}$$
$$1 \text{ yard of linen} = 8 \text{ lbs. of bread, etc.}$$

To be sure, these equations merely denote that equal amounts of universal social labour-time are materialised in 1 yard of linen, 2 lbs. of coffee, 1/2 lb. of tea, etc. But the different kinds of individual labour represented in these particular use-values, in fact, become labour in general, and in this way social labour, only by actually being exchanged for one another in quantities which are proportional to the labour-time contained in them. Social labour-time exists in these commodities in a latent state, so to speak, and becomes evident only in the course of their exchange. The point of departure is not the labour of individuals considered as social labour, but on the contrary the particular kinds of labour of private individuals, *i.e.*, labour which proves that it is universal social labour only by the supersession of its original character in the exchange process. Universal social labour is consequently not a ready-made prerequisite but an emerging result. Thus a new difficulty arises: on the one hand, commodities must enter the exchange process as materialised universal labour-time, on the other hand, the labour-time of individuals becomes materialised universal labour-time only as the result of the exchange process.

It is through the alienation of its use-value, that is of its original form of existence, that every commodity has to acquire its corresponding existence as exchange-value. The commodity must therefore assume a dual form of existence in the exchange process. On the other hand, its second form of existence, exchange-value, can only be represented by another commodity, for only commodities confront one another in the exchange process. How is it possible to present a particular commodity directly as *materialised universal* labour-time, or—which amounts to the same thing—how can the individual labour-time materialised in a particular commodity directly assume a universal character? The concrete expression of the exchange-value of a commodity, *i.e.*, of any commodity considered as universal equivalent, consists of an infinite series of equations such as—

1 yard of linen = 2 lbs. of coffee
1 yard of linen = $\frac{1}{2}$ lb. of tea
1 yard of linen = 8 lbs. of bread
1 yard of linen = 6 yards of calico
1 yard of linen = and so on.

This is a theoretical statement since the commodity is merely *regarded* as a definite quantity of materialised universal labour-time. A particular commodity as a universal equivalent is transformed from a pure abstraction into a *social* result of the exchange process, if one simply reverses the above series of equations. For example—

2 lbs. of coffee = 1 yard of linen
$\frac{1}{2}$ lb. of tea = 1 yard of linen
8 lbs. of bread = 1 yard of linen
6 yards of calico = 1 yard of linen.

Just as the labour-time contained in coffee, tea, bread, calico, in short in all commodities, is expressed in terms of linen, so conversely the exchange-value of linen is reflected in all other commodities which act as its equivalents, and the labour-time materialised in linen becomes direct universal labour-time, which is equally embodied in different volumes of all other commodities. Linen thus becomes the *universal equivalent* in consequence of the *universal action* of all other commodities in relation to it. Every commodity considered as exchange-value became a measure of the value of all other commodities. In this case, on the contrary, because the exchange-value of all commodities is measured in terms of one particular commodity, the excluded commodity becomes the adequate representation of exchange-value as the universal equivalent. On the other hand, the infinite series or the infinite number of equations in which the exchange-value of each commodity was expressed is now reduced to a single equation consisting of two terms. The equation 2 lbs. of coffee = 1 yard of linen is now a comprehensive expression for the exchange-value of coffee, for in this expression it appears as the direct equivalent to a definite quantity of any other commodity. Commodities within the exchange process accordingly exist for one another, or appear to one another, as exchange-values in the form of linen. The fact that all commodities are related to one another as exchange-values, *i.e.*, simply as different quantities of materialised universal labour-time, now appears in the form that all exchange-values represent merely different quantities of one and the *same* article, linen. Universal labour-time thus appears as a specific thing, as a commodity in addition to and apart from all other commodities. At the same time, the equation in which one commodity represents the exchange-value of another commodity, *e.g.*, 2 lbs. of coffee = 1 yard of linen, has still to be realised. Only by being alienated as a use-value—an alienation which depends on whether it is able to prove in the exchange process that it is a needed object—is it really converted from the form of coffee into that of linen, thus becoming a universal equivalent and really representing exchange-value for all other commodities. On the other hand, because as a result of their alienation as use-values all commodities are converted into linen, linen becomes the converted form of all other commodities, and only as a result of this transformation of all other commodities into linen does it become the direct *reification of universal labour-time*, *i.e.*, the product of universal alienation and of the supersession of all individual labour. While commodities thus assume a dual form in order to represent exchange-value for one another, the commodity which has been set apart as universal equivalent acquires a dual use-value. In addition to its particular use-value as an individual commodity it acquires a universal use-value. This latter use-value is itself a determinate form, *i.e.*, it arises from the specific rôle which this commodity plays as a result of the universal action exerted on it by the other commodities in the exchange process. The use-value of each commodity as an object which satisfies particular needs has a different value in different hands, *e.g.*, it has one value for the person who disposes of it and a different value for the person who acquires it. The commodity which has been set apart as the universal equivalent is now an object which satisfies a universal need arising from the exchange process itself, and has the same use-value for everybody—that of being carrier of exchange-value or a universal medium of exchange. Thus the contradiction inherent in the commodity as such, namely that of being a particular use-value and simultaneously universal equivalent, and hence a use-value for everybody or a universal use-value, has been solved in the case of this one commodity. Whereas now the exchange-value of all other commodities is in the first place presented in the form of an ideal equation with the commodity that has been set apart, an equation which has still to be realised; the use-value of this commodity, though real, seems in the exchange process to have merely a formal existence which has still to be realised by conversion into actual use-values. The commodity originally appeared as commodity in general, as universal labour-time materialised in a particular use-value. All commodities are compared in the exchange process with the one excluded commodity which is regarded as com-modity in general, *the commodity*, the embodiment of universal labour-time in a particular use-value. They are therefore as *particular* commodities opposed to one particular commodity considered as being the *universal* commodity.* The fact that commodity-owners treat one another's labour as universal social labour appears in the form of their treating their own commodities as exchange-values; and the interrelation of commodities as exchange-values in the exchange process appears as their universal relation to a particular commodity as the adequate expres-sion of their exchange-value; this in turn appears as the specific relation of this particular commodity to all other commodities and hence as the distinctive, as it were naturally evolved, social character of a thing. The particular commodity which thus represents the exchange-value of all commodities, that is to say, the exchange-value of commodi-ties regarded as a particular, exclusive commodity, consti-tutes *money*. It is a crystallisation of the exchange-value of commodities and is formed in the exchange process. Thus,

---

* The same term is used by Genovesi. [Note in author's copy.]

while in the exchange process commodities become *use-values* for one another by discarding all determinate forms and confronting one another in their immediate physical aspect, they must assume a new determinate form, they must evolve money, so as to be able to confront one another as *exchange-values*. Money is not a symbol, just as the existence of a use-value in the form of a commodity is no symbol. A social relation of production appears as something existing apart from individual human beings, and the distinctive relations into which they enter in the course of production in society appear as the specific properties of a thing—it is this perverted appearance, this prosaically real, and by no means imaginary, mystification that is characteristic of all social forms of labour positing exchange-value. This perverted appearance manifests itself merely in a more striking manner in money than it does in commodities.

The necessary physical properties of the particular commodity, in which the money form of all other commodities is to be crystallised—in so far as they directly follow from the nature of exchange-value—are: unlimited divisibility, homogeneity of its parts and uniform quality of all units of the commodity. As the materialisation of universal labour-time it must be homogeneous and capable of expressing only quantitative differences. Another necessary property is durability of its use-value since it must endure through the exchange process. Precious metals possess these qualities in an exceptionally high degree. Since money is not the result of deliberation or of agreement, but has come into being spontaneously in the course of exchange, many different, more or less unsuitable, commodities were at various times used as money. When exchange reaches a certain stage of development, the need arises to polarise the functions of exchange-value and use-value among various commodities—so that one commodity, for example, shall act as means of exchange while another is disposed of as a use-value. The outcome is that one commodity or sometimes several commodities representing the most common use-value come occasionally to serve as money. Even when no immediate need for these use-values exists, the demand for them is bound to be more general than that for other use-values, since they constitute the most substantial physical element in wealth.

Direct barter, the spontaneous form of exchange, signifies the beginning of the transformation of use-values into commodities rather than the transformation of commodities into money. Exchange-value does not acquire an independent form, but is still directly tied to use-value. This is manifested in two ways. Use-value, not exchange-value, is the purpose of the whole system of production, and use-values accordingly cease to be use-values and become means of exchange, or commodities, only when a larger amount of them has been produced than is required for consumption. On the other hand, they become commodities only within the limits set by their immediate use-value, even when this function is polarised so that the commodities to be exchanged by their owners must be use-values for both of them, but each commodity must be a use-value for its non-owner. In fact, the exchange of commodities evolves originally not within primitive communities,* but on their margins, on their borders, the few points where they come into contact with other communities. This is where barter begins and moves thence into the interior of the community, exerting a disintegrating influence upon it. The particular use-values which, as a result of barter between different communities, become commodities, e.g., slaves, cattle, metals, usually serve also as the first money within these communities. We have seen that the degree to which the exchange-value of a commodity functions as exchange-value is the higher, the longer the series of its equivalents or the *larger* the sphere in which the commodity is exchanged. The gradual extension of barter, the growing number of exchange transactions, and the increasing variety of commodities bartered lead, therefore, to the further development of the commodity as exchange-value, stimulates the formation of money and consequently has a disintegrating effect on direct barter. Economists usually reason that the emergence of money is due to external difficulties which the expansion of barter encounters, but they forget that these difficulties arise from the evolution of exchange-value and

---

* Aristotle makes a similar observation with regard to the individual family considered as the primitive community. But the primitive form of the family is the tribal family, from the historical dissolution of which the individual family develops. "In the first community, indeed, which is the family, this art" (that is, trade) "is obviously of no use" (Aristotle, *loc. cit.*).

hence from that of social labour as universal labour. For example commodities as use-values are not divisible at will, a property which as exchange-values they should possess. Or it may happen that the commodity belonging to A may be use-value required by B; whereas B's commodity may not have any use-value for A. Or the commodity-owners may need each other's commodities but these cannot be divided and their relative exchange-values are different. In other words, on the plea of examining simple barter, these economists display certain aspects of the contradiction inherent in the commodity as being the direct unity of use-value and exchange-value. On the other hand, they then persistently regard barter as a form well adapted to commodity exchange, suffering merely from certain technical inconveniences, to overcome which money has been cunningly devised. Proceeding from this quite superficial point of view, an ingenious British economist has rightly maintained that money is merely a material instrument, like a ship or a steam engine, and not an expression of a social relation of production, and hence is not an economic category. It is therefore simply a malpractice to deal with this subject in political economy, which in fact has nothing in common with technology.*

The world of commodities presupposes a developed division of labour, or rather the division of labour manifests itself directly in the diversity of use-values which confront one another as particular commodities and which embody just as many diverse kinds of labour. The *division of labour* as the aggregate of all the different types of productive activity constitutes the totality of the physical aspects of social labour as labour producing use-values. But it exists as such—as regards commodities and the exchange process—only in its results, in the variety of the commodities themselves.

The exchange of commodities is the process in which the social metabolism, in other words the exchange of particular

---

* "Money is, in fact, only the instrument for carrying on buying and selling" (but could you please explain what you mean by buying and selling?) "and the consideration of it no more forms a part of the science of political economy than the consideration of ships or steam engines, or of any other instruments employed to facilitate the production and distribution of wealth" (Thomas Hodgskin, *Popular Political Economy*, London, 1827, pp. 178, 179).

products of private individuals, simultaneously gives rise to definite social relations of production, into which individuals enter in the course of this metabolism. As they develop, the interrelations of commodities crystallise into distinct aspects of the universal equivalent, and thus the exchange process becomes at the same time the process of formation of money. This process as a whole, which comprises several processes, constitutes *circulation*.

A. Historical Notes on the Analysis of Commodities

The decisive outcome of the research carried on for over a century and a half by classical political economy, beginning with William Petty in Britain and Boisguillebert* in France, and ending with Ricardo in Britain and Sismondi in France, is an analysis of the aspects of the commodity into two forms of labour—use-value is reduced to concrete labour or purposive productive activity, exchange-value to labour-time or homogeneous social labour.

Petty reduces use-value to labour without deceiving himself about the dependence of its creative power on natural factors. He immediately perceives concrete labour in its entire social aspect as *division of labour*.** This

---

* A comparative study of Petty's and Boisguillebert's writings and characters—apart from illuminating the social divergence between Britain and France at the close of the seventeenth century and the beginning of the eighteenth—would explain the origins of those national contrasts that exist between British and French political economy. The same contrast reappears in Ricardo and Sismondi.

** Petty treats the division of labour also as a productive force, and he does so on a much grander scale than Adam Smith. See *An Essay concerning the Multiplication of Mankind*, Third Edition, 1686, pp. 35-36. In this essay he shows the advantages which division of labour has for production not only with the example of the manufacture of a watch—as Adam Smith did later with the example of the manufacture of a pin—but considers also a town and a whole country as large-scale industrial establishments. The *Spectator*[13] of November 26, 1711, refers to this "illustration of the admirable Sir William Petty". McCulloch's conjecture that the *Spectator* confused Petty with a writer forty years his junior is therefore wrong. (See McCulloch, *The Literature of Political Economy, a Classified Catalogue*, London, 1845, p. 102.) Petty regards himself as the founder of a new science. He says that his method "is not yet very usual", "for instead of using only comparative and superlative Words, and intellectual Arguments", he proposes

conception of the source of material wealth does not remain more or less sterile as with his contemporary Hobbes, but leads to the *political arithmetic*, the first form in which

---

to speak "in Terms of *Number, Weight* or *Measure*; to use only Arguments of Sense, and to consider only such Causes, as have visible Foundations in Nature; leaving those that depend upon the mutable Minds, Opinions, Appetites, and Passions of particular Men, to the Consideration of others" (*Political Arithmetick*, etc., London, 1699, Preface). His audacious genius becomes evident for instance in his proposal to transport "all the movables and People of *Ireland,* and of the *Highlands of Scotland* ... into the rest of Great *Britain*". This would result in the saving of labour-time, in increasing productivity of labour, and "the King and his Subjects would thereby become more *Rich* and *Strong*" (*Political Arithmetick*, Chapter 4 [p. 225]). Also in the chapter of his *Political Arithmetick* in which—at a time when Holland was still the predominant trading nation and France seemed to be on the way to becoming the principal trading power—he proves that England is destined to conquer the world market: "That the King of England's Subjects, have Stock competent and convenient, to drive the Trade of the whole Commercial World" (*op. cit.*, Chapter 10 [p. 272]). "That the Impediments of England's greatness, are but contingent and removable" (p. 247 *et seq.*). A highly original sense of humour pervades all his writings. Thus he shows for example that the conquest of the world market by Holland, which was then regarded as the model country by English economists just as Britain is now regarded as the model country by continental economists, was brought about by perfectly natural causes "without such Angelical Wits and Judgments, as some attribute to the Hollanders" (*op. cit.*, pp. 175-76). He champions freedom of conscience as a condition of trade, because the poor are diligent and "believe that Labour and Industry is their Duty towards God" so long as they are permitted "to think they have the more Wit and Understanding, especially of the things of God, which they think chiefly belong to the Poor". "From whence it follows that Trade is not fixt to any Species of Religion as such; but rather ... to the Heterodox part of the whole" (*op. cit.*, pp. 183-86). He recommends special public contribution for rogues, since it would be better for the general public to impose a tax on themselves for the benefit of the rogues than to be taxed by them (*op. cit.*, p. 199). On the other hand, he rejects taxes which transfer wealth from industrious people to those who "do nothing at all, but *Eat* and *Drink, Sing, Play,* and *Dance*: nay such as Study the *Metaphysicks*" [*op. cit.*, p. 198]. Petty's writings have almost become bibliographical curiosities and are only available in old inferior editions. This is the more surprising since William Petty is not only the father of English political economy but also an ancestor of Henry Petty, alias Marquis of Lansdowne, the Nestor of the English Whigs. But the Lansdowne family could hardly prepare a complete edition of Petty's works without prefacing it with his biography, and what is true with regard to the origin of most of the big Whig families, applies also in this case—the less said of it the better. The army surgeon, who was a bold thinker but quite unscrupulous and just as apt to plunder in Ireland under the aegis of Cromwell

political economy is treated as a separate science. But he accepts exchange-value as it *appears* in the exchange of commodities, *i.e.*, as money, and money itself as an existing commodity, as gold and silver. Caught up in the ideas of the Monetary System, he asserts that the labour which determines exchange-value is the particular kind of concrete labour by which gold and silver is extracted. What he really has in mind is that in bourgeois economy labour does not directly produce use-values but commodities, use-values which, in consequence of their alienation in exchange, are capable of assuming the form of gold and silver, *i.e.*, of money, *i.e.*, of exchange-value, *i.e.*, of materialised universal labour. His case is a striking proof that recognition of labour as the source of material wealth by no means precludes misapprehension of the specific social form in which labour constitutes the source of exchange-value.

Boisguillebert for his part, in fact, although he may not be aware of it, reduces the exchange-value of commodities to labour-time, by determining the "true value" (*la juste valeur*) according to the correct proportion in which the labour-time of the individual producers is divided between the different branches of industry, and declaring that free competition is the social process by which this correct proportion is established. But simultaneously, and in contrast with Petty, Boisguillebert wages a fanatical struggle against money, whose intervention, he alleges, disturbs the natural equilibrium or the harmony of the exchange of commodities and, like a fantastic Moloch, demands all physical wealth as a sacrifice. This polemic against money is, on the one hand, connected with definite historical conditions, for Boisguillebert fights against the blindly destructive greed for gold which possessed the court of Louis XIV, his tax-farmers and the aristocracy*; whereas Petty acclaims

---

as to fawn upon Charles II to obtain the title of baronet to embellish his trash, is not a suitable image of an ancestor for public display. In most of the writings published during his lifetime, moreover, Petty seeks to prove that England's golden age was the reign of Charles II, a rather heterodox view for hereditary exploiters of the "glorious revolution".

* As against the "black art of finance" of his time, Boisguillebert says: "The science of finance consists of nothing but a thorough knowledge of the interests of agriculture and commerce" (*Le détail de la France*, 1697. In Eugène Daire's edition of *Economistes financiers du XVIII siècle*, Paris, 1843, Vol. I, p. 241).

the greed for gold as a vigorous force which spurs a nation to industrial progress and to the conquest of the world market; at the same time however it throws into bold relief more profound fundamental differences which recur as a perpetual contrast between typically English and typically French* political economy. Boisguillebert, indeed, sees only the material substance of wealth, its use-value, enjoyment of it,** and regards the bourgeois form of labour, the production of use-values as commodities and the exchange of commodities, as the appropriate social form in which individual labour accomplishes this object. Where, as in money, he encounters the specific features of bourgeois wealth, he therefore speaks of the intrusion of usurping alien factors, and inveighs against one of the forms of labour in bourgeois society, while simultaneously pronouncing utopian eulogies on it in another form.*** Boisguillebert's work proves that it is possible to regard labour-time as the measure of the value of commodities, while confusing the labour which is materialised in the exchange-value of commodities and measured in time units with the direct physical activity of individuals.

It is a man of the New World—where bourgeois relations of production imported together with their representatives sprouted rapidly in a soil in which the superabundance of humus made up for the lack of historical tradition—who for the first time deliberately and clearly (so clearly as to be almost trite) reduces exchange-value to labour-time. This man was *Benjamin Franklin*, who formulated the basic law of modern political economy in an early work,

---

* But not *Romance* political economy, since the contrast of English and French economists is repeated by the Italians in their two schools, one at Naples and the other at Milan; whereas the Spaniards of the earlier period are either simply Mercantilists and modified Mercantilists like Ustáriz, or follow Adam Smith in observing the happy mean like Jovellanos (see his *Obras*, Barcelona, 1839-40).

** "True wealth ... is the complete enjoyment not only of the necessaries of life but also of all the superfluities and of everything that can give pleasure to the senses" (Boisguillebert, *Dissertation sur la nature de la richesse*, etc., p. 403). But whereas Petty was just a frivolous, grasping, unprincipled adventurer, Boisguillebert, although he was one of the intendants of Louis XIV, stood up for the interests of the oppressed classes with both great intellectual force and courage.

*** French socialism as represented by Proudhon suffers from the same national failing.

which was written in 1729 and published in 1731.* He declares it necessary to seek another measure of value than the precious metals, and that this measure is labour.

"By labour may the value of silver be measured as well as other things. As, suppose one man is employed to raise corn, while another is digging and refining silver; at the year's end, or at any other period of time, the complete produce of corn, and that of silver, are the natural price of each other; and if one be twenty bushels, and the other twenty ounces, then an ounce of that silver is worth the labour of raising a bushel of that corn. Now if by the discovery of some nearer, more easy or plentiful mines, a man may get forty ounces of silver as easily as formerly he did twenty, and the same labour is still required to raise twenty bushels of corn, then two ounces of silver will be worth no more than the same labour of raising one bushel of corn, and that bushel of corn will be as cheap at two ounces, as it was before at one, *caeteris paribus*. Thus the riches of a country are to be valued by the *quantity of labour* its inhabitants are able to purchase" (*op. cit.*, p. 265).

From the outset Franklin regards labour-time from a restricted economic standpoint as the measure of value. The transformation of actual products into exchange-values is taken for granted, and it is therefore only a question of discovering a measure of their value.

To quote Franklin again: "Trade in general being nothing else but the exchange of labour for labour, the value of all things is, as I have said before, most justly measured by labour" (*op. cit.*, p. 267).

If in this sentence the term labour is replaced by concrete labour, it is at once obvious that labour in one form is being confused with labour in another form. Because trade may, for example, consist in the exchange of the labour of a shoemaker, miner, spinner, painter and so on, is therefore the labour of the painter the best measure of the value of shoes? Franklin, on the contrary, considers that the value of shoes, minerals, yarn, paintings, etc., is determined by abstract labour which has no particular quality and can thus be measured only in terms of quantity.** But since he does not explain that the labour contained in exchange-value is abstract universal social labour, which is brought

---

* Benjamin Franklin, *A Modest Inquiry into the Nature and Necessity of a Paper Currency*, in *The Works of Benjamin Franklin*, edit. by J. Sparks, Vol. II, Boston, 1836.
** *Remarks and Facts relative to the American Paper Money*, 1764 (*l.c.*).

about by the universal alienation of individual labour, he is bound to mistake money for the direct embodiment of this alienated labour. He therefore fails to see the intrinsic connection between money and labour which posits exchange-value, but on the contrary regards money as a convenient technical device which has been introduced into the sphere of exchange from outside.* Franklin's analysis of exchange-value had no direct influence on the general course of the science, because he dealt only with special problems of political economy for definite practical purposes.

The difference between concrete useful labour and labour which creates exchange-value aroused considerable interest in Europe during the eighteenth century in the following form: what particular kind of concrete labour is the source of bourgeois wealth? It was thus assumed that not every kind of labour which is materialised in use-values or yields products must thereby directly create wealth. But for both the Physiocrats and their opponents the crucial issue was not what kind of labour creates *value* but what kind of labour creates *surplus value*. They were thus discussing a complex form of the problem before having solved its elementary form; just as the historical progress of all sciences leads only through a multitude of contradictory moves to the real point of departure. Science, unlike other architects, builds not only castles in the air, but may construct separate habitable storeys of the building before laying the foundation stone. We shall now leave the Physiocrats and disregard a whole series of Italian economists, whose more or less pertinent ideas come close to a correct analysis of the commodity,** in order to turn at once to Sir *James Steuart*,*** the first Briton to expound a general system of bourgeois economy. The concept of exchange-value like the other

---

* See *Papers on American Politics*, and *Remarks and Facts relative to the American Paper Money*, 1764 (*l.c.*).

** See for instance Galiani, *Della Moneta*, Vol. III, in *Scrittori classici Italiani di Economia Politica* (published by Custodi), *Parte Moderna*, Milano, 1803. He says: "It is only toil" (*fatica*) "which gives value to things", p. 74. The term *"fatica"* for labour is characteristic of the southerner.

*** Steuart's work *An Inquiry into the Principles of Political Economy, Being an Essay on the Science of Domestic Policy in Free Nations* was first published in London in 1767, in two quarto volumes, ten years earlier than Adam Smith's *Wealth of Nations*. I quote from the Dublin edition of 1770.

abstract categories of political economy are in his work still in process of differentiation from their material content and therefore appear to be blurred and ambiguous. In one passage he determines *real value* by labour-time ("what a workman can perform in a day"), but beside it he introduces wages and raw material in a rather confusing way.* His struggle with the material content is brought out even more strikingly in another passage. He calls the physical element contained in a commodity, *e.g.*, the silver in silver filigree, its "*intrinsic worth*", and the labour-time contained in it its "*useful value*".

The first is according to him something "real in itself", whereas "the value of the second must be estimated according to the labour it has cost to produce it.... The labour employed in the modification represents a portion of a man's time."**

His clear differentiation between specifically social labour which manifests itself in exchange-value and concrete labour which yields use-values distinguishes Steuart from his predecessors and his successors.

"Labour," he says, "which through its alienation creates a universal equivalent, I call *industry*."

He distinguishes labour as industry not only from concrete labour but also from other social forms of labour. He sees in it the bourgeois form of labour as distinct from its antique and mediaeval forms. He is particularly interested in the difference between bourgeois and feudal labour, having observed the latter in the stage of its decline both in Scotland and during his extensive journeys on the continent. Steuart knew very well that in pre-bourgeois eras also products assumed the form of commodities and commodities that of money; but he shows in great detail that the commodity as the elementary and primary unit of wealth and alienation as the predominant form of appropriation are characteristic only of the bourgeois period of production, and that accordingly labour which creates exchange-value is a specifically bourgeois feature.***

---

* Steuart, *op. cit.*, Vol. I, pp. 181-83.
** *Ibid.*, pp. 361-62.
*** Steuart therefore declares that the patriarchal form of agriculture, whose direct aim is the production of use-values for the owner of the land, is an abuse, although not in Sparta or Rome or even in Athens,

Various kinds of concrete labour, such as agriculture, manufacture, shipping and commerce, had each in turn been claimed to constitute the real source of wealth, before *Adam Smith* declared that the sole source of material wealth or of use-values is labour in general, that is the entire social aspect of labour as it appears in the *division of labour*. Whereas in this context he completely overlooks the natural factor, he is pursued by it when he examines the sphere of purely social wealth, exchange-value. Although Adam Smith determines the value of commodities by the labour-time contained in them, he then nevertheless transfers this determination of value in actual fact to pre-Smithian times. In other words, what he regards as true when considering simple commodities becomes confused as soon as he examines the higher and more complex forms of capital, wage-labour, rent, etc. He expresses this in the following way: the value of commodities was measured by labour-time in the paradise lost of the bourgeoisie, where people did not confront one another as capitalists, wage-labourers, land-owners, tenant farmers, usurers, and so on, but simply as persons who produced commodities and exchanged them. Adam Smith constantly confuses the determination of the value of commodities by the labour-time contained in them with the determination of their value by the value of labour; he is often inconsistent in the details of his exposition and he mistakes the objective equalisation of unequal quantities of labour forcibly brought about by the social process for the subjective equality of the labours of individuals.* He

---

but certainly in the industrial countries of the eighteenth century. This "abusive agriculture" is not "trade" but a mere means of subsistence. Just as bourgeois agriculture clears the land of superfluous mouths, so bourgeois manufacture clears the factory of superfluous hands.

* Adam Smith writes for instance—"Equal quantities of labour, at all times and places, may be said to be of equal value to the labourer. In his ordinary state of health, strength, and spirits; in the ordinary degree of his skill and dexterity, he must always lay down the same portion of his ease, his liberty, and his happiness. The price which he pays must always be the same, whatever may be the quantity of goods which he receives in return for it. Of these, indeed, it may sometimes purchase a greater and sometimes a smaller quantity; but it is their value which varies, not that of the labour which purchases them.... Labour alone, therefore, never varying in its own value, is alone the ultimate and real standard by which the value of all commodities can ... be estimated.... It is their real price...." [*Wealth of Nations, Book I, Chapter V.*]

tries to accomplish the transition from concrete labour to labour which produces exchange-value, *i.e.*, the basic form of bourgeois labour, by means of the *division of labour*. But though it is correct to say that individual exchange presupposes division of labour, it is wrong to maintain that division of labour presupposes individual exchange. For example, division of labour had reached an exceptionally high degree of development among the Peruvians, although no individual exchange, no exchange of products in the form of commodities, took place.

David Ricardo, unlike Adam Smith, neatly sets forth the determination of the value of commodities by labour-time, and demonstrates that this law governs even those bourgeois relations of production which apparently contradict it most decisively. Ricardo's investigations are concerned exclusively with the *magnitude of value*, and regarding this he is at least aware that the operation of the law depends on definite historical pre-conditions. He says that the determination of value by labour-time applies to

"such commodities only as can be increased in quantity by the exertion of human industry, and on the production of which competition operates without restraint".*

This in fact means that the full development of the law of value presupposes a society in which large-scale industrial production and free competition obtain, in other words, modern bourgeois society. For the rest, the bourgeois form of labour is regarded by Ricardo as the eternal natural form of social labour. Ricardo's primitive fisherman and primitive hunter are from the outset owners of commodities who exchange their fish and game in proportion to the labour-time which is materialised in these exchange-values. On this occasion he slips into the anachronism of allowing the primitive fisherman and hunter to calculate the value of their implements in accordance with the annuity tables used on the London Stock Exchange in 1817. Apart from bourgeois society, the only social system with which Ricardo was acquainted seems to have been the "parallelograms of Mr. Owen".[14] Although encompassed by this bourgeois

---

* David Ricardo, *On the Principles of Political Economy, and Taxation*, Third Edition, London, 1821, p. 3.

horizon, Ricardo analyses bourgeois economy, whose deeper layers differ essentially from its surface appearance, with such theoretical acumen that Lord Brougham could say of him:

"Mr. Ricardo seemed as if he had dropped from another planet."

Arguing directly with Ricardo, *Sismondi* not only emphasises the specifically social character of labour which creates exchange-value,* but states also that it is a "characteristic feature of our economic progress" to reduce value to *necessary* labour-time, to

"the relation between the needs of the whole society and the quantity of labour which is sufficient to satisfy these needs".**

Sismondi is no longer preoccupied with Boisguillebert's notion that labour which creates exchange-value is distorted by money, but just as Boisguillebert denounced money so does Sismondi denounce large industrial capital. Whereas Ricardo's political economy ruthlessly draws its final conclusion and therewith ends, Sismondi supplements this ending by expressing doubt in political economy itself.

Since the determination of exchange-value by labour-time has been formulated and expounded in the clearest manner by Ricardo, who gave to classical political economy its final shape, it is quite natural that the arguments raised by economists should be primarily directed against him. If this polemic is stripped of its mainly trivial*** form it can be summarised as follows:

One. Labour itself has exchange-value and different types of labour have different exchange-values. If one makes exchange-value the measure of exchange-value, one is caught up in a vicious circle, for the exchange-value used as a measure requires in turn a measure. This objection merges

---

* Sismondi, *Etudes sur l'économie politique*, tome II, Bruxelles, 1838. "Trade has reduced the whole matter to the antithesis of use-value and exchange-value." P. 162.
** *Ibid.*, pp. 163-66 *et seq.*
*** It probably assumes the most trivial form in J. B. Say's annotations to the French translation—prepared by Constancio—of Ricardo's work, and the most pedantic and presumptuous in Mr. Macleod's recently published *Theory of Exchange*,[15] London, 1858.

into the following problem: given labour-time as the intrinsic measure of value, how are wages to be determined on this basis. The theory of wage-labour provides the answer to this.

Two. If the exchange-value of a product equals the labour-time contained in the product, then the exchange-value of a working day is equal to the product it yields, in other words, wages must be equal to the product of labour.* But in fact the opposite is true. *Ergo*, this objection amounts to the problem,—how does production on the basis of exchange-value solely determined by labour-time lead to the result that the exchange-value of labour is less than the exchange-value of its product? This problem is solved in our analysis of capital.

Three. In accordance with the changing conditions of demand and supply, the market-price of commodities falls below or rises above their exchange-value. The exchange-value of commodities is, *consequently*, determined not by the labour-time contained in them, but by the relation of demand and supply. In fact, this strange conclusion only raises the question how on the basis of exchange-value a market-price differing from this exchange-value comes into being, or rather, how the law of exchange-value asserts itself only in its antithesis. This problem is solved in the theory of competition.

---

* This objection, which was advanced against Ricardo by bourgeois economists, was later taken up by socialists. Assuming that the formula was theoretically sound, they alleged that practice stood in conflict with the theory and demanded that bourgeois society should draw the practical conclusions supposedly arising from its theoretical principles. In this way at least English socialists turned Ricardo's formula of exchange-value against political economy. The feat of declaring not only that the basic principle of the old society was to be the principle of the new society, but also that he was the inventor of the formula used by Ricardo to summarise the final result of English classical economics, was reserved to M. Proudhon. It has been shown that the utopian interpretation of Ricardo's formula was already completely forgotten in England, when M. Proudhon "discovered" it on the other side of the Channel. (*Cf.* the section on *la valeur constituée*, in my *Misère de la philosophie...*, Paris, 1847.[a])

---

[a] See Karl Marx, *The Poverty of Philosophy*, Moscow, 1962, pp. 43-49.—*Ed.*

Four. The last and apparently the decisive objection, unless it is advanced—as commonly happens—in the form of curious examples, is this: if exchange-value is nothing but the labour-time contained in a commodity, how does it come about that commodities which contain no labour possess exchange-value, in other words, how does the exchange-value of natural forces arise? This problem is solved in the theory of rent.

CHAPTER TWO

MONEY OR SIMPLE CIRCULATION

Gladstone, speaking in a parliamentary debate on Sir Robert Peel's Bank Act of 1844 and 1845, observed that even love has not turned more men into fools than has meditation upon the nature of money. He spoke of Britons to Britons. The Dutch, on the other hand, who in spite of Petty's doubts possessed a divine sense for money speculation from time immemorial, have never lost their senses in speculation about money.

The principal difficulty in the analysis of money is surmounted as soon as it is understood that the commodity is the origin of money. After that it is only a question of clearly comprehending the specific form peculiar to it. This is not so easy because all bourgeois relations appear to be gilded, *i.e.*, they appear to be money relations, and the money form, therefore, seems to possess an infinitely varied content, which is quite alien to this form.

During the following analysis it is important to keep in mind that we are only concerned with those forms of money which arise directly from the exchange of commodities, but not with forms of money, such as credit money, which belong to a higher stage of production. For the sake of simplicity gold is assumed throughout to be the money commodity.

1. MEASURE OF VALUE

The first phase of circulation is, as it were, a theoretical phase preparatory to real circulation. Commodities, which exist as use-values, must first of all assume a form in which they *appear* to one another nominally as exchange-values, as definite quantities of materialised *universal* labour-time.

The first necessary move in this process is, as we have seen, that the commodities set apart a specific commodity, say, *gold*, which becomes the direct reification of universal labour-time or the universal equivalent. Let us return for a moment to the form in which gold is converted into money by commodities.

1 ton of iron	= 2 ounces of gold
1 quarter of wheat	= 1 ounce of gold
1 hundredweight of Mocha coffee	= $1/4$ ounce of gold
1 hundredweight of potash	= $1/2$ ounce of gold
1 ton of Brazil-timber	= $1^1/2$ ounces of gold
Y commodities	= X ounces of gold

In this series of equations iron, wheat, coffee, potash, etc., appear to one another as materialisation of uniform labour, that is labour materialised in gold, in which all distinctive features of the concrete labour represented in the different use-values are entirely obliterated. They are as values identical, *i.e.*, materialisations of the *same* labour or the *same* materialisation of labour—gold. Since they are uniform materialisations of the same labour, they differ only in *one way*, quantitatively: in other words they represent different magnitudes of value, because their use-values contain *unequal* amounts of labour-time. These individual commodities can be compared with one another as embodiments of universal labour-time, since they have been compared with universal labour-time in the shape of the excluded commodity, *i.e.*, gold. The same dynamic relation, as a result of which commodities become exchange-values for one another, causes the labour-time contained in gold to represent universal labour-time, a given amount of which is expressed in different quantities of iron, wheat, coffee, etc., in short in the use-values of all commodities, or it may be displayed directly in the infinite series of commodity equivalents. Since the exchange-value of all commodities is expressed in gold, the exchange-value of gold is directly expressed in all commodities. Because the commodities themselves assume the form of exchange-value for one another, they turn gold into the universal equivalent or into money.

Gold becomes the *measure of value* because the exchange-value of *all* commodities is measured in gold, is expressed in the relation of a definite quantity of gold and a definite quantity of commodity containing equal amounts of labour-time. To begin with, gold becomes the universal equivalent, or money, only because it thus functions as the measure of value and as such its own value is measured directly in all commodity equivalents. The exchange-value of all commodities, on the other hand, is now expressed in gold. One has to distinguish a qualitative and a quantitative aspect in this expression. The exchange-value of the commodity exists as the embodiment of equal uniform labour-time, the value of the commodity is thus fully expressed, for to the extent that commodities are equated with gold they are equated with one another. Their golden equivalent reflects the *universal* character of the labour-time contained in them on the one hand, and its quantity on the other hand. The exchange-value of commodities thus expressed in the form of universal equivalence and simultaneously as the degree of this equivalence in terms of a specific commodity, that is a single equation in which commodities are compared with a specific commodity, constitutes *price*. Price is the converted form in which the exchange-value of commodities *appears* within the circulation process.

Thus as a result of the same process through which the values of commodities are expressed in gold prices, gold is transformed into the measure of value and thence into money. If the values of all commodities were measured in silver or wheat or copper, and accordingly expressed in terms of silver, wheat or copper prices, then silver, wheat or copper would become the measure of value and consequently universal equivalents. Commodities as exchange-values must be antecedent to circulation in order to appear as prices in circulation. Gold becomes the measure of value only because the exchange-value of all commodities is estimated in terms of gold. The universality of this dynamic relation, from which alone springs the capacity of gold to act as a measure, presupposes however that every single commodity is measured in terms of gold in accordance with the labour-time contained in both, so that the real measure of commodity and gold is labour itself, that is commodity and gold are as exchange-values equated by direct exchange. How this equating is carried through in practice cannot be discussed in the context of simple circulation. It is evident, however, that in countries where gold and silver are produced a definite amount of labour-time is directly incorporated in a definite quantity of gold and silver, whereas countries which produce no gold and silver arrive at the same result in a roundabout way, by direct or indirect exchange of their home products, *i.e.*, of a definite portion of their average national labour, for a definite quantity of labour-time embodied in the gold and silver of countries that possess mines. Gold must be in principle a *variable* value, if it is to serve as a measure of value, because only as reification of labour-time can it become the equivalent of other commodities, but as a result of changes in the productivity of concrete labour, the same amount of labour-time is embodied in unequal volumes of the same type of use-values. The valuation of all commodities in terms of gold—like the expression of the exchange-value of any commodity in terms of the use-value of another commodity —merely presupposes that at a given moment gold represents a definite quantity of labour-time. The law of exchange-value set forth earlier applies to changes occurring in the value of gold. If the exchange-value of commodities remains unchanged, then a general rise of their prices in terms of gold can only take place when the exchange-value of gold falls. If the exchange-value of gold remains unchanged, then a general rise of prices in terms of gold is only possible if the exchange-values of all commodities rise. The reverse takes place in the case of a general decline in the prices of commodities. If the value of an ounce of gold falls or rises in consequence of a change in the labour-time required for its production, then it will fall or rise *equally* in relation to all other commodities and will thus for all of them continue to represent a *definite* volume of labour-time. The same exchange-values will now be estimated in quantities of gold which are larger or smaller than before, but they will be estimated in accordance with their values and will therefore maintain the same value relative to one another. The ratio 2:4:8 remains the same whether it becomes 1:2:4 or 4:8:16. The fact that, because of the changing value of gold, exchange-values are represented by varying quantities of gold does not prevent gold from functioning as the measure of value, any more than the fact that the value of silver is one-fifteenth of that of gold prevents silver from taking over this function. Labour-time is the measure of both gold and commodities, and gold becomes the measure of value only because all commodities are measured in terms of gold; it is consequently merely an illusion created by the circulation process to suppose that money makes commodities commensurable.* On the contrary, it is only the commensurability of commodities as material-ised labour-time which converts gold into money.

The concrete form in which commodities enter the process of exchange is as use-values. The commodities will only become universal equivalents as a result of their alienation. The establishment of their price is merely their nominal conversion into the universal equivalent, an equation with gold which still has to be put into practice. But because prices convert commodities only nominally into gold or only into imaginary gold—*i.e.*, the existence of commodities as money is indeed not yet separated from their real existence —gold has been merely transformed into imaginary money, only into the measure of value, and definite quantities of gold serve in fact simply as names for definite quantities of labour-time. The distinct form in which gold crystallises into money depends in each case on the way in which the exchange-values of commodities are represented with regard to one another.

Commodities now confront one another in a dual form, really as use-values and nominally as exchange-values.

---

* Aristotle does indeed realise that the exchange-value of commodi-ties is antecedent to the prices of commodities: "That exchange took place thus before there was money is plain; for it makes no difference whether it is five beds that exchange for a house, or the money value of five beds." On the other hand, since it is only in price that com-modities possess the form of exchange-value in relation to one another, he makes them commensurable by means of money. "This is why all goods must have a price set on them; for then there will always be exchange, and if so, association of man with man. Money, then, acting as a measure, makes goods commensurate and equates them; for neither would there have been association if there were not exchange, nor exchange if there were not equality, nor equality if there were not commensurability." Aristotle is aware of the fact that the different things measured by money are entirely incommensurable magnitudes. What he seeks is the oneness of commodities as exchange-values, and since he lived in ancient Greece it was impossible for him to find it. He extricates himself from this predicament by making essentially incommensurable things commensurable—so far as this is necessary for practical needs—by means of money. "Now in truth it is impossible that things differing so much should become commensurate, but with reference to demand they may become so sufficiently" (Aristoteles, *Ethica Nicomachea*, L. 5, C. 8, edit. Bekkeri, Oxonii, 1837). [The English text is from Aristotle—*Ethica Nicomachea*, Book V, Chapter 8, translation by W. D. Ross, Oxford, 1925, 1133b.]

They represent now for one another the dual form of labour contained in them, since the particular concrete labour actually exists as their use-value, while universal abstract labour-time assumes an imaginary existence in their price, in which they are all alike embodiments of the same substance of value, differing only quantitatively.

The difference between exchange-value and price is, on the one hand, merely nominal; as Adam Smith says, labour is the real price of commodities and money their nominal price. Instead of saying that one quarter of wheat is worth thirty days' labour, one now says it is worth one ounce of gold, when one ounce of gold is produced in thirty working days. The difference is on the other hand so far from being simply a nominal difference that all the storms which threaten the commodity in the actual process of circulation centre upon it. A quarter of wheat contains thirty days' labour, and it therefore does not have to be expressed in terms of labour-time. But gold is a commodity distinct from wheat, and only circulation can show whether the quarter of wheat is actually turned into an ounce of gold as has been anticipated in its price. This depends on whether or not the wheat proves to be a use-value, whether or not the quantity of labour-time contained in it proves to be the quantity of labour-time necessarily required by society for the production of a quarter of wheat. The commodity as such *is* an exchange-value, the commodity *has* a price. This difference between exchange-value and price is a reflection of the fact that the particular individual labour contained in the commodity can only through alienation be represented as its opposite, impersonal, abstract, general—and only in this form social—labour, *i.e.*, money. Whether it can be thus represented or not seems a matter of chance. Although, therefore, the price gives exchange-value a form of existence which is only nominally distinct from the commodity, and the two aspects of the labour contained in the commodity appear as yet only as different modes of expression; while, on the other hand, gold, the embodiment of universal labour-time, accordingly confronts concrete commodities merely as an imaginary measure of value; yet the existence of price as an expression of exchange-value, or of gold as a measure of value, entails the necessity for alienation of commodities in exchange for glittering gold and thus the possibility of their non-alienation. In short, there is here contained in latent form the whole contradiction which arises because the product is a commodity, or because the particular labour of an isolated individual can become socially effective only if it is expressed as its direct opposite, *i.e.*, abstract universal labour. The utopians who wish to retain commodities but not money, production based on private exchange without the essential conditions for this type of production, are therefore quite consistent when they seek to "abolish" money not only in its palpable state but even in the nebulous, chimerical state that it assumes as the measure of value. For beneath the invisible measure of value lurks hard money.

Given the process by which gold has been turned into the measure of value and exchange-value into price, all commodities when expressed in their prices are merely imagined quantities of gold of various magnitudes. Since they are thus various quantities of the same thing, namely gold, they are similar, comparable and commensurable, and thus arises the technical necessity of relating them to a definite quantity of gold as a *unit of measure*. This unit of measure then develops into a scale of measure by being divided into aliquot parts which are in turn subdivided into aliquot parts.* The quantities of gold themselves, however, are measured by weight. The standard weights generally used for metals accordingly provide ready-made standard measures, which originally also served as standard measures of price wherever metallic currency was in use. Since commodities are no longer compared as exchange-values which are measured in terms of labour-time, but as magnitudes of the same denomination measured in terms of gold, gold, the *measure of value*, becomes the *standard of price*. The comparison of commodity-prices in terms of different quantities of gold thus becomes crystallised in figures denoting imaginary quantities of gold and representing gold as a standard measure divided into aliquot parts. Gold as measure of value

---

* The strange fact that the ounce of gold as the standard of money in England is not divided into aliquot parts is accounted for as follows: "Our coinage was originally adapted to the employment of silver only—hence an ounce of silver can always be divided into a certain aliquot number of pieces of coin; but, as gold was introduced at a later period into a coinage adapted only to silver, an ounce of gold cannot be coined into an aliquot number of pieces" (James Maclaren, *A Sketch of the History of the Currency*, London, 1858, p. 16).

and as standard of price has quite distinct specific functions, and the confusion of the one with the other has led to the most absurd theories. Gold as materialised labour-time is a measure of value, as a piece of metal of definite weight it is the standard of price. Gold becomes the measure of value because as an exchange-value it is compared with the exchange-values of other commodities; in its aspect as a standard of price a definite quantity of gold serves as a unit for other quantities of gold. Gold is the measure of value because its value is variable; it is the standard of price because it has been established as an invariable unit of weight. Here, as in all cases of measuring quantities of the same denomination, stability and exactitude of the proportions is essential. The necessity of establishing a quantity of gold as the unit of measure and its aliquot parts as subdivisions of this unit has given rise to the idea that a fixed ratio of values has been set up between a definite quantity of gold, whose value is of course variable, and the exchange-values of commodities. But such a view simply ignores the fact that the exchange-values of commodities are turned into prices, into quantities of gold, before gold becomes the standard of price. Quite irrespective of any changes in the value of gold, different quantities of gold will always represent the same ratio of values with regard to one another. If the value of gold should fall by 1,000 per cent, then the value of twelve ounces of gold would still be twelve times bigger than that of one ounce of gold, and so far as prices are concerned what matters is only the proportion of the different quantities of gold to one another. Since, on the other hand, a rise or fall in the value of an ounce of gold does not in any way affect its weight, the weight of its aliquot parts remains likewise unaffected; gold can thus always serve as a stable standard of price, regardless of any changes in its value.*

---

* "Money may continually vary in value, and yet be as good a measure of value as if it remained perfectly stationary. Suppose, for example, it is reduced in value.... Before the reduction, a guinea would purchase three bushels of wheat or six days' labour; subsequently, it would purchase only two bushels of wheat, or four days' labour. In both these cases, the relations of wheat and labour to money being given, their mutual relations can be inferred; in other words, we can ascertain that a bushel of wheat is worth two days' labour. This, which is all that measuring value implies, is as readily done after the reduction as before. The excellence of any thing as a measure of value is altogether independent of its own variableness in

As a result of an historical process, which, as we shall explain later, was determined by the nature of metallic currency, the names of particular weights were retained for constantly changing and diminishing weights of precious metals functioning as the standard of price. Thus the English pound sterling denotes less than one-third of its original weight, the pound Scots before the Union[16] only $^1/_{36}$, the French livre $^1/_{74}$, the Spanish maravedi less than $^1/_{1,000}$ and the Portuguese rei an even smaller proportion. Historical development thus led to a separation of the money names of certain weights of metals from the common names of these weights.* Because the designation of the unit of measure, its aliquot parts and their names is, on the one hand, purely conventional, and on the other hand must be accepted as universal and indispensable within the sphere of circulation, it had to be established by *legal* means. The purely formal enactment thus devolved upon the government.**

---

value" (Samuel Bailey, *Money and its Vicissitudes*, London, 1837, pp. 9, 10).

* "The coins whose names are now only imaginary are the oldest coins of every nation; all their names were for a time real" (so generally stated the latter assertion is incorrect) "and precisely because they were real they were used for calculation" (Galiani, *Della Moneta, op. cit.*, p. 153).

** The romantic A. Müller says: "According to our views every independent sovereign has the right to introduce metallic currency and ascribe to it a social nominal value, order, position and title" (Adam H. Müller, *Die Elemente der Staatskunst*, Berlin, 1809, Band II, p. 288). The aulic councillor is right as regards the title, but he forgets the *content*. How confused his "views" are becomes evident, for instance, in the following passage: "Everybody realises how important it is to determine the price of coins correctly, especially in a country like England, where the government with *splendid generosity* coins money gratuitously" (Mr. Müller apparently assumes that the members of the British government defray the costs of minting out of their own pocket), "where it does not levy seigniorage, etc., and consequently if it were to fix the mint-price of gold considerably above the market-price, if instead of paying £3 17s. 10½d. for an ounce of gold as at present, it should decide to fix the price of an ounce of gold at £3 19s., all money would flow into the mint and the silver obtained there would be exchanged for the cheaper gold on the market, and then it would again be taken to the mint, thus throwing the monetary system into disorder" (*op. cit.*, pp. 280, 281). Müller throws his ideas into "disorder", so as to preserve order at the mint in England. Whereas shillings and pence are merely names, that is names of definite fractions of an ounce of gold represented by silver and copper tokens, he imagines that an ounce of gold is estimated in terms of gold, silver and copper and thus confers upon the English a triple standard of value. Silver

Which particular metal served as the material of money depended on the given social conditions. The standard of price is of course different in different countries. In England, for example, the ounce as a weight of metal is divided into pennyweights, grains and carats troy; but the ounce of gold as the unit of money is divided into $3^7/_8$ sovereigns, the sovereign into 20 shillings and the shilling into 12 pence, so that 100 pounds of 22-carat gold (1,200 ounces) equal 4,672 sovereigns and 10 shillings. But in the world market, where state frontiers disappear, such national features of the standards of money disappear as well and are replaced by measures of weight generally used for metals.

The price of a commodity, or the quantity of gold into which it is nominally converted, is now expressed therefore in the monetary names of the standard of gold. Thus, instead of saying a quarter of wheat is worth an ounce of gold, one would say in England it is worth £3 17s. $10^1/_2$d. All prices are thus expressed in the same denomination. The specific form which the exchange-value of commodities assumes is converted into *denominations of money*, by which their value is expressed. Money in turn becomes *money of account*.*

The transformation of commodities into money of account in the mind, on paper or in words takes place whenever the aspect of exchange-value becomes fixed in a particular type of wealth.** This transformation needs the material of gold, but only in imagination. Not a single atom of real gold is used to estimate the value of a thousand bales of cotton in terms of a certain number of ounces of gold and then to express this number of ounces in £. s. d., the names

as the standard of money along with gold was formally abolished only in 1816 by 56 George III, C. 68, although it was in fact legally abolished by 14 George II, C. 42 in 1734, and in practice even earlier. Two circumstances in particular enabled *A. Müller* to arrive at a so-called *higher* conception of political economy: first his extensive ignorance of economic facts and second his purely amateurish infatuation with philosophy.

* "When Anacharsis was asked what the Hellenes used money for, he replied—for calculation" (Athenaeus, *Deipnosophistai*, L. IV, 49, v. II, [p. 120], ed. Schweighäuser, 1802).

** G. Garnier, one of the first to translate Adam Smith into French, had the odd idea of establishing the proportion between the use of money of account and that of real money. [According to him] this proportion is 10 to 1 (G. Garnier, *Histoire de la monnaie depuis les temps de la plus haute antiquité*, t. I, p. 78).

of account of the ounce. For instance, not a single ounce of gold was in circulation in Scotland before Sir Robert Peel's Bank Act of 1845, although the ounce of gold, called £3 17s. 10^1/$_2$d. as the British standard of account, served as the legal standard of price. Similarly, silver serves as the standard of price in exchange of commodities between Siberia and China, although this trade is in fact merely barter. It makes no difference, therefore, to gold as money of account whether or not its standard unit or its subdivisions are actually coined. During the reign of William the Conqueror, one pound sterling, at that time a pound of pure silver, and the shilling, ^{1}/$_{20}$ of a pound, existed in England only as money of account, while the penny, ^{1}/$_{240}$ of a pound of silver, was the largest silver coin in existence. On the other hand, there are no shillings or pence in England today, although they are legal names of account for definite fractions of an ounce of gold. Money as money of account may exist only nominally, while actually existing money may be coined according to an entirely different standard. Thus in many of the English colonies in North America, the money in circulation consisted of Spanish and Portuguese coins till late in the eighteenth century, whereas the money of account was everywhere the same as in England.*

Because as standard of price gold is expressed by the same names of account as the prices of commodities—for example £3 17s. 10^1/$_2$d. may denote an ounce of gold just as well as a ton of iron—these names of account are called the *mint-price* of gold. Thus the queer notion arose that gold is estimated in its own material and that, unlike all other commodities, its price is *fixed* by the State. The establishing of names of account for definite weights of gold was mistaken for the establishing of the value of these weights.**

---

* The Act of Maryland of 1723, which made tobacco legal currency but converted its value into English gold money, by declaring a pound of tobacco equal to a penny, recalls the *leges barbarorum*,[17] which on the contrary equated definite sums of money with oxen, cows, etc. In this case the real material of the money of account was neither gold nor silver, but the ox and the cow.

** Thus we read, for example, in the *Familiar Words* of Mr. *David Urquhart*—"The value of gold is to be measured by itself; how can any substance be the measure of its own worth in other things? The worth of gold is to be established by its own weight, under a false denomination of that weight—and an ounce is to be worth so many 'pounds' and fractions of pounds. This is falsifying a measure, not establishing a standard" [pp. 104-05].

Gold has neither a *fixed* price *nor any* price at all, when it is a factor in the determination of prices and therefore functions as money of account. In order to have a price, in other words to be expressed in terms of a *specific* commodity functioning as the *universal* equivalent, this other commodity would have to play the same exclusive role in the process of circulation as gold. But two commodities which exclude all other commodities would exclude each other as well. Consequently, wherever silver and gold exist side by side as legal money, *i.e.*, as measure of value, the vain attempt has always been made to treat them as *one and the same substance*. If one assumes that a given labour-time is invariably materialised in the same proportion in silver and gold, then one assumes, in fact, that silver and gold are the same substance, and that silver, the less valuable metal, represents a constant fraction of gold. The history of the monetary system in England from the reign of Edward III up to the time of George II consists of a continuous series of disturbances caused by conflict between the legally established ratio between the values of gold and silver and the actual fluctuations in their value. Sometimes the value of gold was too high, sometimes that of silver. The metal whose value was estimated at too low a rate was withdrawn from circulation, melted down and exported. The value-ratio of the two metals was then once again changed by law; but soon the new nominal value in its turn clashed with the actual value-ratio. In our own time, the slight and short-lived fall in the value of gold as compared with silver, brought about by the Indian and Chinese demand for silver, produced the same phenomenon on a large scale in France—the export of silver and the elimination of silver from the sphere of circulation by gold. During the years 1855, 1856 and 1857, the excess of France's gold imports over her gold exports amounted to £41,580,000, while the excess of her silver exports over silver imports came to £34,704,000.[a] In countries like France, where both metals are legally sanctioned measures of value and both are accepted as legal tender, where moreover every person can pay in the one or the other metal as he pleases, the metal whose value rises is in fact at a premium, and its price

---

[a] Earlier editions of *A Contribution to the Critique of Political Economy* erroneously gave this figure as £14,704,000.—*Ed.*

like that of any other commodity is measured in terms of the over-rated metal, which thus serves alone as the measure of value. All historical experience in this sphere simply shows that, where two commodities function as legally valid measures of value, it is always one of them only which actually maintains this position.*

B. Theories of the Standard of Money

The fact that commodities are only nominally converted in the form of prices into gold and hence gold is only nominally transformed into money led to the doctrine of the *nominal standard of money*. Because only imaginary gold or silver, *i.e.*, gold and silver merely as money of account, is used in the determination of prices, it was asserted that the terms pound, shilling, pence, thaler, franc, etc., denote ideal particles of value but not weights of gold or silver or any form of materialised labour. If, for example, the value of an ounce of silver were to rise, it would contain more of these particles and would therefore have to be divided or coined into a greater number of shillings. This doctrine, which arose at the close of the seventeenth century, was again advanced during the last commercial crisis in England and was even advocated by Members of Parliament in two special reports appended to the 1858 Report of the Select Committee on the Bank Acts. In England at the time of the accession of William III, the mint-price of an ounce of silver was 5s. 2d., that is $^{1}/_{62}$ of an ounce of silver was called a penny and 12 of these pence were called a shilling. A bar of silver weighing say six ounces would, according to this standard, be coined into 31 coins which would be called shillings. But whereas the *mint-price* of an ounce of silver was 5s. 2d., its *market-price* rose to 6s. 3d., that is to say in order to buy an ounce of uncoined silver 6s. 3d. had to be handed over. How was it possible for the market-price of an ounce of silver to rise

---

* "Money is the measure of commerce ... and therefore ought to be kept (as all other measures) as steady and invariable as may be. But this cannot be, if your money be made of two metals, whose proportion ... constantly varies in respect of one another" (John Locke, *Some Considerations on the Lowering of Interest*, 1691; in his *Works*, 7th Edition, London, 1768, Vol. II, p. 65).

above its mint-price, if the mint-price was merely a name of account for fractions of an ounce of silver? The solution of this riddle was quite simple. Four million of the £5,600,000 of silver money in circulation at that time were worn out or clipped. A trial showed that £57,200 in silver coins, whose weight ought to have been 220,000 ounces, weighed only 141,000 ounces. The mint continued to coin silver pieces according to the same standard, but the lighter shillings which were actually in circulation represented smaller fractions of an ounce than their name denoted. A larger quantity of these reduced shillings had consequently to be paid for an ounce of uncoined silver on the market. When, because of the resulting difficulties, it was decided to recoin all the money, *Lowndes*, the Secretary to the Treasury, claimed that the value of an ounce of silver had risen and that in future accordingly 6s. 3d. would have to be struck from an ounce instead of 5s. 2d. as previously. He thus in effect asserted that, because the value of an ounce of silver had risen, the value of its aliquot parts had fallen. But his false theory was merely designed to make a correct practical measure more palatable. The government debts had been contracted in light shillings, were they to be repaid in coins of standard weight? Instead of saying pay back 4 ounces of silver for every 5 ounces you received nominally but which contained in fact only 4 ounces of silver, he said, on the contrary, pay back nominally 5 ounces but reduce their metal content to 4 ounces and call the amount you hitherto called ⁴/₅ of a shilling a shilling. Lowndes's action, therefore, was in reality based on the metal content, whereas in theory he stuck to the name of account. His opponents on the other hand, who simply clung to the name of account and therefore declared that a shilling of standard weight was identical with a shilling which was 25 to 50 per cent lighter, claimed to be adhering to the metal content. *John Locke*, who championed the new bourgeoisie in every way—he took the side of the manufacturers against the working classes and the paupers, the merchants against the old-fashioned usurers, the financial aristocracy against governments that were in debt; he even demonstrated in a separate work that the bourgeois way of thinking is the normal human way of thinking—took up Lowndes's challenge. John Locke won the day and money borrowed in guineas containing 10 to 14 shillings was repaid in guineas of 20 shillings.* Sir *James Steuart* gives the following ironical summary of this operation:

"...the state gained considerably upon the score of taxes, as well as the creditors upon their capitals and interest; and the nation, which was the principal loser, was pleased; because their *standard*" (the standard of their own value) "was not debased."**

Steuart believed that in the course of further development of commerce the nation would become wiser. But he was wrong. Some 120 years later the same *quid pro quo* was repeated.

Very fittingly it was Bishop *Berkeley*, the advocate of mystical idealism in English philosophy, who gave the doctrine of the nominal standard of money a theoretical

---

* Locke says *inter alia*: "...call that a Crown now, which before ... was but a part of a Crown ... wherein an equal quantity of Silver is always the same Value with an equal quantity of Silver.... For if the abating $^1/_{20}$ of the quantity of Silver of any Coin does not lessen its Value, the abating $^{19}/_{20}$ of the quantity of the Silver of any Coin will not abate its Value. And so ... a single Penny, being called a Crown, will buy as much Spice, or Silk, or any other Commodity, as a Crown-Piece, which contains [20 or] 60 times as much Silver." All you can do is to raise "your Money, ... giving a less quantity of Silver the Stamp and Denomination of a greater", but "'tis Silver and not Names that pay Debts and purchase Commodities". "The raising being but giving of names at pleasure to aliquot parts of any piece, *viz.* that now the sixtieth part of an ounce still be called a penny, may be done with what increase you please." In reply to Lowndes's arguments, Locke declares that the rise of the market-price above the mint-price was not brought about by an increase in the value of silver, but by a decrease in the weight of coins. Seventy-seven clipped shillings did not weigh more than 62 shillings of standard weight. Finally Locke is quite correct in emphasising that, irrespective of the loss of silver suffered by the coins in circulation, a certain rise in the market-price of silver bullion over the mint-price might occur in England, because the export of silver bullion was permitted whereas that of silver coin was prohibited (see *op. cit.*, pp. 54-116 *passim*). Locke takes good care to avoid the vital issue of the National Debt, just as he equally prudently refrains from discussing another ticklish economic problem, *i.e.*, that according to the evidence of both the exchange rate and the ratio of silver bullion to silver coin, the depreciation of the money in circulation was by *no* means proportional to the amount of silver it lost. We shall return to this question in its general form in the section dealing with the medium of circulation. In *A discourse Concerning Coining the New Money Lighter, in Answer to Mr. Locke's Considerations*, London, 1696, Nicholas Barbon vainly sought to entice Locke on to difficult ground.

** Steuart, *op. cit.*, Vol. II, p. 156.

twist, which the practical Secretary to the Treasury had omitted to do. Berkeley asks

"Whether the terms Crown, Livre, Pound Sterling, etc., are not to be considered as Exponents or *Denominations of such Proportions*?" (*i.e.*, proportions of abstract value as such). "And whether Gold, Silver, and Paper are not Tickets or Counters for Reckoning, Recording and Transferring thereof?" (of the proportion of value). "Whether *Power* to command the Industry" (social labour) "of others be not real Wealth? And whether Money be not in Truth, Tickets or Tokens for conveying and recording such Power, and whether it be of great consequence what Materials the Tickets are made of?"*

In this passage, the author, on the one hand, confuses the measure of value with the standard of price, and on the other he confuses gold or silver as measure of value and as means of circulation. Because tokens can be substituted for precious metals in the sphere of circulation, Berkeley concludes that these tokens in their turn represent *nothing*, *i.e.*, the abstract concept of value.

The theory of the nominal standard of money was so fully elaborated by Sir *James Steuart*, that his followers— they are not aware of being followers since they do not know him—can find neither a new expression nor even a new example. He writes:

"Money, which I call of account, is no more than an arbitrary scale of equal parts, invented for measuring the respective value of things vendible. Money of account, therefore, is quite a different thing from money-coin, which is price** and might exist, although there was no such thing in the world as any substance which could become an adequate and proportional equivalent, for every commodity.... Money of account ... performs the same office with regard to the value of things, that degrees, minutes, seconds, etc., do with regard to angles, or as scales do to geographical maps, or to plans of any kind. In all these inventions, there is constantly some denomination taken for the unit.... The usefulness of all these inventions being solely confined to the *marking of proportion*. Just so the unit in money can have no invariable determinate proportion to any part of value, that is to say it cannot be fixed to any particular quantity of gold, silver, or any other commodity whatsoever. The unit once fixed, we can, by multiplying it, ascend to the greatest value.... The value of commodities, there-

---

* *The Querist, loc. cit.* Incidentally, the section "Queries on Money" is rather witty. Among other things it contains the true observation that the development of the North American colonies "makes it plain as daylight, that gold and silver are not so necessary for the wealth of a nation, as the vulgar of all ranks imagine".
** Here, as in the works of seventeenth-century English economists, *price* is used in the sense of a concrete equivalent.

fore, depending upon a general combination of circumstances relative to themselves and to the fancies of men, their value ought to be considered as changing only with respect to one another; consequently, anything which troubles or perplexes the ascertaining those changes of proportion by the means of a general, determinate and invariable scale, must be hurtful to trade.... Money ... is an *ideal scale* of equal parts. If it be demanded what ought to be the standard value of one part? I answer by putting another question: What is the standard length of a degree, a minute, a second? It has none ... but so soon as one part becomes determined by the nature of a scale, all the rest must follow in proportion. Of this kind of money ... we have two examples. The bank of Amsterdam presents us with the one, the coast of Angola with the other."*

Steuart simply considers money *as it appears* in the sphere of circulation, *i.e.*, as *standard of price* and as *money of account*. If different commodities are quoted at 15s., 20s. and 36s. respectively in a price list, then in a comparison of their value both the silver content of the shilling and its name are indeed quite irrelevant. Everything is now expressed in the numerical relations of 15, 20 and 36, and the numeral one has become the sole unit of measure. The purely abstract expression of a proportion is after all only the abstract numerical proportion. In order to be consistent, Steuart therefore had to abandon not only gold and silver but also their legal designations. But since he does not understand how the measure of value is transformed into the standard of price, he naturally thinks that the particular quantity of gold which serves as a unit of measure is, as a measure, related to values as such, and not to other quantities of gold. Because commodities appear to be magnitudes of the same denomination as a result of the conversion of their exchange-values into prices, Steuart denies the existence of the characteristic feature of the measure which reduces commodities to the same denomination, and since in this comparison of different quantities of gold the quantity of gold which serves as a standard is conventionally established, he denies that it must be established at all. Instead of calling a 360th part of a circle a degree, he might call a 180th part a degree; the right angle would then measure not 90 degrees but 45, and the measurements of acute and obtuse angles would change correspondingly. Nevertheless, the measure of the angle would remain firstly a qualitatively determined mathematical figure, the circle,

---

* Steuart, *op. cit.*, Vol. II, pp. 102-07.

and secondly a quantitatively determined section of the circle. As for Steuart's economic examples one of these disproves his own assertions, the other proves nothing at all. The money of the Bank of Amsterdam was in fact only the name of account for Spanish doubloons, which retained their standard weight because they lay idle in the vaults of the bank, while the coins which busily circulated lost weight as a result of intensive friction with their environment. As for the African idealists, we must leave them to their fate until reliable accounts of travellers provide further information about them.* One might say that the French assignat—*"National property, Assignment of 100 francs"*—is nearly ideal money in Steuart's sense. The use-value which the assignat was supposed to represent, *i.e.*, confiscated land, was indeed specified, but the quantitative definition of the unit of measure had been omitted, and "franc" was therefore a meaningless word. How much or little land this franc represented depended on the outcome of public auctions. But in practice the assignat circulated as a token representing silver money, and its depreciation was consequently measured in terms of this silver standard.

The period when the Bank of England suspended cash payments was hardly more prolific of war bulletins than of monetary theories. The depreciation of bank-notes and the rise of the market-price of gold above its mint-price caused some defenders of the Bank to revive the doctrine of the ideal measure of money. Lord *Castlereagh* found the classically confused expression for this confused notion when he declared that the standard of money is "a sense of value in reference to currency as compared with commodities". A few years after the Treaty of Paris when the situation permitted the resumption of cash payments, the problem which Lowndes had broached during the reign of William III arose again in practically the same form. A huge national debt and a mass of private debts, fixed obligations, etc., which had accumulated in the course of over 20 years,

---

* In connection with the last commercial crisis a certain faction in England ardently praised the ideal African money after moving its location on this occasion from the coast into the interior of Barbary. It was declared that because their bars constituted an ideal measure, the Berbers had no commercial and industrial crises. Would it not have been simpler to say that commerce and industry are the *conditio sine qua non* for commercial and industrial crises?

were incurred in depreciated bank-notes. Should they be repaid in bank-notes £4,672 10s. of which represented, not in name but in fact, 100 lbs. of 22-carat gold? *Thomas Attwood*, a Birmingham banker, acted like a resurrected Lowndes. He advocated that as many shillings should be returned to the creditors as they had nominally lent, but whereas according to the old monetary standard, say, $1/_{78}$ of an ounce of gold was known as a shilling, now perhaps $1/_{90}$ of an ounce should be called a shilling. Attwood's supporters are known as the Birmingham school of "little shilling men". The quarrel about the ideal standard of money, which began in 1819, was still carried on in 1845 by Sir Robert Peel and Attwood, whose wisdom in so far as it concerns the function of money as a measure is fully summarised in the following quotation:

During "the recent discussion between Sir Robert Peel and the Birmingham Chamber of Commerce.... The Minister was quite satisfied with asking the question, 'What will your pound note represent?' ....What is to be understood by the present standard of value? Is £3 17s. 10$^1/_2$d. an *ounce* of gold, or is it only of the *value* of an ounce of gold? If £3 17s. 10$^1/_2$d. be an *ounce of gold*, why not call things by their proper names, and, dropping the terms pounds, shillings and pence, say ounces, pennyweights and grains?... If we adopt the terms ounces, pennyweights and grains of gold, as our monetary system, we should pursue a direct system of barter.... But if gold be estimated as of the value of £3 17s. 10$^1/_2$d. per ounce ... how is this ... that much difficulty has been experienced at different periods to check gold from rising to £5 4s. per ounce, and we now notice that gold is quoted at £3 17s. 9d. per ounce?... The expression *pound* has reference to value, but not a fixed standard value.... The term pound is the *ideal unit....* Labour is the parent of cost and gives the relative value to gold or iron. *Whatever denomination of words are used to express the daily or weekly labour of a man,* such words express the cost of the commodity produced."*

The hazy notion about the ideal measure of money fades away in the last words and its real mental content becomes clear. Pound, shilling, etc., the names of account of gold, are said to be names representing definite quantities of labour-time. Since labour-time is the substance and the inherent measure of value, the names thus indeed express the value relations themselves. In other words it is asserted that

---

* *The Currency Question, the Gemini Letters*, London, 1844, pp. 266-72 *passim*.

labour-time is the real standard of money. Here we leave the Birmingham school and merely note in passing that the doctrine of the ideal measure of money has gained new importance in connection with the controversy over the convertibility or non-convertibility of bank-notes. While the denomination of paper is based on gold or silver, the convertibility of the note, *i.e.*, its exchangeability for gold or silver, remains an economic law regardless of what juridical law may say. For instance, a Prussian paper thaler, although legally inconvertible, would immediately depreciate if in everyday commerce it were worth less than a silver thaler, that is if it were not convertible in practice. The consistent advocates of inconvertible paper money in Britain, therefore, had recourse to the ideal standard of money. If the denominations of money, pound, shilling and so on, are names for a determinate amount of particles of value, of which sometimes more, sometimes less are either absorbed or lost by a commodity when it is exchanged for other commodities, then the value of an English £5 note, for instance, is just as little affected by its relation to gold as by its relation to iron and cotton. Since its designation would no longer equate the bank-note in theory to a determinate quantity of gold or of any other commodity, its very concept would preclude the demand for its convertibility, that is for its equation in practice with a determinate quantity of a specific thing.

John Gray was the first to set forth the theory that labour-time is the direct measure of money in a systematic way.* He proposes that a national central bank should ascertain through its branches the labour-time expended in the production of various commodities. In exchange for the commodity, the producer would receive an official certificate of its value, *i.e.*, a receipt for as much labour-time as his

---

* John Gray, *The Social System. A Treatise on the Principle of Exchange*, Edinburgh, 1831. *Cf.* the same author's *Lectures on the Nature and Use of Money*, Edinburgh, 1848. After the February Revolution, Gray sent a memorandum to the French Provisional Government in which he explains that France did not need an "organisation of labour" but an "organisation of exchange", the plan for which was fully worked out in the Monetary System he had invented. The worthy John had no inkling that sixteen years after the publication of *The Social System*, the ingenious Proudhon would be taking out a patent for the same invention.

commodity contains,* and this bank-note of one labour week, one labour day, one labour hour, etc., would serve at the same time as an order to the bank to hand over an equivalent in any of the other commodities stored in its warehouses.** This is the basic principle, which is scrupulously worked out in detail and modelled throughout on existing English institutions. Gray says that under this system

"to sell for money may be rendered, at all times, precisely as easy as it now is to buy with money; ... production would become the uniform and never-failing cause of demand".***

The precious metals would lose their "privileged" position in comparison with other commodities and

"take their proper place in the market beside butter and eggs, and cloth and calico, and then the value of the precious metals will concern us just as little ... as the value of the diamond".****
"Shall we retain our fictitious standard of value, gold, and thus keep the productive resources of the country in bondage? or, shall we resort to the natural standard of value, labour, and thereby set our productive resources free?"*****

Since labour-time is the intrinsic measure of value, why use another extraneous standard as well? Why is exchange-value transformed into price? Why is the value of all commodities computed in terms of an exclusive commodity, which thus becomes the adequate expression of exchange-value, *i.e.*, money? This was the problem which Gray had to solve. But instead of solving it, he assumed that commodities could be directly compared with one another as products of social labour. But they are only comparable as the things they are. Commodities are the direct products of isolated independent individual kinds of labour, and through their

---

* Gray, *The Social System*, p. 63. "Money should be merely a receipt, an evidence that the holder of it has either contributed a certain value to the national stock of wealth, or that he has acquired a right to the said value from some one who has contributed to it."
** "An estimated value being previously put upon produce, let it be lodged in a bank, and drawn out again whenever it is required; merely stipulating, by common consent, that he who lodges any kind of property in the National Bank, may take out of it an equal value of whatever it may contain, instead of being obliged to draw out the self-same thing that he put in." *Op. cit.*, pp. 67-68.
*** *Op. cit.*, p. 16.
**** Gray, *Lectures on Money*, p. 182.
***** *Op. cit.*, p. 169.

84

alienation in the course of individual exchange they must prove that they are general social labour, in other words, on the basis of commodity production, labour becomes social labour only as a result of the universal alienation of individual kinds of labour. But as Gray presupposes that the labour-time contained in commodities is *immediately social* labour-time, he presupposes that it is communal labour-time or labour-time of directly associated individuals. In that case, it would indeed be impossible for a specific commodity, such as gold or silver, to confront other commodities as the incarnation of universal labour and exchange-value would not be turned into price; but neither would use-value be turned into exchange-value and the product into a commodity, and thus the very basis of bourgeois production would be abolished. But this is by no means what Gray had in mind—*goods are to be produced as commodities but not exchanged as commodities*. Gray entrusts the realisation of this pious wish to a national bank. On the one hand, society in the shape of the bank makes the individuals independent of the conditions of private exchange, and, on the other hand, it causes them to continue to produce on the basis of private exchange. Although Gray merely wants "to reform" the money evolved by commodity exchange, he is compelled by the intrinsic logic of the subject-matter to repudiate one condition of bourgeois production after another. Thus he turns capital into national capital,* and land into national property** and if his bank is examined carefully it will be seen that it not only receives commodities with one hand and issues certificates for labour supplied with the other, but that it directs production itself. In his last work, *Lectures on Money*, in which Gray seeks timidly to present his labour money as a purely bourgeois reform, he gets tangled up in even more flagrant absurdities.

Every commodity is immediately money; this is Gray's thesis which he derives from his incomplete and hence incorrect analysis of commodities. The "organic" project of "labour money" and "national bank" and "warehouses" is merely a fantasy in which a dogma is made to appear as a law of universal validity. The dogma that a commodity is

---

* "The business of every nation ought to be conducted on a national capital" (John Gray, *The Social System*, p. 171).
** "The land to be transformed into national property" (*op. cit.*, p. 298).

immediately money or that the particular labour of a private individual contained in it is immediately social labour, does not of course become true because a bank believes in it and conducts its operations in accordance with this dogma. On the contrary, bankruptcy would in such a case fulfil the function of practical criticism. The fact that labour money is a pseudo-economic term, which denotes the pious wish to get rid of money, and together with money to get rid of exchange-value, and with exchange-value to get rid of commodities, and with commodities to get rid of the bourgeois mode of production,—this fact, which remains concealed in Gray's work and of which Gray himself was not aware, has been bluntly expressed by several British socialists, some of whom wrote earlier than Gray and others later.* But it was left to M. *Proudhon* and his school to declare seriously that the degradation of *money* and the exaltation of *commodities* was the essence of socialism and thereby to reduce socialism to an elementary misunderstanding of the inevitable correlation existing between commodities and money.**

2. MEDIUM OF EXCHANGE

When, as a result of the establishing of prices, commodities have acquired the form in which they are able to enter circulation and gold has assumed its function as money, the contradictions latent in the exchange of commodities are both exposed and resolved by circulation. The real exchange of commodities, that is the social metabolic process, constitutes a transformation in which the dual nature of the commodity—commodity as use-value and as exchange-value—manifests itself; but the transformation of the commodity itself is, at the same time, epitomised in certain forms of money. To describe this transformation is to describe circulation. Commodities, as we have seen, constitute fully developed exchange-value only when a world of commodities and consequently a really developed system of division of labour is presupposed; in the same manner circulation

---

* See, *e.g.*, W. Thompson, *An Inquiry into the Distribution of Wealth*, London, 1824; Bray, *Labour's Wrongs and Labour's Remedy*, Leeds, 1839.

** Alfred Darimon, *De la réforme des banques*, Paris, 1856, can be regarded as a compendium of this melodramatic monetary theory.

presupposes that acts of exchange are taking place everywhere and that they are being continuously renewed. It also presupposes that commodities enter into the process of exchange with a *determinate price*, in other words that in the course of exchange they *appear* to confront one another in a dual form—really as use-values and nominally (in the price) as exchange-values.

The busiest streets of London are crowded with shops whose show cases display all the riches of the world, Indian shawls, American revolvers, Chinese porcelain, Parisian corsets, furs from Russia and spices from the tropics, but all of these worldly things bear odious, white paper labels with Arabic numerals and then laconic symbols £ s. d. This is how commodities are presented in circulation.

a. The Metamorphosis of Commodities

Closer examination shows that the circulation process comprises two distinct types of circuit. If commodities are denoted by C and money by M, the two circuits may be represented in the following way:

$$C—M—C$$
$$M—C—M$$

In this section we are solely concerned with the first circuit, that is the one which directly expresses commodity circulation.

The circuit C—M—C may be divided into the movement C—M, the exchange of commodities for money, or *sale*; the opposite movement M—C, the exchange of money for commodities, or *purchase*; and the unity of the two movements C—M—C, exchange of commodities for money so as to exchange money for commodities, in other words, *selling* in order to *purchase*. The outcome in which the transaction terminates is C—C, *i.e.*, exchange of one commodity for another, actual exchange of matter.

C—M—C, when considered from the point of departure of the first commodity, represents its conversion into gold and its reconversion from gold into commodity; that is to say a movement in which at the outset the commodity appears as a particular use-value, then sheds this form of existence and assumes that of exchange-value or universal equivalent—which is entirely distinct from its natural form—finally it sheds this as well and emerges as a real use-value which can serve particular needs. In this last form it drops out of the sphere of circulation and enters that of consumption. Thus to begin with, the whole circuit of C—M—C represents the entire series of metamorphoses through which every individual commodity passes in order to become a direct use-value for its owner. The first metamorphosis takes place in C—M, the first phase of the circuit; the second in M—C, the other phase, and the entire circuit forms the *curriculum vitae* of the commodity. But the cycle C—M—C represents the complete metamorphosis of an individual commodity only because it is at the same time an aggregate of definite partial metamorphoses of other commodities. For each metamorphosis of the first commodity is its transformation into another commodity and therefore the transformation of the second commodity into the first; hence it is a double transformation which is carried through during a single stage of the cycle. To start with, we shall separately examine each of the two phases of exchange into which the cycle C—M—C is resolved.

C—M or *sale*: C, the commodity, enters the sphere of circulation not just as a particular use-value, *e.g.*, a ton of iron, but as a use-value with a definite price, say £3 17s. $10^1/_2$d. or an ounce of gold. The price while on the one hand indicating the amount of labour-time contained in the iron, namely its value, at the same time signifies the pious wish to convert the iron into gold, that is to give the labour-time contained in the iron the form of universal social labour-time. If this transformation fails to take place, then the ton of iron ceases to be not only a commodity but also a product; since it is a commodity only because it is not a use-value for its owner, that is to say his labour is only really labour if it is useful labour for others, and it is useful for him only if it is abstract general labour. It is therefore the task of the iron or of its owner to find that location in the world of commodities where iron attracts gold. But if the sale actually takes place, as we assume in this analysis of simple circulation, then this difficulty, the *salto mortale* of the commodity, is surmounted. As a result of this alienation—that is its transfer from the person for whom it is a non-use-value to the person for whom it is a use-value—the ton of iron proves to be in fact a use-value and its price is simultaneously realised, and merely imaginary gold is converted into real gold. The term "ounce of gold", or £3 17s. 10½d., has now been replaced by an ounce of real gold, but the ton of iron has gone. The sale C—M does not merely transform the commodity—which by means of the price was nominally turned into gold—really into gold, but gold, which as measure of value was only nominally gold and in fact functioned only as the money name of commodities, is through the same process transformed into actual money.* As gold became nominally the universal equivalent, because the values of all commodities were measured in terms of gold, so now, as a result of the universal alienation of commodities in exchange for it—and the sale C—M is the procedure by which this universal alienation is accomplished—does it become the absolutely alienated commodity, *i.e.*, real money. But gold becomes real money through sale, only because the exchange-values of commodities expressed in prices were already converted into nominal gold.

During the sale C—M, and likewise during the purchase M—C, two commodities, *i.e.*, units of exchange-value and use-value, confront each other; but in the case of the commodity exchange-value exists merely nominally as its price, whereas in the case of gold, although it has real use-value, its use-value merely represents exchange-value and is therefore merely a formal use-value which is not related to any real individual need. The contradiction of use-value and exchange-value is thus polarised at the two extreme points of C—M, so that with regard to gold the commodity represents use-value whose nominal exchange-value, the price, still has to be realised in gold; with regard to the commodity, on the other hand, gold represents exchange-value whose formal use-value still has to acquire a material form in the commodity. The contradictions inherent in the exchange of commodities are resolved only by reason of this duplication of the commodity so that it appears as commodity and gold,

---

* "There are two kinds of money, nominal and real; and it can be used in two distinct ways, to measure the value of things and to buy them. Nominal money is as suitable for valuing things as is real money and it may be even better. Money is also used for buying the things which have been valued.... Prices and contracts are calculated in nominal money and are executed in real money" (Galiani, *op. cit.*, p. 112 *et seq.*).

and again by way of the dual and opposite relation in which each extreme is nominal where its opposite is real, and real where its opposite is nominal, in other words they are resolved only by means of presenting commodities as bilateral polar opposites.

So far we have regarded C—M as a sale, as the conversion of a commodity into money. But if we consider it from the other side, then the same transaction appears, on the contrary, as M—C, a purchase, the conversion of money into a commodity. A sale is inevitably and simultaneously its opposite, a purchase; it is the former if one looks at the transaction from one side and the latter if one sees it from the other. In other words, the difference between the transactions is in reality merely that in C—M the initiative comes from the side of the commodity or of the seller while in M—C it comes from the side of money or of the purchaser. When we describe the first metamorphosis of the commodity, its transformation into money, as the result of the first phase of the circuit, we simultaneously presuppose that another commodity has already been converted into money and is therefore now in the second phase of the circuit, M—C. We are thus caught up in a vicious circle of presuppositions. This vicious circle is indeed circulation itself. If we do not regard M in C—M as belonging to the metamorphosis of another commodity, then we isolate the act of exchange from the process of circulation. But if it is separated from the process, the phase C—M disappears and there remain only two commodities which confront each other, for instance iron and gold, whose exchange is not a distinct part of the cycle but is direct barter. At the place where gold is produced, it is a commodity like any other commodity. Its relative value and that of iron or of any other commodity is there reflected in the quantities in which they are exchanged for one another. But this transaction is presupposed in the process of circulation, the value of gold is already given in the prices of commodities. It would therefore be entirely wrong to assume that *within the framework of circulation*, the relation of gold and commodities is that of direct barter and that consequently their relative value is determined by their exchange as simple commodities. It seems as though in the process of circulation gold were exchanged merely as a commodity for other commodities, but this illusion arises simply because a definite quantity of a given commodity is equalised by means of prices with a definite quantity of gold: that is, it is compared with gold as money, the universal equivalent, and *consequently* it can be directly exchanged for gold. In so far as the price of a commodity is *realised* in gold, the commodity is exchanged for gold as a commodity, as a particular materialisation of labour-time; but in so far as it is the *price* of the commodity that is realised in gold, the commodity is exchanged for gold as money and not as a commodity, *i.e.*, for gold as the materialisation of general labour-time. But the quantity of gold for which the commodity is exchanged in the process of circulation is in both cases determined not by means of exchange, but the exchange is determined by the price of the commodity, by its exchange-value calculated in terms of gold.*

Within the process of circulation gold seems to be always acquired as the result of a sale C—M. But since C—M, the sale, is simultaneously M—C, a purchase, it is evident that while C the commodity which begins the process undergoes its first metamorphosis, the other commodity which confronts it as M from the opposite extreme undergoes its second metamorphosis and accordingly passes through the second phase of the circuit while the first commodity is still in the first phase of its cycle.

The outcome of the first stage of circulation, of the sale, provides money, the point of departure of the second stage. The first form of the commodity has now been replaced by its golden equivalent. This outcome may to begin with involve a pause, since the commodity has now assumed a specific durable form. The commodity which was not a use-value in the hands of its owner exists now in a form in which it is always useful because it can always be exchanged, and it depends on circumstances when and at which point in the world of commodities it will again be thrown into circulation. The golden chrysalis state forms an independent phase in the life of the commodity, in which it can remain for a shorter or longer period. The separation and independence of the acts of purchase and sale is a general

---

* This does not, of course, prevent the market-price of commodities from rising above or falling below their value. But this consideration lies outside the sphere of simple circulation and belongs to quite a different sphere to be examined later, in which context we shall discuss the relation of value and market-price.

feature of the labour which creates exchange-value, whereas in barter the exchange of one discrete use-value is directly tied to the exchange of another discrete use-value.

The purchase, M—C, is the reverse movement to C—M and at the same time the second or final metamorphosis of the commodity. Regarded as gold or as the general equivalent, the commodity can be directly expressed in terms of the use-values of all other commodities, all of which through their prices seek gold as their hereafter, and simultaneously they indicate the key note which must be sounded so that their bodies, the use-values, should change over to the money side, while their soul, the exchange-value, is turned into gold. The general result of the alienation of commodities is the absolutely alienated commodity. The conversion of gold into commodities has no qualitative limit but only a quantitative limit, the fact that the amount of gold, or the value it represents, is limited. Everything can be obtained with ready money. Whereas the commodity realises its own price and the use-value of someone else's money through its alienation as a use-value in the movement C—M, it realises its own use-value and the price of the other commodity through its alienation as an exchange-value in the movement M—C. Just as by the realisation of its price, the commodity simultaneously turns gold into real money, so by its retransformation it converts gold into its (the commodity's) own merely transitory money form. Because commodity circulation presupposes an advanced division of labour and therefore also a diversity of wants on the part of the individual, a diversity bearing an inverse relation to the narrow scope of his own production, the purchase M—C will at times consist of an equation with one commodity as the equivalent, and at other times of a series of commodity equivalents determined by the buyer's needs and the amount of money at his disposal. Just as a sale must at the same time be a purchase, so the purchase must at the same time be a sale; M—C is simultaneously C—M, but in this case gold or the purchaser takes the initiative.

Returning to the complete circuit C—M—C, we can see that in it one commodity passes through the entire series of its metamorphoses. But at the same time as this commodity begins the first phase of its circuit and undergoes the first metamorphosis, another commodity commences the second phase of the circuit, passes through its second metamorphosis and drops out of circulation; the first commodity, on the other hand, enters the second phase of the circuit, passes through its second metamorphosis and drops out of circulation, while a third commodity enters the sphere of circulation, passes through the first phase of its cycle and accomplishes the first metamorphosis. Thus the total circuit C—M—C representing the complete metamorphosis of a commodity is simultaneously the end of a complete metamorphosis of a second commodity and the beginning of a complete metamorphosis of a third commodity; it is therefore a series without beginning or end. To demonstrate this and to distinguish the commodities we shall use different symbols to denote C in the two extremes, *e.g.*, C′—M—C″. Indeed, the first term C′—M presupposes that M is the outcome of another C—M, and is accordingly itself only the last term of the circuit C—M—C′, while the second term M—C″ implies that it will result in C″—M, and constitutes the first term of the circuit C″—M—C‴, and so on. It is moreover evident, that, although M is the outcome of a *single* sale, the last term M—C may take the form of M—C′ + M—C″ + M—C‴, and so forth; in other words it may be divided into numerous purchases, *i.e.*, into numerous sales and hence numerous first terms of new complete metamorphoses of commodities. While in this way the complete metamorphosis of a single commodity forms not only a link of just one sequence of metamorphoses without beginning or end, but of many such sequences, the circulation of the world of commodities—since every individual commodity goes through the circuit C—M—C—constitutes an infinitely intricate network of such series of movements, which constantly end and constantly begin afresh at an infinite number of different points. But each individual sale or purchase stands as an independent isolated transaction, whose complementary transaction, which constitutes its continuation, does not need to follow immediately but may be separated from it temporally and spatially. Because every particular cycle C—M or M—C representing the transformation of one commodity into use-value and of another into money, *i.e.*, the first and second phase of the circuit, forms a separate interval for both sides, and since on the other hand all commodities begin their second metamorphosis, that is turn up at the starting point of the circuit's second phase, in the form of gold, the general equivalent, a form common to them all, in the real process of circulation any M—C may follow any particular C—M, *i.e.*, the second section of the life cycle of any commodity may follow the first section of the life cycle of any other commodity. For example, A sells iron for £2, and thus C—M or the first metamorphosis of the commodity iron has taken place, but for the time being A does not buy anything else. At the same time B, who had sold two quarters of wheat for £6 two weeks ago, buys a coat and trousers from Moses and Son with the same £6, and thereby completes M—C or the second metamorphosis of the commodity wheat. The two transactions M—C and C—M appear to be parts of the same sequence only because as M [money or] gold, all commodities look alike and gold does not look any different whether it represents transformed iron or transformed wheat. In the real process of circulation C—M—C, therefore, represents an exceedingly haphazard coincidence and succession of motley phases of various complete metamorphoses. The actual process of circulation *appears*, therefore, not as a complete metamorphosis of the commodity, *i.e.*, not as its movement through opposite phases, but as a mere accumulation of numerous purchases and sales which chance to occur simultaneously or successively. The process accordingly loses its distinct form, especially as each individual transaction, *e.g.*, a sale, is simultaneously its opposite, a purchase, and *vice versa*. On the other hand, the metamorphoses in the world of commodities *constitute* the process of circulation and the former must therefore be reflected in the total movement of circulation. This reflection will be examined in the next section. Here we shall merely observe that the C at each of the two extremes of the circuit C—M—C has a different formal relation to M. The first C is a particular commodity which is compared with money as the universal commodity, whereas in the second phase money as the universal commodity is compared with an individual commodity. The formula C—M—C can therefore be reduced to the abstract logical syllogism P—U—I, where particularity forms the first extreme, universality characterises the common middle term and individuality signifies the final extreme.

The commodity-owners entered the sphere of circulation merely as guardians of commodities. Within this sphere they confront one another in the antithetical rôles of buyer and seller, one personifying a sugar-loaf, the other gold. Just as the sugar-loaf becomes gold, so the seller becomes a buyer. These distinctive social characters are, therefore, by no means due to individual human nature as such, but to the exchange relations of persons who produce their goods in the specific form of commodities. So little does the relation of buyer and seller represent a purely individual relationship that they enter into it only in so far as their individual labour is negated, that is to say, turned into money as *non*-individual labour. It is therefore as absurd to regard buyer and seller, these bourgeois economic types, as eternal social forms of human individuality, as it is preposterous to weep over them as signifying the abolition of individuality.* They are an essential expression of individuality arising at a particular stage of the social process **of production.** The antagonistic nature of bourgeois production is, moreover, expressed in the antithesis of buyer and seller in such a superficial and formal manner that this antithesis exists already in pre-bourgeois social formations, for it requires merely that the relations of individuals to one another should be those of commodity-owners.

An examination of the outcome of the circuit C—M—C shows that it dissolves into the exchange of C—C. Commodity has been exchanged for commodity, use-value for use-value, and the transformation of the commodity into money, or the commodity as money, is merely an intermediary stage which helps to bring about this metabolism. Money

---

* The following extract from M. Isaac Péreire's *Leçons sur l'industrie et les finances*, Paris, 1832, shows that delicate spirits can be deeply hurt even by the quite superficial aspect of antagonism which is represented by purchase and sale. The fact that the same Isaac is the inventor and dictator of the *Crédit mobilier*[18] and as such a notorious wolf of the Paris stock exchange points to the real significance of such sentimental criticism of economics. M. Péreire, at that time an apostle of St. Simon, says: "Since individuals are isolated and separated from one another, whether in their labour or their consumption, they exchange the products of their respective occupations. The necessity of exchanging things entails the necessity of determining their relative value. The ideas of value and exchange are therefore closely linked and in their present form both are expressions of individualism and antagonism. . . . The value of products is determined only because there is sale and purchase, in other words, because there is antagonism between different members of society. Preoccupation with price and value exists only where there is sale and purchase, that is to say, where every individual is compelled to *fight* in order to obtain the things necessary for the maintenance of his existence" (*op. cit.*, pp. 2, 3 *passim*).

emerges thus as a mere *medium of exchange* of commodities, not however as a medium of exchange in general, but a medium of exchange adapted to the process of circulation, *i.e.*, a *medium of circulation.**

If, because the process of circulation of commodities ends in C—C and therefore appears as barter merely mediated by money, or because C—M—C in general does not only fall apart into two isolated cycles but is simultaneously their dynamic unity, the conclusion were to be drawn that only the unity and not the separation of purchase and sale exists, this would display a manner of thinking the criticism of which belongs to the sphere of logic and not of economics. The division of exchange into purchase and sale not only destroys locally evolved primitive, traditionally pious and sentimentally absurd obstacles standing in the way of social metabolism, but it also represents the general fragmentation of the associated factors of this process and their constant confrontation, in short it contains the general possibility of commercial crises, essentially because the contradiction of commodity and money is the abstract and general form of all contradictions inherent in the bourgeois mode of labour. Although circulation of money can occur therefore without crises, crises cannot occur without circulation of money. This simply means that where labour based on individual exchange has not yet evolved a monetary system, it is quite unable of course to produce phenomena that presuppose a full development of the bourgeois mode of production. This displays the profundity of the criticism that proposes to remedy the "shortcomings" of the bourgeois system of production by abolishing the "privileges" of precious metals and by introducing a so-called rational monetary system. A proposition reputed to be exceedingly clever may on the other hand serve as an example of economic apologetics. *James Mill*, the father of the well-known English economist John Stuart Mill, says:

"Whatever ... be the amount of the annual produce, it never can exceed the amount of the annual demand.... Of two men who perform an exchange, the one does not come with only a supply, the other with only a demand; each of them comes with both a demand and a

---

* "Money is only the medium and the agency, whereas commodities that benefit life are the aim and purpose." Boisguillebert, *Le détail de la France*, 1697, in Eugène Daires's *Economistes financiers du XVIIIe siècle*, Vol. I, Paris, 1843, p. 210.

supply.... The supply which he brings is the instrument of his demand; and his demand and supply are of course exactly equal to one another. It is, therefore, impossible that there should ever be in any country a commodity or commodities in quantity greater than the demand, without there being, to an equal amount, some other commodity or commodities in quantity less than the demand."*

Mill establishes equilibrium by reducing the process of circulation to direct barter, but on the other hand he insinuates buyer and seller, figures derived from the process of circulation,—into direct barter. Using Mill's confusing language one may say that there are times when it is impossible to sell all commodities, for instance in London and Hamburg during certain stages of the commercial crisis of 1857/58 there were indeed more buyers than sellers of *one* commodity, *i.e., money,* and more sellers than buyers as regards *all other forms of money, i.e.,* commodities. The metaphysical equilibrium of purchases and sales is confined to the fact that every purchase is a sale and every sale a purchase, but this gives poor comfort to the possessors of commodities who unable to make a sale cannot accordingly make a purchase either.**

---

* A pamphlet by William Spence entitled *Britain Independent of Commerce* was published in London in November 1807; its thesis was further elaborated by William Cobbett in his *Political Register* under the more militant heading "Perish Commerce". Against this James Mill wrote his *Defence of Commerce,* which appeared in 1808; in that work he already advances the argument which is also contained in the passage quoted above from his *Elements of Political Economy.* This ingenious invention has been appropriated by J. B. Say, and used in his polemic against Sismondi and Malthus on the question of commercial crises, and since it was not clear which new idea this comical *prince de la science*—whose merit consists rather in the impartiality with which he consistently misinterpreted his contemporaries Malthus, Sismondi and Ricardo—has contributed to political economy, continental admirers have proclaimed him as the discoverer of the invaluable proposition about a metaphysical equilibrium of purchases and sales.
** The way in which economists describe the different aspects of the commodity may be seen from the following examples:
"With money in possession, we have but one exchange to make in order to secure the object of desire, while with other surplus products we have two, the first of which (securing the money) is infinitely more difficult than the second" (G. Opdyke, *A Treatise on Political Economy,* New York, [1851], pp. 287-88).
"The superior saleableness of money being the exact effect or natural consequence of the less saleableness of commodities" (Thomas Corbet, *An Inquiry into the Causes and Modes of the Wealth of Individuals,* etc., London, 1841, p. 117).
"Money has the ... quality of being always exchangeable for what

The separation of sale and purchase makes possible not only commerce proper, but also numerous *pro forma* transactions, before the final exchange of commodities between producer and consumer takes place. It thus enables large numbers of parasites to invade the process of production and to take advantage of this separation. But this again means only that money, the universal form of labour in bourgeois society, makes the development of the inherent contradictions *possible*.

b. The Circulation of Money

In the first instance real circulation consists of a mass of random purchases and sales taking place simultaneously. In both purchase and sale commodities and money confront each other in the same way; the seller represents the commodity, the buyer the money. As a means of circulation money therefore appears always as a *means of purchase*, and this obscures the fact that it fulfils different functions in the antithetical phases of the metamorphosis of commodities.

Money passes into the hands of the seller in the same transaction which transfers the commodity into the hands of the buyer. Commodity and money thus move in opposite directions, and this change of places—in the course of which the commodity crosses over to one side and money to the other—occurs simultaneously at an indefinite number of points along the entire surface of bourgeois society. But the first move of the commodity in the sphere of circulation is also its last move.* No matter whether the commodity changes its position because gold is attracted by it (C—M) or because it is attracted by gold (M—C), in consequence of the single move, the single change of place, it falls out of the sphere of circulation into that of consumption. Circulation is a perpetual movement of commodities, though always

---

it measures" (Bosanquet, *Metallic, Paper and Credit Currency*, etc., London, 1842, p. 100).

"Money can always buy other commodities, whereas other commodities can not always buy money" (Thomas Tooke, *An Inquiry into the Currency Principle*, Second Ed., London, 1844, p. 10).

* A commodity may be several times bought and sold again. It circulates, in this case, not as a mere commodity, but fulfils a function which does not yet exist from the standpoint of simple circulation and of the simple antithesis of commodity and money.

of different commodities, and each commodity makes but one move. Each commodity begins the second phase of its circuit not as the same commodity, but as a different commodity, i.e., gold. The movement of the metamorphosed commodity is thus the movement of gold. The same coin or the identical bit of gold which in the transaction C—M changed places with a commodity becomes in turn the starting point of M—C, and thus for the second time changes places with another commodity. Just as it passed from the hands of B, the buyer, into those of A, the seller, so now it passes from the hands of A, who has become a buyer, into those of C. The changes in the form of a commodity, its transformation into money and its retransformation from money, in other words the movement of the total metamorphosis of a commodity, accordingly appear as the extrinsic movement of a single coin which changes places twice, with two different commodities. However scattered and fortuitous the simultaneous purchases and sales may be, a buyer is always confronted by a seller in actual circulation, and the money which takes the place of the commodity sold must already have changed places once with another commodity before reaching the hands of the buyer. On the other hand, sooner or later the money will pass again from the hands of the seller who has become a buyer into those of a new seller, and its repeated changes of place express the interlocking of the metamorphoses of commodities. The same coins therefore proceed—always in the opposite direction to the commodities moved—from one point of the circuit to another; some coins move more frequently, others less frequently, thus describing a longer or shorter curve. The different movements of one and the same coin can follow one another only temporally, just as conversely the multiplicity and fragmentation of the purchases and sales are reflected in the simultaneous and spatially concurrent changes of place of commodity and money.

The simple form of commodity circulation, C—M—C, takes place when money passes from the hands of the buyer into those of the seller and from the seller who has become a buyer into the hands of a new seller. This concludes the metamorphosis of the commodity and hence the movement of money in so far as it is the expression of this metamorphosis. But since there are new use-values produced continuously in the form of commodities, which must therefore be thrown continuously afresh into the sphere of circulation, the circuit C—M—C is renewed and repeated by the same commodity-owners. The money they have spent as buyers returns to them when they once more become sellers of commodities. The perpetual renewal of commodity circulation is reflected in the fact that over the entire surface of bourgeois society money not only circulates from one person to another but that at the same time it describes a number of distinct small circuits, starting from an infinite variety of points and returning to the same points, in order to repeat the movement afresh.

As the change of form of the commodity appears as a mere change in place of money, and the continuity of the movement of circulation belongs entirely to the monetary side—because the commodity always makes only one step in the direction opposite to that of money, money however invariably making the second step for the commodity to complete the motion begun by the commodity—so the entire movement *appears* to be initiated by money, although during the sale the commodity causes the money to move, thus bringing about the circulation of the money in the same way as during the purchase the money brings about the circulation of the commodity. Since moreover money always confronts commodities as a *means of purchase* and as such causes commodities to move merely by realising their prices, the entire movement of circulation appears to consist of money changing places with commodities by realising their prices either in separate transactions which occur simultaneously, side by side, or successively when the same coin realises the prices of different commodities one after another. If, for example, one examines C—M—C′—M—C″—M—C‴, etc., and disregards the qualitative aspects, which become unrecognisable in actual circulation, there emerges only the same monotonous operation. After realising the price of C, M successively realises the prices of C′, C″, etc., and the commodities C′, C″, C‴, etc., invariably take the place vacated by money. It thus appears that money causes the circulation of commodities by realising their prices. While it serves to realise prices, money itself circulates continuously, sometimes moving merely to a different place, at other times tracing a curve or describing a small cycle in which the points of departure and of return are identical. As a medium of circulation it has a circulation of its own. The movement and changing forms of the circulating commodities thus appear as the movement of money mediating the exchange of commodities, which are in themselves immobile. The movement of the circulation process of commodities is therefore represented by the movement of money as the medium of circulation, *i.e.*, by the *circulation of money.*

Just as commodity-owners presented the products of individual labour as products of social labour, by transforming a thing, *i.e.*, gold, into the direct embodiment of labour-time in general and therefore into money, so now their own universal movement by which they bring about the exchange of the material elements of their labour confronts them as the specific movement of a thing, *i.e.*, as the circulation of gold. The social movement is for the commodity-owners on the one hand an external necessity and on the other merely a formal intermediary process enabling each individual to obtain different use-values of the same total value as that of the commodities which he has thrown into circulation. The commodity begins to function as a use-value when it leaves the sphere of circulation, whereas the use-value of money as a means of circulation consists in its very circulation. The movement of the commodity in the sphere of circulation is only an insignificant factor, whereas perpetual rotation within this sphere becomes the function of money. The specific function which it fulfils within circulation gives money as the medium of circulation a new and distinctive aspect, which now has to be analysed in more detail.

First of all, it is evident that the circulation of money is an infinitely divided movement, for it reflects the infinite fragmentation of the process of circulation into purchases and sales, and the complete separation of the complementary phases of the metamorphosis of commodities. It is true that a recurrent movement, real circular motion, takes place in the small circuits of money in which the point of departure and the point of return are identical; but in the first place, there are as many points of departure as there are commodities, and their indefinite multitude balks any attempt to check, measure and compute these circuits. The time which passes between the departure from and the return to the starting point is equally uncertain. It is, moreover, quite irrelevant whether or not such a circuit is described in a particular case. No economic fact is more widely known than that somebody may spend money without receiving it back. Money starts its circuit from an endless multitude of points and returns to an endless multitude of points, but the coincidence of the point of departure and the point of return is fortuitous, because the movement C—M—C does not necessarily imply that the buyer becomes a seller again. It would be even less correct to depict the circulation of money as a movement which radiates from one centre to all points of the periphery and returns from all the peripheral points to the same centre. The so-called circuit of money, as people imagine it, simply amounts to the fact that the appearance of money and its disappearance, its perpetual movement from one place to another, is everywhere visible. When considering a more advanced form of money used to mediate circulation, e.g., bank-notes, we shall find that the conditions governing the issue of money determine also its reflux. But as regards simple money circulation it is a matter of chance whether a particular buyer becomes a seller once again. Where actual circular motions are taking place continuously in the sphere of simple money circulation, they merely reflect the more fundamental processes of production, for instance, with the money which the manufacturer receives from his banker on Friday he pays his workers on Saturday, they immediately hand over the larger part of it to retailers, etc., and the latter return it to the banker on Monday.

We have seen that money simultaneously realises a given sum of prices comprising the motley purchases and sales which coexist in space, and that it changes places with each commodity only once. But, on the other hand, in so far as the movements of complete metamorphoses of commodities and the concatenation of these metamorphoses are reflected in the movement of money, the same coin realises the prices of various commodities and thus makes a larger or smaller number of circuits. Hence, if we consider the process of circulation in a country during a definite period, for instance a day, then the amount of gold required for the realisation of prices and accordingly for the circulation of commodities is determined by two factors: on the one hand, the sum total of prices and, on the other hand, the average number of circuits which the individual gold coins make. The number of circuits or the velocity of money circulation is in its turn determined by, or simply reflects, the average velocity of the commodities passing through the various phases of their metamorphosis, the speed with which the metamorphoses constituting a chain follow one another, and the speed with which new commodities are thrown into circulation to replace those that have completed their metamorphosis. Whereas during the determination of prices the exchange-value of all commodities is nominally turned into a quantity of gold of the same value and in the two separate transactions, M—C and C—M, the same value exists twice, on the one hand in the shape of commodities and on the other in the form of gold; yet gold as a medium of circulation is determined not by its isolated relation to individual static commodities, but by its dynamic existence in the fluid world of commodities. The function of gold is to represent the transformation of commodities by its changes of place, in other words to indicate the speed of their transformation by the speed with which it moves from one point to another. Its function in the process as a whole thus determines the actual amount of gold in circulation, or the actual quantity which circulates.

Commodity circulation is the prerequisite of money circulation; money, moreover, circulates commodities which have prices, that is commodities which have already been equated nominally with definite quantities of gold. The determination of the prices of commodities presupposes that the value of the quantity of gold which serves as the standard measure, or the value of gold, is given. According to this assumption, the quantity of gold required for circulation is in the first place determined therefore by the sum of the commodity-prices to be realised. This sum, however, is in its turn determined by the following factors: 1. the price level, the relative magnitude of the exchange-values of commodities in terms of gold, and 2. the quantity of commodities circulating at definite prices, that is the number of purchases and sales at given prices.* If a quarter of wheat costs 60s., then twice as much gold is required to circulate it or to realise its price as would be required if it cost only 30s. Twice as much gold is

---

* The amount of money is a matter of indifference "provided there is enough of it to maintain the prices determined by the commodities." Boisguillebert, *Le détail de la France*, p. 209.

"If the circulation of commodities of four hundred millions required a currency of forty millions, and ... this proportion of one-tenth was the due level ... then, if the value of commodities to be circulated

needed to circulate 500 quarters at 60s. as is needed to circulate 250 quarters at 60s. Finally only half as much gold is needed to circulate 10 quarters at 100s. as is needed to circulate 40 quarters at 50s. It follows therefore that the quantity of gold required for the circulation of commodities can fall despite rising prices, if the mass of commodities in circulation decreases faster than the total sum of prices increases, and conversely the amount of means of circulation can increase while the mass of commodities in circulation decreases provided their aggregate prices rise to an even greater extent. Thus excellent investigations carried out in great detail by Englishmen have shown that in England, for instance, the amount of money in circulation grows during the early stages of a grain shortage, because the aggregate price of the smaller supply of grain is larger than was the aggregate price of the bigger supply of grain, and for some time the other commodities continue to circulate as before at their old prices. The amount of money in circulation decreases, however, at a later stage of the grain shortage, because along with the grain either fewer commodities are sold at their old prices, or the same amount of commodities is sold at lower prices.

But the quantity of money in circulation is, as we have seen, determined not only by the sum of commodity-prices to be realised, but also by the velocity with which money circulates, i.e., the speed with which this realisation of prices is accomplished during a given period. If in one day one and the same sovereign makes ten purchases each consisting of a commodity worth one sovereign, so that it changes hands ten times, it transacts the same amount of business as ten sovereigns each of which makes only one circuit a day.* The velocity of circulation of gold can thus make up for its quantity: in other words, the stock of gold in circulation is determined not only by gold functioning as an equivalent alongside commodities, but also by the function it fulfils in the movement of the metamorphoses of commodities. But

---

increased to four hundred and fifty millions, from natural causes ... the currency, in order to continue at its level, must be increased to forty-five millions." William Blake, *Observations on the Effects Produced by the Expenditure of Government*, etc., London, 1823, pp. 80, 81.

* "It is due to the velocity of the circulation of money and not to the quantity of the metal, that much or little money appears to be available" (Galiani, *op. cit.*, p. 99).

the velocity of currency can make up for its quantity only to a certain extent, for an endless number of separate purchases and sales take place simultaneously at any given moment.

If the aggregate prices of the commodities in circulation rise, but to a smaller extent than the velocity of currency increases, then the volume of money in circulation will decrease. If, on the contrary, the velocity of circulation decreases at a faster rate than the total price of the commodities in circulation, then the volume of money in circulation will grow. A general fall in prices accompanied by an increase in the quantity of the medium of circulation and a general rise in prices accompanied by a decrease in the quantity of the medium of circulation are among the best documented phenomena in the history of prices. But the causes occasioning a rise in the level of prices and at the same time an even larger rise in the velocity of currency, as also the converse development, lie outside the scope of an investigation into simple circulation. We may mention by way of illustration that in periods of expanding credit the velocity of currency increases faster than the prices of commodities, whereas in periods of contracting credit the velocity of currency declines faster than the prices of commodities. It is a sign of the superficial and formal character of simple money circulation that the quantity of means of circulation is determined by factors—such as the amount of commodities in circulation, prices, increases or decreases of prices, the number of purchases and sales taking place simultaneously, and the velocity of currency—all of which are contingent on the metamorphosis proceeding in the world of commodities, which is in turn contingent on the general nature of the mode of production, the size of the population, the relation of town and countryside, the development of the means of transport, the more or less advanced division of labour, credit, etc., in short on circumstances which lie *outside* the framework of simple money circulation and are merely mirrored in it.

If the velocity of circulation is given, then the quantity of the means of circulation is simply determined by the prices of commodities. Prices are thus high or low not because more or less money is in circulation, but there is more or less money in circulation because prices are high or low. This is one of the principal economic laws, and the detailed substantiation of it based on the history of prices is perhaps the only achievement of the post-Ricardian English economists. Empirical data show that, despite temporary fluctuations, and sometimes very intense fluctuations,* over longer periods the level of metallic currency or the volume of gold and silver in circulation in a particular country may remain on the whole stable, deviations from the average level amounting merely to small oscillations. This phenomenon is simply due to the contradictory nature of the factors determining the volume of money in circulation. Changes occurring simultaneously in these factors neutralise their effects and everything remains as it was.

The law that, if the speed of circulation of money and the sum total of the commodity-prices are given, the amount of the medium of circulation is determined, can also be expressed in the following way: if the exchange-values of commodities and the average speed of their metamorphoses are given, then the quantity of gold in circulation depends on its own value. Thus, if the value of gold, *i.e.* the labour-time required for its production, were to increase or to decrease, then the prices of commodities would rise or fall in inverse proportion and, provided the velocity remained unchanged, this general rise or fall in prices would necessitate a larger or smaller amount of gold for the circulation of the same amount of commodities. The result would be similar if the previous standard of value were to be replaced by a more valuable or a less valuable metal. For instance, when, in deference to its creditors and impelled by fear of the effect the discovery of gold in California and Australia might have, Holland replaced gold currency by silver currency, 14 to 15 times more silver was required

---

* An example of a remarkable fall of the metallic currency below its average level occurred in England in 1858 as the following passage from the London *Economist* shows: "From the nature of the case" (*i.e.*, owing to the fragmentation of simple circulation) "very exact data cannot be procured as to the amount of cash that is fluctuating in the market, and in the hands of the not banking classes. But, perhaps, the activity or the inactivity of the mints of the great commercial nations is one of the most likely indications in the variations of that amount. Much will be manufactured when it is wanted; and little when little is wanted. ... At the English mint the coinage was in 1855 £9,245,000; 1856, £6,476,000; 1857, £5,293,858. During 1858 the mint had scarcely anything to do." *Economist*, July 10, 1858. But at the same time about eighteen million pounds sterling were lying in the bank vaults.

than formerly was required of gold to circulate the same volume of commodities.

Since the quantity of gold in circulation depends upon two variable factors, the total amount of commodity-prices and the velocity of circulation, it follows that it must be possible to reduce and expand the quantity of metallic currency; in short, in accordance with the requirements of the process of circulation, gold must sometimes be put into circulation and sometimes withdrawn from it. We shall see later how these conditions are realised in the process of circulation.

c. Coins and Tokens of Value

Gold functioning as a medium of circulation assumes a specific shape, it becomes a *coin*. In order to prevent its circulation from being hampered by technical difficulties, gold is minted according to the standard of the money of account. Coins are pieces of gold whose shape and imprint signify that they contain weights of gold as indicated by the names of the money of account, such as pound sterling, shilling, etc. Both the establishing of the mint-price and the technical work of minting devolve upon the State. Coined money assumes a *local and political character*, it uses different national languages and wears different national uniforms, just as does money of account. Coined money circulates therefore in the *internal* sphere of circulation of commodities, which is circumscribed by the boundaries of a given community and separated from the *universal* circulation of the world of commodities.

But the only difference between gold in the form of bullion and gold in the form of coin is that between the denomination of the coin and denomination of its metal weight. What appears as a difference of denomination in the latter case, appears as a difference of shape in the former. Gold coins can be thrown into the crucible and thus turned again into gold *sans phrase*, just as conversely gold bars have only to be sent to the mint to be transformed into coin. The conversion and reconversion of one form into the other appears as a purely technical operation.

In exchange for 100 pounds or 1,200 ounces troy of 22-carat gold one receives £4,672$\frac{1}{2}$ or 4,672$\frac{1}{2}$ gold sovereigns from the English mint, and if one puts these sovereigns on one side of a pair of scales and 100 pounds of gold bars on the other, the two will balance. This proves that the sovereign is simply a quantity of gold—with a specific shape and a specific imprint—the weight of which is denoted by this name in the English monetary scale. The 4,672½ gold sovereigns are thrown into circulation at different points and, once in the current, they make a certain number of moves each day, some sovereigns more and others less. If the average number of moves made by one ounce of gold during a day were ten, then the 1,200 ounces of gold would realise a total of commodity-prices amounting to 12,000 ounces or 46,725 sovereigns. An ounce of gold, no matter how one may twist and turn it, will never weigh ten ounces. But here in the process of circulation, one ounce does indeed amount to ten ounces. In the process of circulation a coin is equal to the quantity of gold contained in it multiplied by the number of moves it makes. In addition to its actual existence as an individual piece of gold of a certain weight, the coin thus acquires a nominal existence which arises from the function it performs. But whether the sovereign makes one or ten moves, in each particular purchase or sale it nevertheless acts merely as a single sovereign. The effect is the same as in the case of a general who on the day of battle replaces ten generals by appearing at ten different places at the crucial time, but remains the same general at each point. The nominalisation of the medium of circulation, which arises as a result of the replacement of quantity by velocity, concerns only the functioning of coins within the process of circulation but does not affect the status of the individual coins.

But the circulation of money is an external movement and the sovereign, although *non olet*,[a] keeps mixed company. The coin, which comes into contact with all sorts of hands, bags, purses, pouches, tills, chests and boxes, wears away, leaves a particle of gold here and another there, thus losing increasingly more of its intrinsic content as a result of abrasion sustained in the course of its worldly career. While in use it is getting used up. Let us consider a sovereign at a moment when its original solid features are as yet hardly impaired.

---

a   It does not smell.—*Ed.*

"A baker who takes a sovereign one day, and pays it away to his miller the next, does not pay the veritable sovereign itself; it is a little lighter than when he received it...."*

"It being obvious that the coinage, in the very nature of things, must be for ever, unit by unit, falling under depreciation by the mere action of ordinary and unavoidable abrasion ... it is a physical impossibility at any time, even for a single day, utterly to exterminate light coins from circulation."**

Jacob estimates that of the £380 million which existed in Europe in 1809, £19 million had completely disappeared as a result of abrasion by 1829, that is in the course of 20 years.*** Whereas the commodity having taken its first step, bringing it into the sphere of circulation, drops out of it again, the coin, after making a few steps in the sphere of circulation, represents a greater metal content than it actually possesses. The longer a coin circulates at a given velocity, or the more rapidly it circulates in a given period of time, the greater becomes the divergence between its existence as a coin and its existence as a piece of gold or silver. What remains is *magni nominis umbra*, the body of the coin is now merely a shadow. Whereas originally circulation made the coin heavier, it now makes it lighter, but in each individual purchase or sale it still passes for the original quantity of gold. As a *pseudo*-sovereign, or pseudo-gold, the sovereign continues to perform the function of a legal gold coin. Although friction with the external world causes other entities to lose their idealism, the coin becomes increasingly ideal as a result of practice, its golden or silver substance being reduced to a mere pseudo-existence. This second idealisation of metal currency, that is, the disparity between its nominal content and its real content, brought about by the process of circulation itself, has been taken advantage of both by governments and individual adventurers who debased the coinage in a variety of ways. The entire history of the Monetary System from the early Middle

---

* Dodd, *The Curiosities of Industry*, London, 1854 [p. 16].

** *The Currency Theory Reviewed....* By a Banker, Edinburgh, 1845, p. 69. "If a slightly worn coin were to be considered to be worth less than a completely new one, then circulation would be continuously impeded, and not a single payment could be made without argument" (G. Garnier, *Histoire de la monnaie*, tome I, p. 24).

*** William Jacob, *An Historical Inquiry into the Production and Consumption of the Precious Metals*, London, 1831, Vol. II, Chapter XXVI, p. 322.

Ages until well into the eighteenth century is a history of such bilateral and antagonistic counterfeiting, and Custodi's voluminous collection of works of Italian economists is largely concerned with this subject.

But the "ideal" existence of gold within the confines of its function comes into conflict with its real existence. In the course of circulation some gold coins have lost more of their metal content, others less, and one sovereign is now indeed worth more than another. Since they are however equally valid while they function as coin—the sovereign that weighs a quarter of an ounce is valued no more highly than the sovereign which only represents a quarter of an ounce—some unscrupulous owners perform surgical operations on sovereigns of standard weight to achieve the same result artificially which circulation has brought about spontaneously in the case of lighter coins. Sovereigns are clipped and debased and the surplus gold goes into the melting pot. When $4,672\frac{1}{2}$ gold sovereigns placed on the scales weigh on the average only 800 ounces instead of 1,200, they will buy only 800 ounces of gold on the gold market: in other words, the market-price of gold has risen above the mint-price. All sovereigns, even those retaining the standard weight, would be worth less as coin than in the shape of bars. Sovereigns of standard weight would be reconverted into bars, a form in which a greater quantity of gold has a greater value than a smaller quantity of gold. When the decline of the metal content has affected a sufficient number of sovereigns to cause a permanent rise of the market-price of gold over its mint-price, the coins will retain the same names of account but these will henceforth stand for a smaller quantity of gold. In other words, the standard of money will be changed, and henceforth gold will be minted in accordance with this new standard. Thus, in consequence of its idealisation as a medium of circulation, gold in its turn will have changed the legally established relation in which it functioned as the standard of price. A similar revolution would be repeated after a certain period of time; gold both as the standard of price and the medium of circulation in this way being subject to continuous changes, so that a change in the one aspect would cause a change in the other and *vice versa*. This accounts for the phenomenon mentioned earlier, namely that, as the history of all modern nations shows, the same monetary titles continued to stand for a steadily diminishing metal content. The contradiction between gold as coin and gold as the standard of price becomes also the contradiction between gold as coin and gold as the universal equivalent, which circulates not only within the boundaries of a given territory but also on the world market. As a measure of value gold has always retained its full weight, because it has served only nominally as gold. When serving as an equivalent in the separate transaction C—M, gold reverts from movement immediately to a state of rest; but when it serves as a coin its natural substance comes into constant conflict with its function. The transformation of gold sovereigns into nominal gold cannot be entirely prevented, but legislation attempts to preclude the establishment of nominal gold as coin by withdrawing it from circulation when the coins in question have lost a certain percentage of their substance. According to English law, for instance, a sovereign which has lost more than 0.747 grain of weight is no longer legal tender. Between 1844 and 1848, 48 million gold sovereigns were weighed by the Bank of England, which possesses scales for weighing gold invented by Mr. Cotton. This machine is not only able to detect a difference between the weights of two sovereigns amounting to one-hundredth of a grain, but like a rational being it flings the light-weight coin onto a board from which it drops into another machine that cuts it into pieces with oriental cruelty.

Under these conditions, however, gold coins would not be able to circulate at all unless they were confined to a definite sphere of circulation where they wear out less quickly. In so far as a gold coin in circulation is worth a quarter of an ounce, whereas it weighs only a fifth of an ounce, it has indeed become a mere token or symbol for one-twentieth of an ounce of gold, and in this way the process of circulation converts all gold coins to some extent into mere tokens or symbols representing their substance. But a thing cannot be its own symbol. Painted grapes are no symbol of real grapes, but are imaginary grapes. Even less is it possible for a light-weight sovereign to be the symbol of a standard-weight sovereign, just as an emaciated horse cannot be the symbol of a fat horse. Since gold thus becomes a symbol of itself but cannot serve as such a symbol it assumes a symbolic existence—quite separate from its own existence—in the shape of silver or copper counters in those spheres of circulation where it wears out most rapidly, namely where purchases and sales of minute amounts go on continuously. A certain proportion of the total number of gold coins, although not always the same coins, perpetually circulate in these spheres. This proportion of gold coins is replaced by silver or copper tokens. Various commodities can thus serve as coin alongside gold, although only one specific commodity can function as the measure of value and therefore also as money within a particular country. These subsidiary means of circulation, for instance silver or copper tokens, represent definite fractions of gold coins within the circulation. The amount of silver or copper these tokens themselves contain is, therefore, not determined by the value of silver or copper in relation to that of gold, but is arbitrarily established by law. They may be issued only in amounts not exceeding those in which the small fractions of gold coin they represent would constantly circulate, either as small change for gold coin of higher denominations or to realise correspondingly low prices of commodities. The silver tokens and copper tokens will belong to distinct spheres of retail trade. It is self-evident that their velocity of circulation stands in inverse ratio to the price they realise in each individual purchase and sale, or to the value of the fraction of the gold coin they represent. The relatively insignificant total amount of subsidiary coins in circulation indicates the velocity with which they perpetually circulate, if one bears in mind the huge volume of retail trade daily transacted in a country like England. A recently published parliamentary report shows, for instance, that in 1857 the English Mint coined gold to the amount of £4,859,000 and silver having a nominal value of £733,000 and a metal value of £363,000. In the ten-year period ending December 31, 1857, the total amount of gold coined came to £55,239,000 and that of silver to only £2,434,000. The nominal value of copper coins issued in 1857 was only £6,720, while the value of the copper contained in them was £3,492; of this total £3,136 was issued as pennies, £2,464 as halfpennies and £1,120 as farthings. The total nominal value of the copper coin struck during the last ten years came to £141,477, and their metal value to £73,503. Just as gold coin is prevented from perpetually functioning as coin by the statutory provision that on losing a certain quantity of metal it is demonetised, so conversely by laying down the price level which they can legally realise silver and copper counters are prevented from moving into the sphere of gold coin and from establishing themselves as money. Thus for example in England, copper is legal tender for sums up to 6d. and silver for sums up to 40s. The issue of silver and copper tokens in quantities exceeding the requirements of their spheres of circulation would not lead to a rise in commodity-prices but to the accumulation of these tokens in the hands of retail traders, who would in the end be forced to sell them as metal. In 1798, for instance, English copper coins to the amounts of £20, £30 and £50, spent by private people, had accumulated in the tills of shopkeepers and, since their attempts to put the coins again into circulation failed, they finally had to sell them as metal on the copper market.*

The metal content of the silver and copper tokens, which represent gold coin in distinct spheres of home circulation, is determined by law; but when in circulation they wear away, just as gold coins do, and, because of the velocity and constancy of their circulation, they are reduced even faster to a merely imaginary, or shadow existence. If one were to establish that silver and copper tokens also, on losing a certain amount of metal, should cease to function as coin, it would be necessary to replace them in turn in certain sections of their own sphere of circulation by some other symbolic money, such as iron or lead; and in this way the representation of one type of symbolic money by other types of symbolic money would go on for ever. The needs of currency circulation itself accordingly compel all countries with a developed circulation to ensure that silver and copper tokens function as coin independently of the percentage of metal they lose. It thus becomes evident that they are, by their very nature, symbols of gold coin not because they are made of silver or copper, not because they have value, but they are symbols in so far as they have no value.

Relatively worthless things, such as *paper*, can function as symbols of gold coins. Subsidiary coins consist of metal, silver, copper, etc., tokens principally because in most countries the less valuable metals circulated as money— *e.g.*, silver in England, copper in the ancient Roman

* David Buchanan, *Observations on the Subjects Treated of in Doctor Smith's Inquiry into the Nature and Causes of the Wealth of Nations*, Edinburgh, 1814, p. 31.

Republic, Sweden, Scotland, etc.—before the process of circulation reduced them to the status of small coin and put a more valuable metal in their place. It is in the nature of things moreover that the monetary symbol which directly arises from metallic currency should be, in the first place, once again a metal. Just as the portion of gold which would constantly have to circulate as small change is replaced by metal tokens, so the portion of gold which as coin remains always in the sphere of home circulation, and must therefore circulate perpetually, can be replaced by tokens without intrinsic value. The level below which the volume of currency never falls is established in each country by experience. What was originally an insignificant divergence of the nominal content from the actual metal content of metallic currency can therefore reach a stage where the two things are completely divorced. The names of coins become thus detached from the substance of money and exist apart from it in the shape of worthless scraps of paper. In the same way as the exchange-value of commodities is crystallised into gold money as a result of exchange, so gold money in circulation is sublimated into its own symbol, first in the shape of worn gold coin, then in the shape of subsidiary metal coin, and finally in the shape of worthless counters, scraps of paper, mere *tokens of value*.

But the gold coin gave rise first to metallic and then to paper substitutes only because it continued to function as a coin despite the loss of metal it incurred. It circulated not because it was worn, but it was worn to a symbol because it continued to circulate. Only in so far as in the process of circulation gold currency becomes a mere token of its own value can mere tokens of value be substituted for it.

In so far as the circuit C—M—C is the dynamic unity of the two aspects C—M and M—C, which directly change into each other, or in so far as the commodity undergoes the entire metamorphosis, it evolves its exchange-value into price and into money, but immediately abandons these forms again to become once more a commodity, or rather a use-value. The exchange-value of the commodity thus acquires *only a seemingly independent existence*. We have seen, on the other hand, that gold, when it functions only as specie, that is when it is perpetually in circulation, does indeed represent merely the interlinking of the metamorphoses of commodities and *their ephemeral existence as money.* Gold realises the price of one commodity only in order to realise that of another, but it never appears as exchange-value in a state of rest or even a commodity in a state of rest. The reality which in this process the exchange-value of commodities assumes, and which is expressed by gold in circulation, is merely the reality of an electric spark. Although it is real gold, it functions merely as apparent gold, and in this function therefore a token of itself can be substituted for it.

The token of value, say a piece of paper, which functions as a coin, represents the quantity of gold indicated by the name of the coin, and is thus a *token of gold.* A definite quantity of gold as such does not express a value relation, nor does the token which takes its place. The gold token represents value in so far as a definite quantity of gold, because it is materialised labour-time, possesses a definite value. But the amount of value which the token represents depends in each case upon the value of the quantity of gold represented by it. As far as commodities are concerned, the token of value represents the *reality of their price* and constitutes a token of their price and a token of their value only because their value is expressed in their price. In the circuit C—M—C, in so far as it expresses merely the dynamic unity of the two metamorphoses or the direct transformation of one metamorphosis into the other—and this is how it appears in the sphere of circulation, within which the token of value operates—the exchange-value of commodities assumes in the price merely a nominal existence and in money merely an imaginary or symbolic existence. Exchange-value thus appears to be something *purely* conceptual or an imagined entity but possessing no *reality* except in the commodities, in so far as a definite amount of labour-time is materialised in them. The token of value therefore *seems* to represent the value of commodities *directly*, since it appears to be not a token of gold but a token of the exchange-value which exists solely in the commodity and is merely expressed in the price. But the appearance is deceptive. The token of value is directly only a *token of price,* that is a *token of gold,* and only indirectly a token of the value of the commodity. Gold, unlike Peter Schlemihl,[19] has not sold its shadow, but uses its shadow as a means of purchase. Thus the token of value is effective only when in the process of exchange it signifies the price

115

of one commodity compared with that of another or when it *represents gold* with regard to every commodity-owner. First of all custom turns a certain, relatively worthless object, a piece of leather, a scrap of paper, etc., into a token of the material of which money consists, but it can maintain this position only if its function as a symbol is guaranteed by the general intention of commodity-owners, in other words if it acquires a legal conventional existence and hence a legal rate of exchange. Paper money issued by the state and given a legal rate is an advanced form of the *token of value*, and the only kind of paper money which directly arises from metallic currency or from simple commodity circulation itself. *Credit money* belongs to a more advanced stage of the social process of production and conforms to very different laws. Symbolic paper money indeed does not differ at all from subsidiary metal coin except in having a wider sphere of circulation. Even the merely technical development of the standard of price, or of the mint-price, and later the external transformation of gold bars into gold coin led to state intervention and consequently to a visible separation of internal circulation from the general circulation of commodities, this division being completed by the transformation of coin into a token of value. Money as a simple medium of circulation can after all acquire an independent existence only within the sphere of internal circulation.

Our exposition has shown that gold in the shape of coin, that is tokens of value divorced from gold substance itself, originates in the process of circulation itself and does not come about by arrangement or state intervention. Russia affords a striking example of a spontaneously evolved token of value. At a time when hides and furs served as money in that country, the contradiction between the perishable and unwieldy material and its function as a medium of circulation led to the custom of substituting small pieces of stamped leather for it; these pieces thus became money orders payable in hides and furs. Later they were called kopeks and became mere tokens representing fractions of the silver ruble and as such were used here and there until 1700, when Peter the Great ordered their replacement by small copper coins issued by the State.* In antiquity writers,

---

* Henry Storch, *Cours d'économie politique* ... avec des notes par J. B. Say, Paris, 1823, tome IV, p. 79. Storch published his work in

who were able to observe only the phenomena of metallic currency, among them Plato* and Aristotle** already understood that gold coin is a symbol or token of value. Paper money with a legal rate of exchange arises early in countries such as China, which have not evolved a credit system.*** Later advocates of paper money also refer expressly

French in St. Petersburg. J. B. Say immediately brought out a reprint in Paris, supplemented by so-called notes, which in fact contain nothing but platitudes. Storch's reaction to the annexation of his work by the *"prince de la science"* was not at all polite (see his *Considérations sur la nature du revenu national*, Paris, 1824).

* Plato, *De Republica*, L. II. "The coin is a token of exchange" (*Opera omnia* etc., ed. G. Stallbaumius, London, 1850, p. 304). Plato analyses only two aspects of money, *i.e.*, money as a standard of value and a token of value; apart from the token of value circulating within the country he calls for another token of value serving in the commerce of Greece with other countries (*cf.* book 5 of his *Laws*).

** Aristoteles, *Ethica Nicomachea*, L. 5, C. 8 [p. 98]. "But money has become by convention a sort of representative of demand; and this is why it has the name 'money' (νόμισμα)—because it exists not by nature but by 'law' (νόμω), and it is in our power to change it and make it useless." [The English translation is from Aristotle, *Ethica Nicomachea*, Oxford, 1925, 1133a.] Aristotle's conception of money was considerably more complex and profound than that of Plato. In the following passage he describes very well how as a result of barter between different communities the necessity arises of turning a specific commodity, that is a substance which has itself value, into money. "When the inhabitants of one country became more dependent on those of another, and they imported what they needed, and exported what they had too much of, money *necessarily* came into use ... and hence men agreed to employ in their dealings with each other something which was *intrinsically useful* and easily applicable to the purposes of life, for example, iron, silver and the like." (Aristoteles, *De Republica*, L. I, C. 9, *loc. cit* [p. 14]. [The English translation is from Aristotle, *Politica*, by Benjamin Jowett, Oxford, 1966, 1257a.])

Michel Chevalier, who has either not read or not understood Aristotle, quotes this passage to show that according to Aristotle the medium of circulation must be a substance which is itself valuable. Aristotle, however, states plainly that money regarded simply as medium of circulation is merely a conventional or legal entity, as even its name (νόμισμα) indicates, and its use-value as specie is in fact only due to its function and not to any intrinsic use-value. "Others maintain that coined money is a mere sham, a thing not natural, but conventional only, because, if the users substitute another commodity for it, it is worthless, and because it is not useful as a means to any of the necessities of life." (Aristoteles, *De Republica* [p. 15]. [The English translation is from Aristotle, *Politica*, 1257b.])

*** Sir John Mandeville, *Voyages and Travels*, London, 1705, p. 105: "This Emperor (of Cattay or China) may dispende ols muche as he wile withouten estymacion. For he despendethe not, nor makethe no money, but of lether emprendeth, or of papyre. And when that money

117

to the transformation of the metal coin into a token of value which is brought about by the circulation process itself. Such references occur in the works of Benjamin Franklin[*] and Bishop Berkeley.[**]

How many reams of paper cut into fragments can circulate as money? In this form the question is absurd. Worthless tokens become tokens of value only when they represent gold within the process of circulation, and they can represent it only to the amount of gold which would circulate as coin, an amount which depends on the value of gold if the exchange-value of the commodities and the velocity of their metamorphoses are given. The number of pieces of paper with a denomination of £5 which could be used in circulation would be one-fifth of the number of pieces of paper with a denomination of £1, and if all payments were to be transacted in shilling notes, then twenty times more shilling notes than pound notes would have to circulate. If gold coin were represented by notes of different denomination, e.g., £5 notes, £1 notes and 10s. notes, the number of the different types of tokens of value needed would not just be determined by the quantity of gold required in the sphere of circulation as a whole, but by the quantity needed in the sphere of circulation of each particular type of note. If £14 million were the level below which the circulation of a country never fell (this is the presupposition of English Banking legislation, not however with

---

hathe ronne so longe that it begynethe to waste, then men beren it to the Emperoure Tresorye, and then they taken newe Money for the old. And that money gothe thorghe out all the contree, and thorge out all his Provynces. . . . They make no money nouther of Gold nor of Sylver", and Mandeville adds, "therefore he may despende ynew and outrageously."

[*] Benjamin Franklin, *Remarks and Facts Relative to the American Paper Money*, 1764, *op. cit.*, p. 348: "At this very time, even the silver money in England is obliged to the legal tender for part of its value; that part which is the difference between its real weight and its denomination. Great part of the shillings and sixpences now current are by wearing become 5, 10, 20, and some of the sixpences even 50%, too light. For this difference between the *real* and the *nominal* you have no intrinsic value; you have not so much as paper, you have nothing. It is the legal tender, with the knowledge that it can easily be repassed for the same value, that makes three pennyworth of silver pass for a sixpence."

[**] Berkeley, *op. cit.* [p. 3]. "Whether the denominations being retained, although the bullion were gone . . . might not nevertheless . . . a circulation of commerce (be) maintained?"

regard to coin but to credit money), then 14 million pieces of paper, each a token of value representing £1, could circulate. If the value of gold decreased or increased because the labour-time required for its production had fallen or risen then the number of pound notes in circulation would increase or decrease in inverse ratio to the change in the value of gold, provided the exchange-value of the same mass of commodities remained unchanged. Supposing gold were superseded by silver as the standard of value and the relative value of silver to gold were 1:15, then 210 million pound notes would have to circulate henceforth instead of 14 million, if from now on each piece of paper was to represent the same amount of silver as it had previously represented of gold. The number of pieces of paper is thus determined by the quantity of gold currency which they represent in circulation, and as they are tokens of value only in so far as they take the place of gold currency, their value is simply determined by their *quantity*. Whereas, therefore, the quantity of gold in circulation depends on the prices of commodities, the value of the paper in circulation, on the other hand, depends solely on its own quantity.

The intervention of the State which issues paper money with a legal rate of exchange—and we speak only of this type of paper money—seems to invalidate the economic law. The State, whose mint price merely provided a definite weight of gold with a name and whose mint merely imprinted its stamp on gold, seems now to transform paper into gold by the magic of its imprint. Because the pieces of paper have a legal rate of exchange, it is impossible to prevent the State from thrusting any arbitrarily chosen number of them into circulation and to imprint them at will with any monetary denomination such as £1, £5, or £20. Once the notes are in circulation it is impossible to drive them out, for the frontiers of the country limit their movement, on the one hand, and on the other hand they lose all value, both use-value and exchange-value, *outside* the sphere of circulation. Apart from their function they are useless scraps of paper. But this power of the State is mere illusion. It may throw any number of paper notes of any denomination into circulation but its control ceases with this mechanical act. As soon as the token of value or paper money enters the sphere of circulation it is subject to the inherent laws of this sphere.

Let us assume that £14 million is the amount of gold required for the circulation of commodities and that the State throws 210 million notes each called £1 into circulation: these 210 million would then stand for a total of gold worth £14 million. The effect would be the same as if the notes issued by the State were to represent a metal whose value was one-fifteenth that of gold or that each note was intended to represent one-fifteenth of the previous weight of gold. This would have changed nothing but the nomenclature of the standard of prices, which is of course purely conventional, quite irrespective of whether it was brought about directly by a change in the monetary standard or indirectly by an increase in the number of paper notes issued in accordance with a new lower standard. As the name pound sterling would now indicate one-fifteenth of the previous quantity of gold, all commodity-prices would be fifteen times higher and 210 million pound notes would now be indeed just as necessary as 14 million had previously been. The decrease in the quantity of gold which each individual token of value represented would be proportional to the increased aggregate value of these tokens. The rise of prices would be merely a reaction of the process of circulation, which forcibly placed the tokens of value on a par with the quantity of gold which they are supposed to replace in the sphere of circulation.

One finds a number of occasions in the history of the debasement of currency by English and French governments when the rise in prices was not proportionate to the debasement of the silver coins. The reason was simply that the increase in the volume of currency was not proportional to its debasement; in other words, if the exchange-value of commodities was in future to be evaluated in terms of the lower standard of value and to be realised in coins corresponding to this lower standard, then an inadequate number of coins with lower metal content had been issued. This is the solution of the difficulty which was not resolved by the controversy between Locke and Lowndes. The rate at which a token of value—whether it consists of paper or bogus gold and silver is quite irrelevant—can take the place of definite quantities of gold and silver calculated according to the mint-price depends on the number of tokens in circulation and by no means on the material of which they are made. The difficulty in grasping this relation is due to the fact that the two functions of money—as a standard of value and a medium of circulation—are governed not only by conflicting laws, but by laws which appear to be at variance with the antithetical features of the two functions. As regards its function as a standard of value, when money serves solely as money of account and gold merely as nominal gold, it is the physical material used which is the crucial factor. Exchange-values expressed in terms of silver, or as silver prices, look of course quite different from exchange-values expressed in terms of gold, or as gold prices. On the other hand, when it functions as a medium of circulation, when money is not just imaginary but must be present as a real thing side by side with other commodities, its material is irrelevant and its quantity becomes the crucial factor. Although whether it is a pound of gold, of silver or of copper is decisive for the standard measure, mere number makes the coin an adequate embodiment of any of these standard measures, quite irrespective of its own material. But it is at variance with common sense that in the case of purely imaginary money everything should depend on the physical substance, whereas in the case of the corporeal coin everything should depend on a numerical relation that is nominal.

The rise or fall of commodity-prices corresponding to an increase or decrease in the volume of paper notes—the latter where paper notes are the sole medium of circulation—is accordingly merely a forcible assertion by the process of circulation of a law which was mechanically infringed by extraneous action; i.e., the law that the quantity of gold in circulation is determined by the prices of commodities and the volume of tokens of value in circulation is determined by the amount of gold currency which they replace in circulation. The circulation process will, on the other hand, absorb or as it were digest any number of paper notes, since, irrespective of the gold title borne by the token of value when entering circulation, it is compressed to a token of the quantity of gold which could circulate instead.

In the circulation of tokens of value all the laws governing the circulation of real money seem to be reversed and turned upside down. Gold circulates because it has value, whereas paper has value because it circulates. If the exchange-value of commodities is given, the quantity of gold in circulation depends on its value, whereas the value of paper tokens depends on the number of tokens in circulation. The amount of gold in circulation increases or decreases with the rise or fall of commodity-prices, whereas commodity-prices seem to rise or fall with the changing amount of paper in circulation. The circulation of commodities can absorb only a certain quantity of gold currency, the alternating contraction and expansion of the volume of money in circulation manifesting itself accordingly as an inevitable law, whereas any amount of paper money seems to be absorbed by circulation. The State which issues coins even $1/100$ of a grain below standard weight debases gold and silver currency and therefore upsets its function as a medium of circulation, whereas the issue of worthless pieces of paper which have nothing in common with metal except the denomination of the coinage is a perfectly correct operation. The gold coin obviously represents the value of commodities only after the value has been assessed in terms of gold or expressed as a price, whereas the token of value seems to represent the value of commodities directly. It is thus evident that a person who restricts his studies of monetary circulation to an analysis of the circulation of paper money with a legal rate of exchange must misunderstand the inherent laws of monetary circulation. These laws indeed appear not only to be turned upside down in the circulation of tokens of value but even annulled; for the movements of paper money, when it is issued in the appropriate amount, are not characteristic of it as token of value, whereas its specific movements are due to infringements of its correct proportion to gold, and do not directly arise from the metamorphosis of commodities.

3. MONEY

Money as distinguished from coin is the result of the circuit C—M—C and constitutes the starting point of the circuit M—C—M, that is the exchange of money for commodities so as to exchange commodities for money. In the form C—M—C it is the commodity that is the beginning and the end of the transaction; in the form M—C—M it is money. Money mediates the exchange of commodities in the first circuit, the commodity mediates the evolution of money into money in the second circuit. Money, which serves solely as a medium in the first circuit, appears as the goal of circulation in the second, whereas the commodity, which was the goal in the first circuit, appears simply as a means in the second. Because money itself is already the result of the circuit C—M—C, the result of circulation appears to be also its point of departure in the form M—C—M. The exchange of material is the content of C—M—C, whereas the real content of the second circuit, M—C—M, is the commodity in the form in which it emerged from the first circuit.

In the formula C—M—C the two extremes are commodities of the same value, which are at the same time however qualitatively different use-values. Their exchange, C—C, is real exchange of material. On the other hand, in the formula M—C—M both extremes are gold and moreover gold of the same value. But it seems absurd to exchange gold for commodities in order to exchange commodities for gold, or if one considers the final result M—M, to exchange gold for gold. But if one translates M—C—M into the formula—to *buy* in order to *sell*, which means simply to exchange gold for gold with the aid of an intermediate movement, one will immediately recognise the predominant form of bourgeois production. Nevertheless, in real life people do not buy in order to sell, but they buy at a low price in order to sell at a high price. They exchange money for commodities in order then to exchange these for a larger amount of money, so that the extremes M, M are quantitatively different, even if not qualitatively. This quantitative difference presupposes the *exchange of non-equivalents*, whereas commodities and money as such are merely antithetical forms of the commodity, in other words, different forms of existence of the same value. Money and commodity in the circuit M—C—M therefore imply more advanced relations of production, and within simple circulation the circuit is merely a reflection of movement of a more complex character. Hence money as distinct from the medium of circulation must be derived from C—M—C, the immediate form of commodity circulation.

Gold, *i.e.*, the specific commodity which serves as standard of value and medium of circulation, becomes *money* without any special effort on the part of society. Silver has not become money in England, where it is neither the standard of value nor the predominant medium of circulation, similarly gold ceased to be money in Holland as soon as it was deposed from its position of standard of value. In the first place, a commodity in which the functions of standard of value and medium of circulation are united accordingly becomes money, or the unity of standard of value and medium of circulation is money. But as such a unity gold in its turn possesses an independent existence which is distinct from these two functions. As the standard of value gold is merely nominal money and nominal gold; purely as a medium of circulation it is symbolic money and symbolic gold, but in its simple metallic corporeality gold is money or money is real gold.

Let us for a moment consider the commodity gold, that is money, in a state of rest and its relations with other commodities. All prices of commodities signify definite amounts of gold; they are thus merely notional gold or notional money, *i.e.*, *symbols* of gold, just as, on the other hand, money considered as a token of value appeared to be merely a symbol of the prices of commodities.* Since all commodities are therefore merely notional money, money is the only real commodity. Gold is *the material aspect of abstract wealth* in contradistinction to commodities which only represent the independent form of exchange-value, of universal social labour and of abstract wealth. So far as use-value is concerned, each commodity represents only one element of physical wealth, only one separate facet of wealth, through its relation to a particular need. But money satisfies any need since it can be immediately turned into the object of any need. Its own use-value is realised in the endless series of use-values which constitute its equivalents. All the physical wealth evolved in the world of commodities is contained in a latent state in this solid piece of metal. Thus whereas the prices of commodities represent gold, the universal equivalent or abstract wealth, the use-value of gold represents the use-values of all commodities. Gold is, therefore, *the material symbol of physical wealth.* It is the "epitome of all things" (Boisguillebert), the compendium of social wealth. As regards its form, it is the direct incarnation of universal labour, and as regards its content the quintessence of all

---

* "Not only are precious metals tokens of things ... but alternatively things ... are also tokens of gold and silver." A. Genovesi, *Lezioni di Economia Civile*, 1765, in Custodi, *Parte Moderna*, t. VIII, p. 281.

concrete labour. It is universal wealth in an individual form.* Functioning as a medium of circulation, gold suffered all manner of injuries, it was clipped and even reduced to a purely symbolical scrap of paper. Its golden splendour is restored when it serves as money. The servant becomes the master.** The mere underling becomes the god of commodities.***

a. Hoarding

Gold as money was in the first place divorced from the medium of circulation because the metamorphosis of the commodity was interrupted and the commodity remained in the form of gold. This happens whenever a sale is not immediately turned into a purchase. The fact that gold as money assumes an independent existence is thus above all a tangible expression of the separation of the process of circulation or of the metamorphosis of commodities into two discrete and separate transactions which exist side by side. The coin itself becomes money as soon as its movement is interrupted. In the hands of the seller who receives it in return for a commodity it is money, and not coin; but when it leaves his hands it becomes a coin once more. Everybody sells the particular commodity which he

---

* Gold and silver are "universal wealth". Petty, *Political Arithmetick*, p. 242.

** E. Misselden, *Free Trade, or the Means to Make Trade Florish*, London, 1622. "The natural matter of Commerce is Merchandize, which Merchants from the end of Trade have stiled Commodities. The Artificiall matter of Commerce is Money, which hath obtained the title of sinewes of Warre and of State. ... Money, though it be in nature and time after Merchandize, yet forasmuch as it is now in use become the chiefe" (p. 7). He compares the position of commodity and money with that of the descendents of "Old Jacob", who "blessing his Grandchildren, crost his hands, and laide his right hand on the yonger, and his left hand on the elder" (*l.c.*). Boisguillebert, *Dissertation sur la nature des richesses*. "Thus the slave of commerce has become its master.... The misery of the peoples is due to the fact that the slave has been turned into a master or rather into a tyrant" (pp. 395, 399).

*** "These metals (gold and silver) have been turned into idols, and disregarding the goal and purpose they were intended to fulfil in commerce, *i.e.*, to serve as tokens in exchange and reciprocal transfer, they were allowed to abandon this service almost entirely in order to be transformed into *divinities* to whom more goods, important needs and even human beings were sacrificed and continue to be sacrificed, than were ever sacrificed to the false divinities even in blind antiquity..." (Boisguillebert, *op. cit.*, p. 395).

125

produces, but he buys all other commodities that he needs as a social being. How often he appears on the market as a seller depends on the labour-time required to produce his commodity, whereas his appearance as a buyer is determined by the constant renewal of his vital requirements. In order to be able to buy without selling, he must have sold something without buying. The circuit C—M—C is indeed the dynamic unity of sale and purchase only in so far as it is simultaneously the continuous process of their separation. So that money as coin may flow continuously, coin must continuously congeal into money. The continual movement of coin implies its perpetual stagnation in larger or smaller amounts in reserve funds of coin which arise everywhere within the framework of circulation and which are at the same time a condition of circulation. The formation, distribution, dissolution and re-formation of these funds constantly changes; existing funds disappear continuously and their disappearance is a continuous fact. This unceasing transformation of coin into money and of money into coin was expressed by Adam Smith when he said that, in addition to the particular commodity he sells, every commodity-owner must always keep in stock a certain amount of the general commodity with which he buys. We have seen that M—C, the second member of the circuit C—M—C, splits up into a series of purchases, which are not effected all at once but successively over a period of time, so that one part of M circulates as coin, while the other part remains at rest as money. In this case, money is in fact only *suspended coin* and the various component parts of the coinage in circulation appear, constantly changing, now in one form, now in another. The first transformation of the medium of circulation into money constitutes therefore merely a technical aspect of the circulation of money.*

The first spontaneously evolved form of wealth consists

---

* *Boisguillebert* suspects that the first immobilisation of the *perpetuum mobile, i.e.*, the negation of its function as the medium of circulation, will immediately render it independent in relation to commodities. Money, he says, must be "in constant motion, which is only the case so long as it moves, but as soon as it becomes immobile all is lost" (Boisguillebert, *Le détail de la France*, p. 213). What he overlooks is that this inactivity is the prerequisite of its movement. What he actually wants is that the value form of commodities should be a quite insignificant aspect of their metabolism, but should never become an end in itself.

of an overplus or excess of products, *i.e.* of the portion of products which are not directly required as use-values, or else of the possession of products whose use-value lies outside the range of mere necessity. When considering the transition from commodity to money, we saw that at a primitive stage of production it is this overplus or excess of products which really forms the sphere of commodity exchange. Superfluous products become exchangeable products or commodities. The adequate form of this surplus is gold and silver, the first form in which wealth as abstract social wealth is kept. It is not only possible to store commodities in the form of gold and silver, *i.e.*, in the material shape of money, but gold and silver constitute wealth in preserved form. Every use-value fulfils its function while it is being consumed, that is destroyed, but the use-value of gold as money is to represent exchange-value, to be the embodiment of universal labour-time as an amorphous raw material. As amorphous metal exchange-value possesses an imperishable form. Gold or silver as money thus immobilised constitutes *a hoard*. In the case of nations with purely metallic currency, such as the ancients, hoarding becomes a universal practice extending from the individual to the State, which guards its State hoard. In Asia and Egypt, during their early period, these hoards were in the custody of kings and priests and served mainly as evidence of their power. In Greece and Rome the creation of State hoards became a principle of public policy, for excess wealth in this form is always safe and can be used at any moment. The rapid transfer of such hoards by conquerors from one country to another and their sudden effusion in part into the sphere of circulation are characteristics of the economy of antiquity.

As *materialised labour-time* gold is a pledge for its own magnitude of value, and, since it is the embodiment of *universal* labour-time, its continuous function as exchange-value is vouched for by the process of circulation. The simple fact that the commodity-owner is able to retain his commodities in the form of exchange-value, or to retain the exchange-value as commodities, makes the exchange of commodities, in order to recover them transformed into gold, the specific motive of circulation. The metamorphosis of commodities C—M takes place for the sake of their metamorphosis, for the purpose of transforming particular physical wealth into general social wealth. Change of form—instead of exchange of matter—becomes an end in itself. Exchange-value, which was merely a form, is turned into the content of the movement. Commodities remain wealth, that is commodities, only while they keep within the sphere of circulation, and they remain in this liquid state only in so far as they ossify into silver and gold. They remain liquid as the crystallisation of the process of circulation. But gold and silver establish themselves as money only in so far as they do not function as means of circulation. *They become money as non-means of circulation.* The withdrawal of commodities from circulation in the form of gold is thus the only means of keeping them continuously in circulation.

The owner of commodities can recover as money from circulation only as much as he put into it in the form of commodities. Looked at from the standpoint of the circulation of commodities, the first condition of hoarding is constant selling, the incessant throwing of commodities into circulation. On the other hand, money as a medium of circulation constantly disappears in the process of circulation itself, since it is all the time being realised in use-values and dissolved in ephemeral enjoyments. It must, therefore, be withdrawn from the stream of circulation; in other words commodities must be retained in the first stage of their metamorphosis in order to prevent money from functioning as means of purchase. The owner of commodities who has now become a hoarder of money must sell as much as possible and buy as little as possible, as even old Cato preached—*patrem familias vendacem, non emacem esse.*[a] Parsimony is the negative pre-condition of hoarding, just as industry is its positive pre-condition. The smaller the proportion that is withdrawn from circulation as an equivalent for the commodities [thrown into it] consisting of particular commodities or use-values, the larger the proportion that consists of money or exchange-value.* The appropriation of wealth in its general form therefore implies renunciation of the material reality of wealth. Hence the motive power of hoarding is *avarice*, which desires not

---

* "The more the stock ... is ... encreased in wares, the more it decreaseth in treasure." E. Misselden, *op. cit.*, p. 23.

---

[a] The head of the family should be eager to sell, not eager to buy. Cato The Elder, *De re rustica.—Ed.*

128

commodities as use-values, but exchange-value as a commodity. So as to take possession of superfluous wealth in its general form, particular needs must be treated as luxuries and superfluities. For instance, in 1593 the Cortes sent a petition to Philip II, which among other matters contains the following passage:

"The Cortes of Valladolid requested Your Majesty in 1586 not to permit the further importation into this kingdom of candles, glass-ware, jewellery, knives and similar articles coming from abroad, which, though they are of no use to human life, have to be exchanged for gold, as though the Spaniards were *Indians*."[a]

The hoarder of money scorns the worldly, temporal and ephemeral enjoyments in order to chase after the eternal treasure which can be touched neither by moths nor by rust, and which is wholly celestial and wholly mundane.

In the above-quoted work Misselden writes: "The general remote cause of our want of money is the great excesse of this Kingdom in consuming the Commodities of Forreine Countries, which prove to us discommodities, in hindering us of so much treasure, which otherwise would bee brought in, in lieu of those toyes.... Wee ... consume amongst us, that great abundance of the Wines of Spaine, of France, of the Rhene, of the Levant ... the Raisins of Spaine, the Corints of the Levant, the Lawnes and Cambricks of Hannaults ... the Silkes of Italie, the Sugers and Tobaco of the West Indies, the Spices of the East Indies: All which are of *no necessetie* unto us, and yet are bought with ready mony."[*]

Wealth in the shape of gold and silver is imperishable because exchange-value is represented by an indestructible metal and especially because gold and silver are prevented from functioning as means of circulation and thus from becoming a merely transient monetary aspect of commodities. The perishable content is thus sacrificed to the non-perishable form.

"Suppose that Money be taken (by means of Taxation) from one who spendeth the same ... in superfluous eating and drinking, or any other perishing Commodity; and the same transferred to one that bestoweth it on Cloaths; I say, that even in this case the Commonwealth hath some little advantage; because Cloaths do not altogether perish so soon as Meats and Drinks. But if the same be spent in Furniture of

---

[*] E. Misselden, *op. cit.*, pp. 11-13 *passim*.

[a] Sempéré, *Considérations sur les causes de la grandeur et de la décadence de la Monarchie Espagnole*, Vol. I, pp. 275-76.—*Ed.*

Houses, the advantage is yet a little more; if in Building of Houses, yet more; if in improving of Lands, working of Mines, Fishing, etc., yet more; but most of all, in bringing Gold and Silver into the Country; because those things are not only not perishable, but are esteemed for Wealth at all times and every where; whereas other Commodities [which are perishable, or whose value depends upon the Fashion; or which are contingently scarce and plentiful,] are Wealth, but *pro hic et nunc.*ᵃ"*

An outward expression of the desire to withdraw money from the stream of circulation and to save it from the social metabolism is the *burying* of it, so that social wealth is turned into an imperishable subterranean hoard with an entirely furtive private relationship to the commodity-owner. Doctor Bernier, who spent some time at Aurangzeb's court at Delhi, relates that merchants, especially non-Moslem heathens, in whose hands nearly the entire commerce and all money are concentrated—secretly bury their money deep in the ground,

"being held in thrall to the belief that the money they hide during their lifetime will serve them in the next world after their death".**

Incidentally, in so far as the hoarder of money combines asceticism with assiduous diligence he is intrinsically a Protestant by religion and still more a Puritan.

"It cannot be denied that buying and selling are necessary practices, which cannot be dispensed with and may surely be used in a Christian manner, especially as regards things that serve necessity and honour; for thus cattle, wool, corn, butter, milk and other goods were bought and sold by the patriarchs. These are gifts of God, which He produces from the soil and divides among men. But foreign trade, which brings merchandise from Calicut and India and other places— merchandise such as precious silks and jewellery and spices, which are used only for display and serve no need—and drains money from the country and the people, should not be permitted if we had a government and princes. But I do not want to write of this now, for I consider that in the end when we have no more money, it will have to be abandoned, and finery and gluttony as well; for all writing and preaching will be in vain until we are compelled by necessity and poverty."***

---

* Petty, *Political Arithmetick*, p. 196.

** François Bernier, *Voyages contenant la description des états du Grand Mogol*, Paris edition of 1830, t. 1, *cf.* pp. 312-14.

*** Doctor Martin Luther, *Bücher vom Kaufhandel und Wucher*, 1524. Luther writes in the same passage: "God has brought it about that we

---

ᵃ At a particular place and a particular time.—*Ed.*

Even in advanced bourgeois societies hoards of money are buried at times of upheaval in the social metabolic process. This is an attempt to save social cohesion—for the commodity-owner this cohesion is represented by the commodity and the adequate embodiment of the commodity is money—in its compact form from the social movement. The social sinews of things are buried alongside the body whose sinews they are.

If the hoard were not constantly in tension with circulation, it would now simply be a heap of useless metal, its monetary soul would have disappeared and nothing but burnt-out ashes of circulation, its *caput mortuum*, would remain. Money, *i.e.*, exchange-value which has assumed an independent existence, is by nature the embodiment of abstract wealth; but, on the other hand, any given sum of money is a quantitatively finite magnitude of value. The quantitative delimitation of exchange-value conflicts with its qualitative universality, and the hoarder regards the limi-

---

Germans must thrust our gold and silver into foreign countries making all the world rich while we ourselves remain beggars. England would surely have less gold if Germany refused to take her cloth, and the King of Portugal, too, would have less, if we refused to take his spices. If you calculate how much money is extracted, without need or cause, from the German territories during one fair at Frankfurt, you will wonder how it comes about that even a single farthing is still left in Germany. Frankfurt is the silver and gold drain through which everything that arises and grows, that is minted or struck here flows out of the country; if this hole were plugged one would not hear the present complaint that there is everywhere unmitigated debts and no money, that the entire country and all the towns are despoilt by usury. But never mind, things will nevertheless continue in this way: we Germans have to remain Germans, we do not desist unless we have to." [Pp. 4-5.]

In the above-quoted work *Misselden* wants gold and silver to be retained at all events within the bounds of Christendom: "The other forreine remote causes of the want of money, are the Trades maintained out of Christendome to Turky, Persia and the East Indies, which trades are maintained for the most part with ready money, yet in a different manner from the trades of Christendome within it selfe. For although the trades within Christendome are driven with ready monies, yet those monies are still contained and continued within the bounds of Christendome. There is indeede a fluxus and refluxus, a flood and ebbe of the monies of Christendome traded within it selfe; for sometimes there is more in one part of Christendome, sometimes there is lesse in another, as one Countrey wanteth and another aboundeth: It cometh and goeth, and wirleth about the Circle of Christendome, but is still contained within the compasse thereof. But the money that is traded out of Christendome into the parts aforesaid is continually issued out and never returneth againe." [Pp. 19-20.]

tation as a restriction, which in fact becomes also a qualitative restriction, *i.e.*, the hoard is turned into a merely limited representation of material wealth. Money as the universal equivalent may be directly expressed, as we have seen, in terms of an equation, in which it forms one side while the other side consists of an endless series of commodities. The degree in which the realisation of exchange-value approaches such an infinite series, in other words how far it corresponds to the concept of exchange-value, depends on its magnitude. After all, movement of exchange-value as such, as an automaton, can only be expansion of its quantitative limits. But in passing one set of quantitative limits of the hoard new restrictions are set up, which in turn must be abolished. What appears as a restriction is not a particular limit of the hoard, but any limitation of it. The formation of hoards therefore has no intrinsic limits, no bounds in itself, but is an unending process, each particular result of which provides an impulse for a new beginning. Although the hoard can only be increased by being preserved, on the other hand it can only be preserved by being increased.

Money is not just *an* object of the passion for enrichment, it is *the* object of it. This urge is essentially *auri sacra fames*.[a] The passion for enrichment by contrast with the urge to acquire particular material wealth, *i.e.*, use-values, such as clothes, jewellery, herds of cattle, etc., becomes possible only when general wealth as such is represented by a specific thing and can thus be retained as a particular commodity. Money therefore appears both as the object and the source of the desire for riches.[*] The underlying reason is in fact that exchange-value as such becomes the goal, and consequently also an expansion of exchange-value. Avarice clings to the hoard and does not allow money to become a medium of circulation, but greed for gold preserves the monetary soul of the hoard and maintains it in constant tension with circulation.

The activity which amasses hoards is, on the one hand, the withdrawal of money from circulation by constantly

---

[*] "But from money first springs avarice ... this grows by stages into a kind of madness, no longer merely avarice but a positive hunger for gold." (Plinius, *Historia naturalis*, L. XXXIII, C. III.) [The English translation is from Pliny, *Natural History*, Vol. IX, Book XXXIII, pp. 39-49, London, 1952.]

---

[a] The accursed greed for gold.—*Ed.*

repeated sales, and on the other, simple piling up, *accumulation*. It is indeed only in the sphere of simple circulation, and specifically in the form of hoards, that accumulation of wealth as such takes place, whereas the other so-called forms of accumulation, as we shall see later, are quite improperly, and only by analogy with simple accumulation of money, regarded as accumulation. All other commodities are accumulated either as use-values, and in this case the manner of their accumulation is determined by the specific features of their use-value. Storing of corn, for example, requires special equipment; collecting sheep makes a person a shepherd; accumulation of slaves and land necessitates relations of domination and servitude, and so on. Unlike the simple act of piling things up, the formation of stocks of particular types of wealth requires special methods and develops special traits in the individual. Or wealth in the shape of commodities may be accumulated as exchange-value, and in this case accumulation becomes a commercial or specifically economic operation. The one concerned in it becomes a corn merchant, a cattle-dealer, and so forth. Gold and silver constitute money not as the result of any activity of the person who accumulates them, but as crystals of the process of circulation which takes place without his assistance. He need do nothing but put them aside, piling one lot upon another, a completely senseless activity, which if applied to any other commodity would result in its devaluation.*

---

* Horace, therefore, knows nothing of the philosophy of hoarding treasures, when he says (*Satir.* L. II, Satir. III): "If a man were to buy harps, and soon as bought were to pile them together, though feeling no interest in the harp or any Muse; if, though no cobbler, he did the same with shoes, knives and lasts; with ships' sails, though set against a trader's life—everyone would call him crazy and mad, and rightly too. How differs from these the man who hoards up silver and gold, though he knows not how to use his store, and fears to touch it as though hallowed?" [Horace, *Satires, Epistles, Ars Poetica*, London, 1942, p. 163.]

Mr. *Senior* knows more about the subject:

"Money seems to be the only object for which the desire is universal; and it is so, because money is *abstract wealth.* Its possessor may satisfy at will his requirements whatever they may be." *Principes fondamentaux de l'économie politique,* traduit par le Comte Jean Arrivabene, Paris, 1836, p. 221. [The English passage is taken from Senior, *Political Economy*, 1850, p. 27.]. And *Storch* as well: "As money represents all other forms of wealth, one needs only to accumulate it in order to obtain all other kinds of wealth that exist on earth" (*op. cit.*, t. II, p. 135).

Our hoarder is a martyr to exchange-value, a holy ascetic seated at the top of a metal column. He cares for wealth only in its social form, and accordingly he hides it away from society. He wants commodities in a form in which they can always circulate and he therefore withdraws them from circulation. He adores exchange-value and he consequently refrains from exchange. The liquid form of wealth and its petrification, the elixir of life and the philosophers' stone are wildly mixed together like an alchemist's apparitions. His imaginary boundless thirst for enjoyment causes him to renounce all enjoyment. Because he desires to satisfy all social requirements, he scarcely satisfies the most urgent physical wants. While clinging to wealth in its metallic corporeality the hoarder reduces it to a mere chimaera. But the accumulation of money for the sake of money is in fact the barbaric form of production for the sake of production, *i.e.*, the development of the productive powers of social labour beyond the limits of customary requirements. The less advanced is the production of commodities, the more important is hoarding—the first form in which exchange-value assumes an independent existence as money—and it therefore plays an important role among ancient nations, in Asia up to now, and among contemporary agrarian nations, where exchange-value has not yet penetrated all relations of production. Before, however, examining the specific economic function that hoarding fulfils in relation to metallic currency, let us note another form of hoarding.

Gold and silver articles, quite irrespective of their aesthetic properties, can be turned into money, since the material of which they consist is the material of money, just as gold coins and gold bars can be transformed into such articles. Since gold and silver are the material of abstract wealth, their employment as concrete use-values is the most striking manifestation of wealth, and although at certain stages of production the commodity-owner hides his treasures, he is impelled to show to other commodity-owners that he is a rich man, whenever he can safely do so. He bedecks himself and his house with gold.* In Asia, and India in particular,

---

* How little the inner man of the individual owner of commodities has changed even when he has become civilised and turned into a capitalist is for instance proved by a London representative of an international banking house who displayed a framed £100,000 note as an

where the formation of hoards does not play a subordinate part in the total mechanism of production, as it does in bourgeois economy, but where this form of wealth is still considered a final goal, gold and silver articles are in fact merely hoards in an aesthetic form. The law in mediaeval England treated gold and silver articles simply as a kind of treasure-hoard, since the rough labour applied to them added little to their value. They were intended to be thrown again into circulation and the fineness of the metal of which they were made was therefore specified in the same way as that of coin. The fact that increasing wealth leads to an increased use of gold and silver in the form of luxury articles is such a simple matter that ancient thinkers* clearly understood it, whereas modern economists put forward the incorrect proposition that the use of silver and gold articles increases not in proportion to the rise in wealth but in proportion to the fall in the value of precious metals. There is therefore always a flaw in their otherwise accurate explanations regarding the use of Californian and Australian gold, for according to their views the increased employment of gold as raw material is not justified by a corresponding fall in its value. As a result of the fight between the American colonies and Spain[20] and the interruption of mining by revolutions, the average annual output of precious metals decreased by more than one-half between 1810 and 1830. The amount of coin circulating in Europe decreased by almost one-sixth in 1829 as compared with 1809. Although the output thus decreased and the costs of production (provided they changed at all) increased, nevertheless an exceptionally rapid rise in the use of precious metals as articles of luxury took place in England even during the war and on the continent following the Treaty of Paris. Their use increased with the growth of wealth in general.** It may be regarded as a general law that the conversion of gold and silver coin into luxury goods predominates in times of peace, while their reconversion into bars and also into coin only predominates in turbulent periods.*** How considerable a

appropriate family coat of arms. The point in this case is the derisory and supercilious air with which the note looks down upon circulation.
* See the passage from Xenophon quoted later.
** Jacob, op. cit., Vol. II, ch. 25 and 26.
*** "In times of great agitation and insecurity, especially during internal commotions or invasions, gold and silver articles are rapidly con-

proportion of the gold and silver stock exists in the shape of luxury articles compared with the amount used as money is shown by the fact that in 1829, according to Jacob, the ratio was as 2 to 1 in England, while in Europe as a whole and America, 25 per cent more precious metal was used in luxury goods than in coins.

We have seen that the circulation of money is merely a manifestation of the metamorphosis of commodities, or of the transformation which accompanies the social metabolism. The total quantity of gold in circulation must therefore perpetually increase or decrease in accordance with the varying aggregate price of the commodities in circulation, that is in accordance, on the one hand, with the volume of their metamorphoses which take place simultaneously and, on the other hand, with the prevailing velocity of their transformation. This is only possible provided that the proportion of money in circulation to the total amount of money in a given country varies continuously. Thanks to the formation of hoards this condition is fulfilled. If prices fall or the velocity of circulation increases, then the money ejected from the sphere of circulation is absorbed by the reservoirs of hoarders; if prices rise or the velocity of circulation decreases, then these hoards open and a part of them streams back into circulation. The solidification of circulating money into hoards and the flowing of the hoards into circulation is a continuously changing and oscillating movement, and the prevalence of the one or the other trend is solely determined by variations in the circulation of commodities. The hoards thus act as channels for the supply or withdrawal of circulating money, so that the amount of money circulating as coin is always just adequate to the immediate requirements of circulation. If the total volume of circulation suddenly expands and the fluid unity of sale and purchase predominates, so that the total amount of prices to be realised grows even faster than does the velocity of circulation of money, then the hoards dwindle visibly; whenever an abnormal stagnation prevails in the movement as a whole, that is when the separation of sale from purchase predominates, then the medium of circulation solidifies into money to a remarkable extent and the reservoirs of the

---

verted into money; whilst, during periods of tranquillity and prosperity, money is converted into plate and jewellery" (*op. cit.*, Vol. II, p. 357).

hoarders are filled far above their average level. In countries which have purely metallic currency or are at an early stage of development of production, hoards are extremely fragmented and scattered throughout the country, whereas in advanced bourgeois countries they are concentrated in the reservoirs of banks. Hoards must not be confused with reserve funds of coin, which form a constituent element of the total amount of money always in circulation, whereas the active relation of hoard and medium of circulation presupposes that the total amount of money decreases or increases. As we have seen, gold and silver articles also act both as channels for the withdrawal of precious metals and latent sources of supply. Under ordinary circumstances only the former function plays an important rôle in the economy of metallic currency.*

b. Means of Payment

Up to now two forms of money which differ from the medium of circulation have been considered, namely *suspended coin* and *hoard*. The first form, the temporary transformation of coins into money, reflects the fact that in a

---

* In the following passage *Xenophon* discusses money and hoard, two specific and distinct aspects of money: "Of all operations with which I am acquainted, this is the only one in which no sort of jealousy is felt at a further development of the industry ... the larger the quantity of ore discovered and the greater the amount of silver extracted, the greater the number of persons ready to engage in the operation.... No one when he has got sufficient furniture for his house dreams of making further purchases on this head, but of silver no one ever yet possessed so much that he was forced to cry 'Enough'. On the contrary, if ever anybody does become possessed of an immoderate amount he finds as much pleasure in digging a hole in the ground and hoarding it as an actual employment of it.... When a state is prosperous there is nothing which people so much desire as silver. The men want money to expend on beautiful armour and fine horses, and houses and sumptuous paraphernalia of all sorts. The women betake themselves to expensive apparel and ornaments of gold. Or when states are sick, either through barrenness of corn and other fruits, or through war, the demand for current coin is even more imperative (whilst the ground lies unproductive), to pay for necessaries or military aid." (Xenophon, *De Vectigalibus*, C. IV [transl. by H. G. Dakyns, London, 1892, Vol. II, pp. 335-36].) In Ch. 9, Book I of his *Politics*, Aristotle sets forth the two circuits of circulation C—M—C and M—C—M, which he calls "economics" and "Chrematistics", and their differences. The two forms under the names δίχη and χέρδος are contrasted with each other by the Greek tragedians, especially Euripides.

certain sphere of circulation, the second term of C—M—C, that is M—C the purchase, must break up into a series of successive purchases. Hoarding, however, is either simply due to the separation of the transaction C—M which does not proceed to M—C, or it is merely an independent development of the first metamorphosis of commodities, money, or the alienated form of existence of all commodities as distinct from means of circulation, which represents the always saleable form of the commodity. Coin held in reserve and hoards constitute money only as non-means of circulation, and are non-means of circulation merely because they do not circulate. The distinctive form of money which we now consider circulates or enters circulation, but does not function as means of circulation. Money as means of circulation was always means of purchase, but now it does not serve in that capacity.

When as a result of hoarding money becomes the embodiment of abstract social wealth and the material representative of physical wealth, this aspect of money acquires specific functions within the process of circulation. When money circulates simply as a means of circulation and hence as a means of purchase, this presupposes that commodity and money confront each other simultaneously; in other words, that the same value is available twice, as a commodity in the hands of the seller at one pole, and as money in the hands of the buyer at the other pole. The simultaneous existence of the two equivalents at opposite poles and their simultaneous change of place, or their mutual alienation, presupposes in its turn that seller and buyer enter into relation with each other only as owners of actually existing commodities. But the metamorphosis of commodities, in the course of which the various distinct forms of money are evolved, transforms the commodity-owners as well, and alters the social rôle they play in relation to one another. In the course of the metamorphosis of commodities the keeper of commodities changes his skin as often as the commodity undergoes a change or as money appears in a new form. Commodity-owners thus faced each other originally simply as commodity-owners; then one of them became a seller, the other a buyer; then each became alternately buyer and seller; then they became hoarders and finally rich men. Commodity-owners emerging from the process of circulation are accordingly different from those entering the process.

The different forms which money assumes in the process of circulation are in fact only crystallisations of the transformation of commodities, a transformation which is in its turn only the objective expression of the changing social relations in which commodity-owners conduct their exchange. New relations of intercourse arise in the process of circulation, and commodity-owners, who represent these changed relations, acquire new economic characteristics. In the same way as within the sphere of internal circulation money becomes nominal, and a mere piece of paper representing gold is able to function as money, so a buyer or seller who comes forward as a mere representative of money or commodities, namely one who represents future money or future commodities, is enabled by the same process to operate as a real buyer or seller.

All the distinct forms evolved by gold as money are merely manifestations of aspects latent in the metamorphosis of commodities, but these aspects did not assume a separate form in the simple circulation of money, in money as it appears as coin and the circuit C—M—C as a dynamic unity, or else they emerged merely as potentialities, as did for example the interruption of the matamorphosis of commodities. We have seen that in the course of the transaction C—M the commodity as a real use-value and nominal exchange-value is brought into relation with money as a real exchange-value and only nominal use-value. By alienating the commodity as use-value the seller realises its exchange-value and the use-value of money. In contrast, by alienating money as exchange-value, the buyer realises its use-value and the price of the commodity. Commodity and money, accordingly, change places. The active process of this bilateral polar antithesis is in its turn separated while it is being carried through. The seller actually alienates the commodity but realises its price in the first place only nominally. He has sold the commodity at its price, but the price will only be realised at a predetermined later date. The buyer buys as the representative of future money, whereas the seller sells as the owner of a commodity available here and now. On the one hand, the seller actually hands over the commodity as use-value without actually realising its price; on the other hand, the buyer actually realises his money in the use-value of the commodity without actually handing over the money as exchange-value.

Just as formerly money was represented by a token of value, so now it is symbolically represented by the buyer himself. Just as formerly the value-token as a universal symbol entailed a State guarantee and a legal rate, so now the buyer as a personal symbol gives rise to private, legally enforcible, contracts among commodity-owners.

Conversely, in the transaction M—C, money as a real means of purchase may be alienated, thus realising the price of the commodity before the use-value of the money is realised, or before the commodity is handed over. This happens, for instance, in the well-known form of advance-payment; also in the form of payment used by the English government to buy opium from Indian ryots, and is largely used by foreign merchants living in Russia to buy goods produced in that country. In these cases, however, money functions only in the familiar form of means of purchase and therefore requires no new definition,* or any further discussion. With regard to the changed form which the two transactions M—C and C—M assume here, we shall only note that the purely conceptual distinction of purchase and sale as it appears directly in circulation becomes now a real distinction, since there is only money in one case and only commodity in the other; in each of them, however, only the extreme is actually available from which the initiative comes. Both forms, moreover, have in common the fact that in each of them one equivalent exists only by common decision of buyer and seller, a decision which is mutually binding and is given a distinct legal form.

Seller and buyer become creditor and debtor. Whereas the commodity-owner as the guardian of a hoard was a rather comical figure, he now becomes terrifying, because he regards, not himself, but his neighbour as the embodiment of a definite sum of money, and turns his neighbour and not himself into a martyr to exchange-value. The former believer becomes a creditor,[a] and turns from religion to jurisprudence.

"I stay here on my bond!"[21]

---

* Of course capital, too, is advanced in the form of money and it is possible that the money advanced is capital advanced, but this aspect does not lie within the scope of simple circulation.

---

[a] In German a pun on the words "der Gläubige", the believer, and "der Gläubiger", the creditor.—*Ed.*

In the changed form of C—M, in which the commodity is actually on hand and the money is merely represented, money functions first as the measure of value. The exchange-value of the commodity is assessed in money as its measure, but the exchange-value assessed by contract, that is the price, exists not merely in the mind of the seller, but is also the measure of the liabilities of the buyer. Secondly, money functions here as means of purchase, although it is merely its future existence which casts its shadow before it, for it causes the commodity to move from the hands of the seller into those of the buyer. On the settlement day of the contract, money enters circulation, for it moves from the hands of the former buyer into those of the former seller. But it does not come into the sphere of circulation as means of circulation or means of purchase. It fulfilled these functions before it existed, and it appears on the scene after ceasing to perform these functions. It enters circulation as the only adequate equivalent of the commodity, as the absolute embodiment of exchange-value, as the last word of the exchange process, in short as money, and moreover as money functioning as the *universal means of payment*. Money functioning as means of payment appears to be the absolute commodity, but it remains within the sphere of circulation, not outside it as with the hoard. The difference between means of purchase and means of payment becomes very conspicuous, and unpleasantly so, at times of commercial crises.*

The conversion of products into money in the sphere of circulation appears originally simply as an individual necessity for the commodity-owner when his own product does not constitute use-value for himself, but has still to become a use-value through alienation. In order to make payment on the contractual settlement day, however, he must already have sold commodities. The evolution of the circulation process thus turns selling into a social necessity for him, quite irrespective of his individual needs. As a former buyer of commodities he is forced to become a seller of other commodities so as to obtain money, not as a means of purchase, but as a means of payment, as the absolute form of exchange-value. The conversion of commodities into money as a final act, or the first metamorphosis of commodities as the ulti-

---

* Luther emphasises the distinction which exists between means of purchase and means of payment. [Note in author's copy.]

mate goal, which in hoarding appeared to be the whim of the commodity-owner, has now become an economic function. The motive and the content of selling for the sake of payment constitutes the content of the circulation process, a content arising from its very form.

In this type of sale, the commodity moves from one position to another, although its first metamorphosis, its conversion into money, is deferred. On the buyer's side, however, the second metamorphosis is carried through, *i.e.*, money is reconverted into commodities, before the first metamorphosis has taken place, *i.e.*, before the conversion of the commodities into money. In this case, therefore, the first metamorphosis appears to take place later than the second. Hence money, the form of the commodity in its first metamorphosis, acquires a new distinctive aspect. Money, that is the independent development of exchange-value, is no longer an intermediary phase of commodity circulation, but its final result.

No proof in detail is needed to show that such *purchases on credit,* in which the two poles of the transaction are separated in time, evolve spontaneously on the basis of simple circulation of commodities. At first it happens that in the course of circulation certain commodity-owners confront one another repeatedly as buyers and sellers. Such repeated occurrences do not remain merely accidental, but commodities may, for example, be ordered for a future date at which they are to be delivered and paid for. The sale in this case takes place only nominally, *i.e.*, juridically, without the actual presence of commodities and money. The two forms of money, means of circulation and means of payment, are here still identical, since on the one hand commodities and money change places simultaneously, and on the other, money does not purchase commodities but realises the price of commodities previously sold. Moreover, owing to the specific nature of a number of use-values they are really alienated not by being in fact handed over but only by being leased for a definite period. For example, when one sells the use of a house for a month, its use-value is delivered only at the expiration of the month, although the house changes hands at the beginning of the month. Because in this case the actual transfer of the use-value and its real alienation are separated in time, the realisation of its price also takes place later than the date on which it changes hands. Finally, owing to differences in the period and length of time required for the production of different commodities, one producer comes to the market as a seller before the other can act as a buyer, and if the same commodity-owners repeatedly buy and sell one another's products, the two aspects of the transaction are separated according to the conditions of production of their commodities. This gives rise to relations of creditor and debtor among commodity-owners. These relations can be fully developed even before the credit system comes into being, although they are the natural basis of the latter. It is evident however that the evolution of the credit system, and therefore of the bourgeois mode of production in general, causes money to function increasingly as a means of payment to the detriment of its function both as a means of purchase and even more as an element of hoarding. For instance in England, coin is almost entirely confined to the sphere of retail trade and to petty transactions between producers and consumers, whereas money as means of payment predominates in the sphere of large commercial transactions.*

Money as the universal means of payment becomes the *universal commodity* of contracts, though at first only within the sphere of commodity circulation.** But as this function of money develops, all other forms of payment are gradually converted into payments in money. The extent to which money functions as the exclusive means of payment

---

* Despite Mr. Macleod's doctrinaire priggishness about definitions, he misinterprets the most elementary economic relations to such an extent that he asserts that money in general arises from its most advanced form, that is means of payment. He says *inter alia* that since people do not always require each other's services at the same time and to the same value, "there would remain a certain difference or amount of service due from the first to the second, and this would constitute a debt". The owner of this debt may need the services of a third person who does not immediately require his services, and "what could be more natural than for the second to transfer to the third the debt due to him from the first". The "evidence of a debt, would pass from hand to hand;... what is called a currency. ...when a person receives an obligation expressed by a metallic currency, he is able to command the services not only of the original debtor, but also those of the whole of the industrious community." H. D. Macleod, *The Theory and Practice of Banking*, Vol. I, London, 1855, Ch. I [pp. 24, 29].

** "Money is the general commodity of contract, or that in which the majority of bargains about property, to be completed at a future time, are made." Bailey, *op. cit.*, p. 3.

indicates how deep-seated and widespread the domination of production by exchange-value is.*

The volume of money in circulation as means of payment is first of all determined by the amount of payments due, that is by the aggregate prices of the commodities which have been sold, not of the commodities that are to be sold as is the case with simple money circulation. But the amount thus determined is subject to modification by two factors: first by the velocity with which a coin repeats the same operation, or the number of payments which constitute a dynamic chain of payments. A pays B, then B pays C and so on. The velocity with which the same coin can act repeatedly as means of payment depends, on the one hand, on the interconnection of the commodity-owners' relations as creditors and debtors, in which the same commodity-owner who is a creditor in relation to one person is a debtor in relation to another, and so forth; and on the other hand, on the period of time separating the various dates on which payments are due. The series of payments, or of first metamorphoses carried out subsequently, is qualitatively different from the series of metamorphoses represented by the movement of money as means of circulation. The second series does not only appear in temporal succession, but it *comes into being* in this way. A commodity is turned into money, then into a commodity again, thus making it possible for another commodity to be turned into money, and so on: in other words, a seller becomes a buyer and another commodity-owner thereby becomes a seller. This sequence arises fortuitously in the course of commodity exchange itself. But

---

* Senior (*op. cit.*, p. 221) says: "Since the value of everything changes within a certain period of time, people select as a means of payment an article whose value changes least and which retains longest a given average ability to buy things. Thus, money becomes the expression or representative of values." On the contrary, gold, silver, etc., become general means of payment, because they have become money, that is the independent embodiment of exchange-value. It is precisely when the stability of the value of money, mentioned by Mr. Senior, is taken into account, *i.e.*, in periods when force of circumstances establishes money as the universal means of payment, that people become aware of variations in the value of money. Such a period was the Elizabethan age in England, when, because of the manifest depreciation of the precious metals, an Act was shepherded through Parliament by Lord Burleigh and Sir Thomas Smith to compel the universities of Oxford and Cambridge to provide for the payment of one-third of the rent of their lands in wheat and malt.

the fact that the money which A pays to B is then used by B to pay C, and then by C to pay D, etc., and that moreover payments rapidly succeed one another—this external relation is but a manifestation of a previously existing social relation. The same coin passes through various hands not because it acts as means of payment; but it is passed on as means of payment because these hands have already been joined. A far more extensive integration of the individual into the process of circulation is accordingly signified by the velocity of money as means of payment, than by the velocity of money as coin or means of purchase.

The aggregate of prices of simultaneous, and therefore spatially coexisting, purchases and sales is the limit beyond which the velocity of currency cannot be substituted for its volume. But this barrier does not exist when money functions as means of payment. If payments falling due simultaneously are concentrated at one place, which occurs at first spontaneously at the large foci of commodity circulation, then payments offset one another like negative and positive quantities: A who has to pay B may receive a payment from C at the same time, and so on. The amount of money required as means of payment thus depends not on the aggregate amount of payments which are due to be made simultaneously, but on the degree of their concentration and on the size of the balance left over after the negative and positive amounts have been offset against one another. Special devices for this type of balancing arise even if no credit system has been evolved, as was the case in ancient Rome. But consideration of them is no more relevant here than is consideration of the usual settlement dates, which in every country become established among people of certain social strata. Here we shall merely note that scholarly investigations of the specific influence exerted by these dates on the periodic variations in the quantity of money in circulation have been undertaken only in recent times.

When payments cancel one another as positive and negative quantities, no money need actually appear on the scene. Here money functions merely as measure of value with respect to both the price of the commodity and the size of mutual obligations. Apart from its nominal existence, exchange-value does not therefore acquire an independent existence in this case, even in the shape of a token of value, in other words money becomes purely nominal money of account. Money functioning as means of payment thus contains a contradiction: on the one hand, when payments balance, it acts merely as a nominal measure; on the other hand, when actual payments have to be made, money enters circulation not as a transient means of circulation, but as the static aspect of the universal equivalent, as the absolute commodity, in short, as money. Where chains of payments and an artificial system for adjusting them have been developed, any upheaval that forcibly interrupts the flow of payments and upsets the mechanism for balancing them against one another suddenly turns money from the nebulous chimerical form it assumed as measure of value into hard cash or means of payment. Under conditions of advanced bourgeois production, when the commodity-owner has long since become a capitalist, knows his Adam Smith and smiles superciliously at the superstition that only gold and silver constitute money or that money is after all the absolute commodity as distinct from other commodities— money then suddenly appears not as the medium of circulation but once more as the only adequate form of exchange-value, as a unique form of wealth just as it is regarded by the hoarder. The fact that money is the sole incarnation of wealth manifests itself in the actual devaluation and worthlessness of all physical wealth, and not in purely imaginary devaluation as for instance in the Monetary System. This particular phase of world market crises is known as monetary crisis. The *summum bonum*, the sole form of wealth for which people clamour at such times, is money, hard cash, and compared with it all other commodities—just because they are use-values—appear to be useless, mere baubles and toys, or as our Doctor Martin Luther says, mere ornament and gluttony. This sudden transformation of the credit system into a monetary system adds theoretical dismay to the actually existing panic, and the agents of the circulation process are overawed by the impenetrable mystery surrounding their own relations.*

---

* *Boisguillebert*, who wishes to prevent bourgeois relations of production from being pitted against the bourgeoisie themselves, prefers to consider those forms of money in which money appears as a purely nominal or transitory phenomenon. Previously he regarded means of circulation from this point of view and now means of payment. He fails to notice, however, the sudden transformation of the nominal form of money into external reality, and the fact that even the purely concep-

Payments in their turn necessitate reserve funds, accumulations of money as means of payment. The formation of reserve funds, unlike hoarding, no longer seems an activity extraneous to circulation, or, as in the case of coin reserves, a purely technical stagnation of coin; on the contrary money has to be gradually accumulated so as to be available at definite dates in the future when payments become due. Although with the development of bourgeois production, therefore, the abstract form of hoarding regarded as enrichment decreases, the form of hoarding necessitated by the exchange process itself increases; a part of the wealth which generally accumulates in the sphere of commodity circulation being drawn into reserve funds of means of payment. The more advanced is bourgeois production, the more these funds are restricted to the indispensable minimum. Locke's work on the lowering of the rate of interest* contains interesting information about the size of these reserve funds in his time. It shows how substantial a proportion of the money in circulation in England was absorbed by the reserves of means of payment precisely during the period when banking began to develop.

The law regarding the quantity of money in circulation as it emerged from the examination of simple circulation of money is significantly modified by the circulation of means of payment. If the velocity of money, both as means of circulation and as means of payment, is given, then the aggregate amount of money in circulation during a particular period is determined by the total amount of commodity-prices to be realised [plus] the total amount of payments falling due during this period minus the payments that balance one another. This does not affect at all the general principle that the amount of money in circulation depends upon commodity-prices, for the aggregate amount of payments is itself determined by the prices laid down in the contracts. It is however quite obvious that the aggregate prices of the commodities in circulation during a definite period, say a day, are by no means commensurate with the

tual measure of value latently contains hard cash. Boisguillebert says, wholesale trade—in which, after "the appraisal of the commodities", exchange is accomplished without the intervention of money—shows that money is simply an aspect of the commodities themselves. *Le détail de la France*, p. 210.

* Locke, *Some Considerations on the Lowering of Interest*, pp. 17, 18.

volume of money in circulation on the same day, even if the velocity of circulation and the economic methods of payment are assumed to remain unchanged; since a certain quantity of commodities is in circulation whose prices will only be realised in money at a later date, and a certain amount of money in circulation corresponds to commodities which have left the sphere of circulation a long time ago. This amount of money depends in its turn on the value of the payments that fall due on this day, although the relevant contracts were concluded at widely varying dates.

We have seen that changes in the value of gold and silver do not affect their functions as measure of value and money of account. But with regard to hoarded money these changes are of decisive importance, since with the rise or fall in the value of gold and silver the value of the hoard of gold or silver will rise or fall. Such changes are of even greater importance for money as means of payment. The payment is effected at a date subsequent to the sale of the commodities; that is to say, money performs two different functions at two different periods, acting first as a measure of value, and then as the means of payment appropriate to this measure. If meanwhile a change has occurred in the value of the precious metals, or in the labour-time needed for their production, the same quantity of gold or silver will have a greater or smaller value when it functions as means of payment than at the time it served as measure of value, when the contract was signed. The function which a specific commodity, such as gold or silver, performs as money, or as exchange-value that has assumed an independent form, comes here into conflict with the nature of the specific commodity, whose value depends on variations in its costs of production. It is well-known that the fall in the value of precious metals in Europe gave rise to a great social revolution, just as the ancient Roman Republic at an early stage of its history experienced a reverse revolution caused by a rise in the value of copper, the metal in which the debts of the plebeians were contracted. Even without further examination of the influence which fluctuations in the value of precious metals exert on the system of bourgeois economy, it is clear that a fall in the value of precious metals favours debtors at the expense of creditors, while a rise in their value favours creditors at the expense of debtors.

c. World Money

Gold becomes money, as distinct from coin, first by being withdrawn from circulation and hoarded, then by entering circulation as a non-means of circulation, finally however by breaking through the barriers of domestic circulation in order to function as universal equivalent in the world of commodities. It thus becomes *world money*.

In the same way as originally the commonly used weights of precious metals served as measures of value, so on the world market the monetary denominations are reconverted into corresponding denominations of weight. Just as amorphous crude metal (*aes rude*) was the original form of means of circulation, and originally the coined form was simply the official indication of metallic weight, so precious metal serving as universal coin discards its specific shape and imprint and reverts to neutral bullion form; that is when national coins, such as Russian imperials, Mexican thalers and English sovereigns, circulate abroad their titles become unimportant and what counts is only their substance. Finally, as international money the precious metals once again fulfil their original function of means of exchange: a function which, like commodity exchange itself, originated at points of contact between different primitive communities and not in the interior of the communities. Money functioning as world money reverts to its original natural form. When it leaves domestic circulation, money sheds the particular forms occasioned by the development of exchange within particular areas, or the local forms assumed by money as measure of price—specie, small change, and token of value.

We have seen that only one commodity serves as a measure of value in the internal circulation of any country. But since in one country gold performs this function, in another silver, a double standard of value is recognised on the world market, and all functions of money are duplicated. The translation of the values of commodities from gold prices into silver prices and *vice versa* always depends on the relative value of the two metals; this relative value varying continuously and its determination appearing accordingly as a continuous process. Commodity-owners in every country are compelled to use gold and silver alternately for foreign commerce thus exchanging the metal current as money within the country for the metal which they happen to require as money in a foreign country. Every nation thus employs both gold and silver as world money.

Gold and silver in the sphere of international commodity circulation appear not as means of circulation but as *universal means of exchange*. The universal means of exchange act however merely as *means of purchase* and *means of payment*, two forms which we have already described, but their relations are reversed on the world market. When in the sphere of internal circulation money was used as coin, *i.e.*, as the intermediary link in the dynamic unity C—M—C or as the merely transitory form of exchange-value during the perpetual motion of commodities—it functioned exclusively as means of purchase. The reverse is the case on the world market. Here gold and silver act as means of purchase if the interchange is only unilateral and therefore purchase and sale are separated. For example, the border trade at Kyakhta is in fact and according to treaty stipulations[22] barter, in which silver is only used as a measure of value. The war of 1857-58[23] induced the Chinese to sell without buying. Thereupon silver suddenly appeared as means of purchase. In deference to the letter of the treaty, the Russians turned French five-franc coins into crude silver articles which were used as means of exchange. Silver has always served as means of purchase for Europe and America, on the one side, and Asia, where it congeals into hoards, on the other. Precious metals, moreover, serve as international means of purchase when the usual equilibrium in the interchange of products between two nations is suddenly disturbed, *e.g.*, when a bad harvest compels one of them to buy on an extraordinary scale. Precious metals, finally, are used as international means of purchase by the gold and silver producing countries, where they are direct products and also commodities, and not a converted form of commodities. With the development of commodity exchange between different national spheres of circulation, the function which world money fulfils as *means of payment* for settling international balances develops also.

International circulation, like domestic circulation, requires a constantly changing amount of gold and silver. Part of the accumulated hoards is consequently used by every nation as a reserve fund of world money, a fund which is sometimes diminished, sometimes replenished according to fluctuations in commodity exchange.* In addition to particular move-ments of world money which flows backwards and for-wards between national spheres of circulation, there is a general movement of world money; the points of departure being the sources of production, from which gold and silver flow in various directions to all the markets of the world. Thus gold and silver as commodities enter the sphere of world circulation and in proportion to the labour-time contained in them they are exchanged for commodity equivalents before reaching the area of domestic circulation. They ac-cordingly already have a definite value when they turn up in these areas. Their relative value on the world market is therefore uniformly affected by every fall or rise in their costs of production and is quite independent of the degree to which gold or silver is absorbed by the various national spheres of circulation. One branch of the stream of metal which is caught up in a particular area of the world of com-modities immediately enters the domestic circulation of money as replacement of worn-out coins; another is diverted into various reservoirs where coin, means of payment and world money accumulate; a third is used to make luxury articles and the rest, finally, is turned simply into hoards. Where the bourgeois mode of production has reached an advanced stage the formation of hoards is reduced to the minimum needed by the different branches of the circula-tion process for the free action of their mechanism. Under these conditions hoards as such consist only of wealth lying idle, unless they represent a temporary surplus in the balance of payments, the result of an interruption in the interchange of products and therefore commodities congealed in their first metamorphosis.

Just as in theory gold and silver as money are universal commodities, so world money is the appropriate form of existence of the universal commodity. In the same propor-tion as all commodities are exchanged for gold and silver these become the transmuted form of all commodities and hence universally exchangeable commodities. They are realised as embodiments of universal labour-time in the degree that the interchange of the products of concrete labour becomes

---

* "The accumulated money is added to the sum which, to be really in circulation and satisfy the possibilities of trade, departs and *leaves the sphere of circulation itself.*" (G. R. Carli, Note on Verri, *Meditazio-ni sulla Economia Politica*, p. 192, t. XV, Custodi, *l.c.*)

world-wide. They become universal equivalents in proportion to the development of the series of particular equivalents which constitute their spheres of exchange. Because the exchange-value of commodities is universally developed in international circulation, it appears transformed into gold and silver as international money. Since as a result of their versatile industry and all-embracing commerce the nations of commodity-owners have turned gold into adequate money, they regard industry and commerce merely as means enabling them to withdraw money in the form of gold and silver from the world market. Gold and silver as international money are therefore both the products of the universal circulation of commodities and the means to expand its scope. Just as the alchemists, who wanted to make gold, were not aware of the rise of chemistry, so commodity-owners, chasing after a magical form of the commodity, are not aware of the sources of world industry and world trade that are coming into being. Gold and silver help to create the world market by anticipating its existence in their concept of money. Their magical effect is by no means confined to the infancy of bourgeois society, but is the inevitable consequence of the inverted way in which their own social labour appears to the representatives of the world of commodities; a proof of this being the remarkable influence which the discovery of gold in various new areas exerted on international trade in the middle of the nineteenth century.

As money develops into international money, so the commodity-owner becomes a cosmopolitan. The cosmopolitan relations of men to one another originally comprise only their relations as commodity-owners. Commodities as such are indifferent to all religious, political, national and linguistic barriers. Their universal language is price and their common bond is money. But together with the development of international money as against national coins, there develops the commodity-owner's cosmopolitanism, a cult of practical reason, in opposition to the traditional religious, national and other prejudices which impede the metabolic process of mankind. The commodity-owner realises that nationality "is but the guinea's stamp", since the same amount of gold that arrives in England in the shape of American eagles is turned into sovereigns, three days later circulates as napoleons in Paris and may be encountered as ducats in Venice a few weeks later. The sublime idea in which for him the whole world merges is that of a market, the *world market.**

At first the process of bourgeois production takes possession of metallic currency as an existing and ready-made instrument, which, although it has been gradually reorganised, in its basic structure has nevertheless been retained. The question why gold and silver, and not other commodities, are used as the material of money lies outside the confines of the bourgeois system. We shall therefore do no more than summarise the most important aspects.

Because universal labour-time itself can only display quantitative differences, the object to be recognised as its specific embodiment must be able to express purely quantitative differences, thus presupposing identical, homogeneous quality. This is the first condition that has to be fulfilled if a commodity is to function as a measure of value. If, for instance, one evaluates all commodities in terms of oxen, hides, corn, etc., one has in fact to measure them in ideal average oxen, average hides, etc., since there are qualitative differences between one ox and another, one lot of corn and another, one hide and another. Gold and silver, on the other hand, as simple substances are always uniform and consequently equal quantities of them have equal values.** Another condition that has to be fulfilled by the commodity which is to serve as universal equivalent and that follows directly from its function of representing purely quantitative differences, is its divisibility into any desired number of parts and the possibility of combining these again, so that money of account can be represented in palpable form too. Gold and silver possess these qualities to an exceptional degree.

---

* "Intercourse between nations spans the whole globe to such an extent that one may almost say all the world is but a single city in which a permanent fair comprising all commodities is held, so that by means of money all the things produced by the land, the animals and human industry can be acquired and enjoyed by any person in his own home. A wonderful invention." Montanari, *Della Moneta* (1683), p. 40.

** "A peculiar feature of metals is that in them alone all relations are reduced to a single one, that is their quantity, for by nature they are not distinguished by differences in quality either in their internal composition or in their external form and structure" (Galiani, *op. cit.*, pp. 126-27).

As means of circulation gold and silver have an advantage over other commodities in that their high specific gravity—representing considerable weight in a relatively small space—is matched by their economic specific gravity, in containing much labour-time, *i.e.*, considerable exchange-value, in a relatively small volume. This facilitates transport, transfer from one hand to another, from one country to another, enabling gold and silver suddenly to appear and just as suddenly to disappear—in short these qualities impart physical mobility, the *sine qua non* of the commodity that is to serve as the *perpetuum mobile* of the process of circulation.

The high specific value of precious metals, their durability, relative indestructibility, the fact that they do not oxidise when exposed to the air and that gold in particular is insoluble in acids other than *aqua regia*—all these physical properties make precious metals the natural material for hoarding. Peter Martyr, who was apparently a great lover of chocolate, remarks, therefore, of the sacks of cocoa which in Mexico served as a sort of money.

"Blessed money which furnishes mankind with a sweet and nutritious beverage and protects its innocent possessors from the infernal disease of avarice, since it cannot be long hoarded, nor hidden underground!" (*De orbe novo* [Alcala, 1530, dec. 5, cap. 4].[24])

Metals in general owe their great importance in the direct process of production to their use as instruments of production. Gold and silver, quite apart from their scarcity, cannot be utilised in this way because, compared with iron and even with copper (in the hardened state in which the ancients used it), they are very soft and, therefore, to a large extent lack the quality on which the use-value of metals in general depends. Just as the precious metals are useless in the direct process of production, so they appear to be unnecessary as means of subsistence, *i.e.*, as articles of consumption. Any quantity of them can thus be placed at will within the social process of circulation without impairing production and consumption as such. Their individual use-value does not conflict with their economic function. Gold and silver, on the other hand, are not only negatively superfluous, *i.e.*, dispensable objects, but their aesthetic qualities make them the natural material for pomp, ornament, glamour, the requirements of festive occasions, in short, the positive expression of supra-abundance and wealth. They appear, so to speak, as solidified light raised from a subterranean world, since all the rays of light in their original composition are reflected by silver, while red alone, the colour of the highest potency, is reflected by gold. Sense of colour, moreover, is the most popular form of aesthetic perception in general. The etymological connection between the names of precious metals and references to colour in various Indo-European languages has been demonstrated by Jakob Grimm (see his *History of the German Language*).

Finally the fact that it is possible to transform gold and silver from coin into bullion, from bullion into articles of luxury and *vice versa*, the advantage they have over other commodities of not being confined to the particular useful form they have once been given makes them the natural material for money, which must constantly change from one form into another.

Nature no more produces money than it does bankers or a rate of exchange. But since in bourgeois production, wealth as a fetish must be crystallised in a particular substance, gold and silver are its appropriate embodiment. Gold and silver are not by nature money, but money consists by its nature of gold and silver. Gold or silver as crystallisation of money is, on the one hand, not only the product of the circulation process but actually its sole stable product; gold and silver are, on the other hand, finished primary products, and they directly represent both these aspects, which are not distinguished by specific forms. The universal product of the social process, or the social process itself considered as a product, is a particular natural product, a metal, which is contained in the earth's crust and can be dug up.*

We have seen that gold and silver cannot comply with the demand that as money they should have an invariable value. Their value is nevertheless more stable than that of other commodities on the average, as even Aristotle noted. Apart from the general effect of an appreciation or depre-

---

* In the year 760 a crowd of poor people turned out to wash gold from the sand of the river south of Prague, and three men were able in a day to extract a mark [half a pound] of gold; and so great was the consequent rush to "the diggings" and the number of hands attracted from agriculture so great, that in the next year the country was visited by famine. (See M. G. Körner, *Abhandlung von dem Alterthum des böhmischen Bergwerks*, Schneeberg, 1758 [p. 37 *seq.*].)

ciation of the precious metals, variations in the relative value of gold and silver are of particular importance, since both are used side by side as monetary material on the world market. The purely economic reasons of such changes in value—conquests and other political upheavals, which exerted a substantial influence on the value of metals in antiquity, have merely a local and temporary effect—must be attributed to changes in the labour-time required for the production of these metals. This labour-time itself will depend on the relative scarcity of natural deposits and the difficulties involved in procuring them in a purely metallic state. Gold is in fact the first metal that man discovered. On the one hand, it occurs in nature in pure crystalline form, as a separate substance not chemically combined with other substances, or in a virgin state, as the alchemists said; on the other hand, nature herself performs the technical work by washing gold on a large scale in rivers. Only the crudest labour is required on the part of man for extracting gold either from rivers or from alluvial deposits; whereas production of silver requires mining and in general a relatively high level of technical development. The value of silver is therefore originally higher than that of gold, although it is absolutely less scarce. Strabo's statement that an Arabian tribe gave ten pounds of gold for one pound of iron, and two pounds of gold for one pound of silver, is by no means incredible. But the value of silver tends to fall in relation to that of gold, as the productive powers of social labour develop and consequently the product of simple labour becomes more expensive compared with that of complex labour, and with the earth's crust being increasingly opened up the original surface-sources of gold are liable to be exhausted. Finally, at a given stage of development of technology and of the means of communication, the discovery of new territories containing gold or silver plays an important rôle. The ratio of gold to silver in ancient Asia was 6 to 1 or 8 to 1; the latter ratio was prevalent in China and Japan even in the early nineteenth century; 10 to 1, the ratio obtaining in Xenophon's time, can be regarded as the average ratio of the middle period of antiquity. The working of the Spanish silver mines by Carthage and later by Rome exerted a rather similar influence on the ancient world to that of the discovery of the American mines on modern Europe. During the era of the Roman emperors, 15 or 16 to

1 can be taken as the rough average, although the value of silver in Rome often sank even lower. During the following period reaching from the Middle Ages to modern times, a similar movement which begins with a relative depreciation of gold and ends with a fall in the value of silver takes place. The average ratio in the Middle Ages, as in Xenophon's time, was 10 to 1, and as a result of the discovery of mines in America the ratio once again becomes 16 or 15 to 1. The discovery of gold in Australia, California and Colombia will probably lead to another fall in the value of gold.*

C. Theories of the Medium of Circulation and of Money

Just as in the sixteenth and seventeenth centuries, when modern bourgeois society was in its infancy, nations and princes were driven by a general desire for money to embark on crusades to distant lands in quest of the golden grail,** so the first interpreters of the modern world, the originators

---

* The relative value of gold and silver up to now has not been affected by the Australian and other discoveries. Michel Chevalier's contention that the opposite is the case is worth no more than the socialism of this ex-St.-Simonist. Quotations on the London market show, indeed, that between 1850 and 1858 the average price of silver in terms of gold was nearly 3 per cent higher than in the period between 1830 and 1850; but this rise was simply due to the demand of Asian countries for silver. Silver prices between 1852 and 1858 change in different years and months *solely* in accordance with this *demand* and by no means in accordance with the supply of gold from the newly discovered sources. The following is a summary of silver prices in terms of gold quoted on the London market.

Price of an Ounce of Silver

Year	March	July	November
1852	$60^{1}/_{8}$ pence	$60^{1}/_{4}$ pence	$61^{7}/_{8}$ pence
1853	$61^{3}/_{8}$ „	$61^{1}/_{2}$ „	$61^{7}/_{8}$ „
1854	$61^{7}/_{8}$ „	$61^{3}/_{4}$ „	$61^{1}/_{2}$ „
1855	$60^{7}/_{8}$ „	$61^{1}/_{2}$ „	$60^{7}/_{8}$ „
1856	60 „	$61^{1}/_{4}$ „	$62^{1}/_{8}$ „
1857	$61^{3}/_{4}$ „	$61^{5}/_{8}$ „	$61^{1}/_{2}$ „
1858	$61^{5}/_{8}$		

** "Gold is a wonderful thing. Its owner is master of everything he desires. Gold can even enable souls to enter paradise." (Columbus in a letter from Jamaica written in 1503.) [Note in author's copy.]

of the Monetary System—the Mercantile System is merely a variant of it—declared that gold and silver, *i.e.*, money, alone constitutes wealth. They quite correctly stated that the vocation of bourgeois society was the making of money, and hence, from the standpoint of simple commodity production, the formation of permanent hoards which neither moths nor rust could destroy. It is no refutation of the Monetary System to point out that a ton of iron whose price is £3 has the same value as £3 in gold. The point at issue is not the magnitude of the exchange-value, but its adequate form. With regard to the special attention paid by the Monetary and Mercantile systems to international trade and to individual branches of national labour that lead directly to international trade, which are regarded by them as the only real source of wealth or of money, one has to remember that in those times national production was for the most part still carried on within the framework of feudal forms and served as the immediate source of subsistence for the producers themselves. Most products did not become commodities; they were accordingly neither converted into money nor entered at all into the general process of the social metabolism; hence they did not appear as materialisation of universal abstract labour and did not indeed constitute bourgeois wealth. Money as the end and object of circulation represents exchange-value or abstract wealth, not any physical element of wealth, as the determining purpose and driving motive of production. It was consistent with the rudimentary stage of bourgeois production that those misunderstood prophets should have clung to the solid, palpable and glittering form of exchange-value, to exchange-value in the form of the universal commodity as distinct from all particular commodities. The sphere of commodity circulation was the strictly bourgeois economic sphere at that time. They therefore analysed the whole complex process of bourgeois production from the standpoint of that basic sphere and confused money with capital. The unceasing fight of modern economists against the Monetary and Mercantile systems is mainly provoked by the fact that the secret of bourgeois production, *i.e.*, that it is dominated by exchange-value, is divulged in a naïvely brutal way by these systems. Although drawing the wrong conclusions from it, Ricardo observes somewhere that, even during a famine, corn is imported because the corn-merchant thereby makes money, and not because the nation is starving. Political economy errs in its critique of the Monetary and Mercantile systems when it assails them as mere illusions, as utterly wrong theories, and fails to notice that they contain in a primitive form its own basic presuppositions. These systems, moreover, remain not only historically valid but retain their full validity within certain spheres of the modern economy. At every stage of the bourgeois process of production when wealth assumes the elementary form of commodities, exchange-value assumes the elementary form of money, and in all phases of the productive process wealth for an instant reverts again to the universal elementary form of commodities. The functions of gold and silver as money, in contradistinction to their functions as means of circulation and in contrast with all other commodities, are not abolished even in the most advanced bourgeois economy, but merely restricted; the Monetary and Mercantile systems accordingly remain valid. The catholic fact that gold and silver as the direct embodiment of social labour, and therefore as the expression of abstract wealth, confront other profane commodities, has of course violated the protestant code of honour of bourgeois economists, and from fear of the prejudices of the Monetary System, they lost for some time any sense of discrimination towards the phenomena of money circulation, as the following account will show.

It was quite natural that, by contrast with the Monetary and Mercantile systems, which knew money only as a crystalline product of circulation, classical political economy in the first instance should have understood the fluid form of money, that is the form of exchange-value which arises and vanishes within the metamorphosis of commodities. Because commodity circulation is looked at exclusively in the form C—M—C, and this in its turn solely as the dynamic unity of sale and purchase, the specific aspect of money as means of circulation is upheld against its specific aspect as money. If the function of means of circulation in serving as coin is isolated, then, as we have seen, it becomes a value-token. But since classical political economy was at first confronted with metallic currency as the predominant form of currency, it regarded metallic money as coin, and coin as a mere token of value. In accordance with the law relating to the circulation of value-tokens, the proposition is then advanced that the prices of commodities depend on the volume of money in circulation, and not that the volume of money in circulation depends on the prices of commodities. This view is more or less clearly outlined by Italian economists of the seventeenth century; it is sometimes accepted, sometimes repudiated by *Locke*, and firmly set forth in the *Spectator* (in the issue of October 19, 1711) as well as in the works of *Montesquieu* and *Hume*. Since *Hume* is by far the most important exponent of this theory in the eighteenth century, we shall begin our survey with him.

Under certain conditions, an increase or decrease in the quantity of either specie in circulation, or tokens of value in circulation, seems to have a *similar* effect upon commodity-prices. If there is a fall or rise in the *value* of gold and silver, in which the exchange-value of commodities is measured as price, then prices rise or fall because a change has taken place in their standard of value; and an increased or diminished amount of gold and silver is in circulation as coin because the prices have risen or fallen. The observable phenomenon, however, is that with an increasing or diminishing volume of means of circulation, prices change while the exchange-value of commodities remains constant. If, on the other hand, the amount of value-tokens in circulation falls below the requisite level, or rises above it, then it is forcibly reduced to that level by a fall or rise of commodity-prices. The effect in both cases appears to be brought about by the same cause, and *Hume* holds fast to this appearance.

Any scholarly investigation of the relation between the volume of means of circulation and movements in commodity-prices must assume that the value of the monetary material is given. Hume, however, considers exclusively periods when revolutionary changes in the value of the precious metals take place, that is revolutions in the standard of value. The rise in commodity-prices that occurred simultaneously with the increase in the amount of specie consequent upon the discovery of the American mines forms the historical background of his theory, and its practical motive was the polemic that he waged against the Monetary and Mercantile systems. It is, of course, quite possible to increase the supply of precious metals while their costs of production remain unchanged. On the other hand, a decrease in their value, that is in the labour-time required to produce them, will in the first place be attested only by an increase in their supply. Hume's disciples accordingly stated subsequently that the diminished value of the precious metals was reflected in the growing volume of means of circulation, and the growing volume of the means of circulation was reflected in increased commodity-prices. But there is in reality an increase only in the prices of exported commodities which are exchanged for gold and silver as commodities and not as means of circulation. The price of those commodities, which are measured in gold and silver of reduced value, thus rises in relation to all other commodities whose exchange-value continues to be measured in gold and silver in accordance with the scale of their former costs of production. Such a dual evaluation of exchange-values of commodities in a given country can of course occur only temporarily; gold and silver prices must be adjusted to correspond with the exchange-values themselves, so that finally the exchange-values of all commodities are assessed in accordance with the new value of monetary material. This is not the place for either a description of this process or an examination of the ways in which the exchange-value of commodities prevails within the fluctuations of market-prices. Recent critical investigations of the movement of commodity-prices during the sixteenth century have conclusively demonstrated that in the early stages of the evolution of the bourgeois mode of production, such adjustment proceeds only very gradually, extending over long periods, and does not by any means keep in step with the increase of ready money in circulation.* Quite inappropriate are references—in vogue among Hume's disciples—to rising prices in ancient Rome brought about by the conquest of Macedonia, Egypt and Asia Minor. The sudden and forcible transfer of hoarded money from one country to another is a specific feature of the ancient world; but the temporary lowering of the production costs of precious metals achieved in a particular country by the simple method of plunder does not affect the inherent laws of monetary circulation, any more than, for instance, the distribution of Egyptian and Sicilian corn free of charge in Rome affects the general law which regulates corn prices. For a detailed analysis of the circulation of money, Hume, like all other eighteenth-century

---

* Incidentally, Hume admits that the adjustment takes place gradually, although this does not accord with his principle. See David Hume, *Essays and Treatises on Several Subjects*, London, 1777, Vol. I, p. 300.

writers, lacked the necessary material, *i.e.*, on the one hand a reliable history of commodity-prices, and on the other hand, official and continuous statistics regarding the expansion and contraction of the medium of circulation, the influx or withdrawal of precious metals, etc., in other words material which on the whole only becomes accessible when banking is fully developed. The following propositions summarise Hume's theory of circulation. 1. Commodity-prices in a given country are determined by the amount of money (real or token money) existing therein. 2. The money circulating in a given country represents all commodities which are in that country. As the amount of money grows, each unit represents a correspondingly larger or smaller proportion of the things represented. 3. If the volume of commodities increases, then their prices fall or the value of money rises. If the amount of money increases, then, on the contrary, commodity-prices rise and the value of money falls.*

"The dearness of everything," says Hume, "from plenty of money, is a disadvantage, which attends an established commerce, and sets bounds to it in every country, by enabling the poorer states to undersell the richer in all foreign markets."** "Where coin is in greater plenty; as a greater quantity of it is required to represent the same quantity of goods; it can have no effect, either good or bad, taking a nation within itself; any more than it would make an alteration on a merchant's books, if, instead of the Arabian method of notation, which requires few characters, he should make use of the Roman, which requires a great many. Nay, the greater quantity of money, like the Roman characters, is rather inconvenient, and requires greater trouble both to keep and transport it."***

If this example were to prove anything, Hume would have to show that in a *given* system of notation the quantity of characters employed does not depend on the numerical value, but that on the contrary the numerical value is determined by the quantity of characters employed. It is quite true that there is no advantage in evaluating or "counting" commodity values in gold or silver of diminished value; and as the value of the commodities in circulation increased, therefore, nations invariably decided that it was more convenient to count in silver than in copper, and in gold than in silver. In the proportion that nations grew richer, they turned

---

* *Cf.* Steuart, *op. cit.*, Vol. I, pp. 394-400.
** David Hume, *op. cit.*, p. 300.
*** David Hume, *op. cit.*, pp. 302-03.

the less valuable metals into subsidiary coin and the more valuable metals into money. Hume, moreover, forgets that in order to calculate values in terms of gold and silver, neither gold nor silver need be "present". Money of account and means of circulation are for him identical phenomena and he regards both as coin. Because a change in the value of the standard of value, *i.e.* in the precious metals which function as money of account, causes a rise or fall in commodity-prices, and hence, provided the velocity of money remains unchanged, an increase or decrease in the volume of money in circulation, Hume infers that increases or decreases of commodity-prices are determined by the quantity of money in circulation. Hume could have deduced from the closing down of European mines that not only the quantity of gold and silver grew during the sixteenth and seventeenth centuries, but that simultaneously their cost of production diminished. Along with the volume of imported American gold and silver commodity-prices rose in Europe in the sixteenth and seventeenth centuries; commodity-prices are consequently in every country determined by the volume of gold and silver which the country contains. This was the first "necessary consequence" drawn by Hume.* Prices in the sixteenth and seventeenth centuries did not rise in step with the increased amount of precious metals; more than half a century elapsed before *any* change at all was noticeable in the prices of commodities, and even after this a considerable time elapsed before the prices of commodities in general were revolutionised, that is before the exchange-values of commodities were generally estimated according to the diminished value of gold and silver. Hume—who quite contrary to the principles of his own philosophy uncritically turns unilaterally interpreted facts into general propositions —concludes that, in consequence, the price of commodities or the value of money is determined not by the absolute amount of money present in a country, but rather by the amount of gold and silver actually in circulation; in the long run, however, all the gold and silver present in the country must be absorbed as coin in the sphere of circulation.** It

---

* David Hume, *op. cit.*, p. 303.
** "It is evident, that the prices do not so much depend on the absolute quantity of commodities, and that of money, which are in a nation, as on that of the commodities, which can or may come to market, and of the money which circulates. If the coin be locked up in chests,

is clear, that, if gold and silver themselves have value, quite irrespective of all other laws of circulation, only a definite quantity of gold and silver can circulate as the equivalent of a given aggregate value of commodities. Thus, if without reference to the total value of commodities, all the gold and silver that happens to be in the country must participate as means of circulation in the exchange of commodities, then gold and silver have no intrinsic value and are indeed not real commodities. This is Hume's third "necessary consequence". According to Hume, commodities without price and gold and silver without value enter the process of circulation. He, therefore, never mentions the value of commodities and the value of gold, but speaks only of their reciprocal quantity. Locke had already said that gold and silver have a purely imaginary or conventional value; this was the first blunt opposition to the contention of the Monetary System that only gold and silver have genuine value. The fact that gold and silver are money only as the result of the function they perform in the social process of exchange is thus taken to mean that their specific value and hence the magnitude of their value is due to their social function.*
Gold and silver are thus things without value, but in the process of circulation, in which they *represent commodities*, they acquire a fictitious value. This process turns them not into money but into value: a value that is determined by the proportion of their own volume to the volume of commodities, for the two volumes must balance. Although then, according to Hume, gold and silver enter the world of commodities as non-commodities, as soon as they function as coin he transforms them into plain commodities, which are exchanged for other commodities by simple barter. Provided the world of commodities consisted of a single commodity, *e.g.*, one million quarters of corn, it would be quite simple to imagine that, if two million ounces of gold existed, one quarter of corn would be exchanged for two

---

it is the same thing with regard to prices, as if it were annihilated; if the commodities be hoarded in magazines and granaries, a like effect follows. As the money and commodities, in these cases, never meet, they cannot affect each other.... The whole (of prices) at last reaches *a just proportion with the new quantity of specie which is in the kingdom."* David Hume, *op. cit.*, pp. 303, 307, 308.

* See *Law* and *Franklin* on the surplus value which gold and silver are said to acquire from the function they perform as money. *Forbonnais* too. [Note in author's copy.]

ounces of gold or, if twenty million ounces of gold existed, one quarter would be exchanged for twenty ounces of gold; the price of the commodity and the value of money would thus rise or fall in inverse ratio to the available quantity of money.* But the world of commodities consists of an infinite variety of use-values, whose relative value is by no means determined by their relative quantities. How then does Hume envisage this exchange of commodities for gold? He confines himself to the vague abstract conception that every commodity being a portion of the total volume of commodities is exchanged for a commensurate portion of the existing volume of gold. The dynamic movement of commodities—a movement, which originates in the contradiction of exchange-value and use-value contained in the commodities, which is reflected in the circulation of money and epitomised in the various distinct aspects of the latter— is thus obliterated and replaced by an imaginary mechanical equalisation of the amount of precious metals present in a particular country and the volume of commodities simultaneously available.

Sir James Steuart begins his investigation of specie and money with a detailed criticism of Hume and Montesquieu.** He is indeed the first to ask whether the amount of money in circulation is determined by the prices of commodities, or the prices of commodities determined by the amount of money in circulation. Although his exposition is tarnished by his fantastic notion of the measure of value, by his inconsistent treatment of exchange-value in general and by arguments reminiscent of the Mercantile System, he discovers the essential aspects of money and the general laws of circulation of money, because he does not mechanically place commodities on one side and money on the other, but really deduces its various functions from different moments in commodity exchange.

"These uses" (of money in internal circulation) "may be comprehended under two general heads. The first, payment of what one owes; the second, buying what one has occasion for; the one and the other may be called by the general term of ready-money demands.... Now the state of trade, manufactures, modes of living, and the customary expence of the inhabitants, when taken all together, regulate and

---

* This invention can actually be found in Montesquieu's works. [Note in author's copy.]
** Steuart, *op. cit.*, Vol. I, p. 394 *et seq.*

determine what we may call the mass of ready-money demands, that is, of alienation. To operate this multiplicity of payments, a certain proportion of money is necessary. This proportion again may increase or diminish according to circumstances; although the quantity of alienation should continue the same.... From this we may conclude, that the circulation of a country can only absorb a determinate quantity of money."*

"The standard price of every thing" is determined by "the complicated operations of demand and competition", which "bear no determined proportion whatsoever to the quantity of gold and silver in the country". "What then will become of the additional quantity of coin?"—"It will be hoarded up in treasures" or converted into luxury articles. "If the coin of a country ... falls below the proportion of the produce of industry offered for sale ... inventions such as symbolical money will be fallen upon to provide an equivalent for it."

"When a favourable balance pours in a superfluity of coin, and at the same time cuts off the demands of trade for sending it abroad, it frequently falls into coffers; where it becomes as useless as if it were in the mine."**

The second law discovered by *Steuart* is that currency based on credit returns to its point of departure. Finally he analyses the consequences produced by the diversity in the rate of interest obtaining in different countries on the export and import of precious metals. The last two aspects are mentioned here only for the sake of a complete picture, since they are remote from our subject, namely simple circulation.*** Symbolical money or credit money—Steuart does not

---

* James Steuart, *op. cit.*, Vol. II, pp. 377-79 *passim.*

** *Op. cit.*, pp. 380 and 397-407 *passim.*

*** "The additional coin will probably be locked up, or converted into plate.... As for the paper money, so soon as it has served the first purpose of supplying the demand of him who borrowed it ... it will return upon the debtor in it, and become realised;... Let the specie of a country, therefore, be augmented or diminished in ever so great a proportion, commodities will still rise and fall according to the principles of demand and competition, and these will constantly depend upon the inclinations of those who have property or any kind of equivalent whatsoever to give; but never upon the quantity of coin they are possessed of.... Let it" (*i.e.*, the quantity of specie in a country) "be diminished ever so low, while there is real property of any denomination in the country, and a competition to consume in those who possess it, prices will be high, by the means of barter, symbolical money, mutual prestations, and a *thousand* other inventions.... Is it not plain, that if this country has a communication with other nations, there must be a proportion between the prices of many kinds of merchandise, there and elsewhere, and that the sudden augmentation or diminution of the specie, supposing it could *of itself* operate the effects of raising or sinking prices, would be *restrained* in its operation by foreign competition?" (*Op. cit.*, Vol. I, pp. 400-01.) "The circulation of every

yet distinguish these two forms of money—can function as means of purchase and means of payment in place of the precious metals in domestic circulation, but not on the world market. Paper notes are consequently "money of the society", whereas gold and silver are "money of the world".*

It is a characteristic of nations with an "historical" development, in the sense given to this term by the Historical School of Law,[25] that they always forget their own history. Thus although during this half century the issue of the relation between commodity-prices and the quantity of currency has agitated Parliament continuously and has caused thousands of pamphlets, large and small, to be published in England, Steuart remained even more of "a dead dog" than Spinoza appeared to be to Moses Mendelssohn in Lessing's time. Even the most recent historiographer of "currency", Maclaren, makes Adam Smith the inventor of Steuart's theory, and Ricardo the inventor of Hume's theory.** Whereas Ricardo improves upon Hume's theory, Adam Smith records the results of Steuart's research as dead facts. The Scottish proverb that if one has gained a little it is often easy to gain much, but the difficulty is to

---

country ... must ever be in proportion to the industry of the inhabitants, producing the commodities which come to market.... If the coin of a country, therefore, falls below the proportion of the produce of industry offered to sale ... inventions, such as symbolical money, will be fallen upon to provide an equivalent for it. But if the specie be found above the proportion of the industry, it will have no effect in raising prices, nor will it enter into circulation: *it will be hoarded up in treasures*.... Whatever be the quantity of money in any nation, in correspondence with the rest of the world, there never can remain, *in circulation*, but a quantity nearly proportional to the consumption of the rich, and to the labour and industry of the poor inhabitants" and this proportion is not determined "by the quantity of money actually in the country" (*op. cit.*, p. 407). "All nations will endeavour to throw their ready money, not necessary for their own circulation, into that country where the interest of money is high with respect to their own" (*op. cit.*, Vol. II, p. 5). "The richest nation in Europe may be the poorest in circulating specie" (*op. cit.*, Vol. II, p. 6). [Note in author's copy:] See polemic against Steuart in Arthur Young's work.

* Steuart, *op. cit.*, Vol. II, p. 370. Louis Blanc transforms the "money of the society", which simply means internal, national money, into socialist money, which means nothing at all, and quite consistently turns John Law into a socialist. (See the first volume of his History of the French Revolution.)

** Maclaren, *op. cit.*, p. 43 *seq.* A German writer (Gustav Julius), who died prematurely, was induced by patriotism to oppose the old Büsch as an authority to the Ricardian school. The honourable Büsch

gain a little, has been applied by *Adam Smith* to intellectual wealth as well, and with meticulous care he accordingly keeps the sources secret to which he is indebted for the little, which he turns indeed into much. More than once he prefers to take the sharp edge off a problem when the use of precise definitions might have forced him to settle accounts with his predecessors. This is, for instance, the case with the theory of money. Adam Smith tacitly accepts Steuart's theory by relating that a part of gold and silver available in a country is used as coin, a part is accumulated as reserve funds for merchants in countries which have no banks and as bank reserves in countries with a credit system, a part serves as a stock for the adjustment of international payments, and a part is converted into luxury articles. He quietly eliminates the question about the amount of coin in circulation by quite improperly regarding money as a simple commodity.* This not entirely artless slip of Adam Smith was with much pomposity fashioned into a dogma** by his vulgariser, the insipid *J. B. Say*, whom the French have designated *prince de la science*, just as Johann Christoph Gottsched calls his Schönaich a Homer and Pietro Aretino calls himself *terror principum* and *lux mundi*. The tension caused by the struggle against the illusions of the Mercantile System prevented Adam Smith, moreover, from objectively considering the phenomena of metallic currency, whereas his views on paper money are original and profound. Just as the palaeontological theories of the eighteenth century inevitably contain an undercurrent which arises from a critical or an apologetic consideration of the biblical tradition of the Deluge, so behind the façade of all monetary theories of the eighteenth century a hidden struggle is waged against the Monetary System, the spectre which stood guard

---

has translated Steuart's brilliant English into the Low-German dialect of Hamburg and distorted the original whenever it was possible.

* This is inaccurate. On the contrary, in some passages the law is correctly expressed by Smith. [Note in author's copy.]

** The distinction between "currency" and "money", *i.e.*, between means of circulation and money, does not therefore occur in the *Wealth of Nations*. Misled by the apparent ingenuousness of Adam Smith, who had studied Hume and Steuart closely, honest Maclaren observes: "The theory of the dependence of prices on the extent of the currency had not, as yet, attracted attention; and Dr. Smith, like Mr. Locke" (Locke's views vary), "considers metallic money nothing but a commodity." Maclaren, *op. cit.*, p. 44.

over the cradle of bourgeois economy and still cast its heavy shadow over legislation.

Investigations of monetary matters in the nineteenth century were stimulated directly by phenomena attending the circulation of bank-notes, rather than by those of metallic currency. The latter was merely referred to for the purpose of discovering the laws governing the circulation of bank-notes. The suspension of cash payments by the Bank of England in 1797, the rise in price of many commodities which followed, the fall in the mint-price of gold below its market-price, and the depreciation of bank-notes especially after 1809 were the immediate practical occasion for a party contest within Parliament and a theoretical encounter outside it, both waged with equal passion. The historical background of the debate was furnished by the evolution of paper money in the eighteenth century, the fiasco of Law's bank,[26] the growing volume of value-tokens which was accompanied by a depreciation of provincial bank-notes of the British colonies in North America from the beginning to the middle of the eighteenth century; after which came the legally-imposed paper money, the Continental bills issued by the American Government during the War of Independence, and finally the French assignats, an experiment conducted on an even larger scale. Most English writers of that period confuse the circulation of bank-notes, which is determined by entirely different laws, with the circulation of value-tokens or of government bonds which are legal tender and, although they pretend to explain the phenomena of this forced currency by the laws of metallic currency, in reality they derive the laws of metallic currency from the phenomena of the former. We omit the numerous writers whose works appeared between 1800 and 1809 and turn at once to Ricardo, because he not only summarises his predecessors and expresses their ideas with greater precision, but also because monetary theory in the form he has given it has dominated British banking law up to the present time. Like his predecessors, Ricardo confuses the circulation of bank-notes or of credit money with the circulation of simple tokens of value. The fact which dominates his thought is the depreciation of paper money and the rise in commodity-prices that occurred simultaneously. The printing presses in Threadneedle Street which issue paper notes played the same rôle for Ricardo as the American mines played for Hume; and in one passage Ricardo explicitly equates these two causes. His first writings, which deal only with monetary matters, originated at a time when a most violent controversy raged between the Bank of England, which was backed by the Ministers and the war party, and its adversaries around whom were grouped the parliamentary opposition, the Whigs and the peace party. These writings appeared as the direct forerunners of the famous Report of the Bullion Committee of 1810, which adopted Ricardo's ideas.* The odd fact that Ricardo and his supporters, who maintained that money was merely a token of value, were called bullionists was due not only to the name of the Committee but also to the content of Ricardo's theory. Ricardo restated and further elaborated the same ideas in his work on political economy, but he has nowhere examined money as such in the way in which he has analysed exchange-value, profit, rent, etc.

To begin with, Ricardo determines the value of gold and silver, like the value of all other commodities, by the quantity of labour-time materialised in them.** The value of other commodities is measured in terms of the precious metals, which are commodities of a determinate value.*** The quantity of means of circulation employed in a country is thus determined by the value of the standard of money on the one hand, and by the aggregate of the exchange-values of commodities on the other. This quantity is modified by the economy with which payments are effected.**** Since, therefore, the quantity in which money of a given value can be circulated is determined, and within the framework of

---

* David Ricardo, *The High Price of Bullion, a Proof of the Depreciation of Bank-notes*, 4th Edition, London, 1811 (the first edition was published in 1809). Also: *Reply to Mr. Bosanquet's Practical Observations on the Report of the Bullion Committee*, London, 1811.
** David Ricardo, *On the Principles of Political Economy and Taxation*, p. 77. "The same general rule which regulates the value of raw produce and manufactured commodities, is applicable also to the metals, their value depending ... on the total quantity of labour necessary to obtain the metal, and to bring it to market."
*** *Op. cit.*, pp. 77, 180, 181.
**** Ricardo, *op. cit.*, p. 421. "The quantity of money that can be employed in a country must depend on its value: if gold alone were employed for the circulation of commodities, a quantity would be required, one fifteenth only of what would be necessary, if silver were made use of for the same purpose." See also Ricardo, *Proposals for an*

circulation its value manifests itself only in its quantity, money within the sphere of circulation can be replaced by simple value-tokens, provided that these are issued in the amount determined by the value of money. Moreover

"a currency is in its most perfect state when it consists wholly of paper money, but of paper money of an equal value with the gold which it professes to represent."[*]

So far, therefore, Ricardo has assumed that the value of money is given, and has determined the amount of means of circulation by the prices of commodities: for him money as a token of value is a token which stands for a determinate quantity of gold and is not a valueless symbol representing commodities, as it was for Hume.

When Ricardo suddenly interrupts the smooth progress of his exposition and adopts the opposite view, he does so in order to deal with the international movement of precious metals and thus complicates the problem by introducing extraneous aspects. Following his own train of thought, let us first of all leave aside all artificial and incidental aspects and accordingly locate the gold and silver mines within the countries in which the precious metals circulate as money. The only proposition which follows from Ricardo's analysis up to now is that if the value of gold is given, the amount of money in circulation is determined by the prices of commodities. The volume of gold circulating in a country therefore is simply determined by the exchange-value of the commodities in circulation at the given time. Now supposing that the aggregate amount of these exchange-values decreases, because either a smaller amount of commodities is produced at the old exchange-values, or the same amount of commodities is produced but the commodities represent less exchange-value as a result of an increase in the productivity of labour. Or let us assume by contrast that the aggregate exchange-value has increased, because a larger volume

---

Economical and Secure Currency, London, 1816, p. 8, where he writes: "The quantity of metal for which paper money is the substitute, if paper money be partly or wholly used, must depend on three things: first, on its value;—secondly, on the amount or value of the payments to be made;—and, thirdly, on the degree of economy practised in effecting those payments."

[*] Ricardo, *Principles of Political Economy*, pp. 432, 433.

of commodities has been produced while production costs remain constant, or because either the same or a smaller volume of commodities has a larger value as a result of a decline in the productivity of labour. What happens to the *existing* quantity of metal in circulation in these two cases? If gold is money only because it circulates as a medium of circulation, if it is forced to stay in the sphere of circulation, like paper money with forced currency issued by the State (and Ricardo implies this), then the quantity of money in circulation will, in the first case, be excessive in relation to the exchange-value of the metal, and it will stand below its normal level in the second case. Although endowed with a specific value, gold thus becomes a token which, in the first case, represents a metal with a lower exchange-value than its own, and in the second case represents a metal which has a higher value. Gold as a token of value will fall below its real value in the first case, and rise above it in the second case (once more a deduction made from paper money with forced currency). The effect would be the same as if, in the first case, all commodities were evaluated in metal of lower value than gold, and in the second case as if they were evaluated in metal of a higher value. Commodity-prices would therefore rise in the first case, and fall in the second. The movement of commodity-prices, their rise or fall, in either case would be due to the relative expansion or contraction in the amount of gold in circulation occasioning a rise above or a fall below the level corresponding to its own value, *i.e.*, the normal quantity determined by the relation between its own value and the value of the commodities which are to be circulated.

The same process would take place if the aggregate price of the commodities in circulation remained constant, but the amount of gold in circulation either fell below or rose above the proper level; the former might occur if gold coin worn out in circulation were not replaced by sufficient new output from the mines, the latter if the new supply from the mines surpassed the requirements of circulation. In both cases it is assumed that the production cost of gold, or its value, remains unchanged.

To recapitulate: if the exchange-values of the commodities are given, the money in circulation is at its proper level when its quantity is determined by its own metallic value. It exceeds this level, gold falls below its own metallic value and the prices of commodities rise, whenever the aggregate exchange-value of commodities decreases or the supply of gold from the mines increases. The quantity of money sinks below its appropriate level, gold rises above its own metallic value and commodity-prices fall, whenever the aggregate exchange-value of commodities increases or the supply of gold from the mines is insufficient to replace worn-out gold. In these two cases the gold in circulation is a token of value representing either a larger or a smaller value than it actually possesses. It can become an appreciated or depreciated token of itself. When commodities are generally evaluated in conformity with the new value of money, and commodity-prices in general have risen or fallen accordingly, the amount of gold in circulation will once more be commensurate with the needs of circulation (a result which Ricardo emphasises with special satisfaction), but it will be at variance with the production costs of precious metals, and hence with the relations of precious metals as commodities to other commodities. According to Ricardo's general theory of exchange-value, the rise of gold above its exchange-value, in other words above the value which is determined by the labour-time it contains, would lead to an enlarged output of gold until the increased supply reduced it again to its proper value. Conversely, a fall of gold below its value would lead to a decline in the output of gold until its value rose again to its proper level. These opposite movements would resolve the contradiction between the metallic value of gold and its value as a medium of circulation; the amount of gold in circulation would reach its proper level and commodity-prices would once more be in accordance with the standard of value. These fluctuations in the value of gold would in equal measure affect gold bullion, since according to the assumption all gold that is not used as luxury articles is in circulation. Seeing that even gold in the form of coin or bullion can become a value-token representing a larger or smaller value than its own, it is obvious that any convertible bank-notes that are in circulation must share the same fate. Although bank-notes are convertible and their real value accordingly corresponds to their nominal value, "the aggregate currency consisting of metal and of convertible notes" may appreciate or depreciate if, for reasons described earlier, the total quantity either rises above or falls below the level which is determined by the exchange-value of the commodities in circulation and the metallic value of gold. According to this point of view, inconvertible paper money has only one advantage over convertible paper money, i.e., it can be depreciated in two ways. It may fall below the value of the metal which it professes to represent, because too much of it has been issued, or it may fall because the metal it represents has fallen below its own value. This depreciation, not of notes in relation to gold, but of gold and notes taken together, i.e., of the aggregate means of circulation of a country, is one of Ricardo's main discoveries, which Lord Overstone and Co. pressed into their service and turned into a fundamental principle of Sir Robert Peel's bank legislation of 1844 and 1845.

What should have been demonstrated was that the price of commodities or the value of gold depends on the amount of gold in circulation. The proof consists in postulating what has to be proved, i.e., that any quantity of the precious metal serving as money, regardless of its relation to its intrinsic value, must become a medium of circulation, or coin, and thus a token of value for the commodities in circulation regardless of the total amount of their value. In other words, this proof rests on disregarding all functions performed by money except its function as a medium of circulation. When driven into a corner, as for instance in his controversy with Bosanquet, Ricardo—entirely dominated by the phenomenon of value-tokens depreciating because of their quantity,—resorts to dogmatic assertion.*

If Ricardo had presented his theory in abstract form, as we have done, without introducing concrete circumstances and incidental aspects which represent digressions from the main problem, its hollowness would have been quite obvious. But he gives the whole analysis an *international* veneer. It is easy to show, however, that the apparent magnitude of scale can in no way alter the insignificance of the basic ideas.

The first proposition, therefore, was: the quantity of specie in circulation is normal if it is determined by the

---

* David Ricardo, *Reply to Mr. Bosanquet's Practical Observations,* p. 49. "That commodities would rise or fall in price, in proportion to the increase or diminution of money, *I assume as a fact which is incontrovertible.*"

aggregate value of commodities in circulation estimated in terms of the metallic value of specie. Adjusted for the international scene this reads: when circulation is in a normal state, the amount of money in each country is commensurate with its wealth and industry. The value of money in circulation corresponds to its real value, *i.e.*, its costs of production: in other words, money has the same value in *all countries*.* Money therefore would never be transferred (exported or imported) from one country to another.** A state of equilibrium would thus prevail between the currencies (the total volume of money in circulation) of different countries. The appropriate level of national currency is now expressed in the form of international currency-equilibrium, and this means in fact simply that nationality does not affect the general economic law at all. We have now reached again the same crucial point as before. In what way is the appropriate level upset, which now reads as follows: in what way is the international equilibrium of currencies upset, or why does money cease to have the same value in all countries, or finally why does it cease to have its specific value in each country? Just as previously the appropriate level was upset because the volume of gold in circulation increased or decreased while the aggregate value of commodities remained unchanged, or because the quantity of money in circulation remained constant while the exchange-value of commodities increased or decreased; so now the international level, which is determined by the value of the metal, is upset because the amount of gold is augmented in one country as a result of the discovery of new gold mines in that country,*** or because the aggregate exchange-value of the commodities in circulation in a particular country increases or decreases. Just as previously the output of precious metals was diminished or enlarged in accordance with the need for reducing or expanding the currency, and in accordance with it to lower or raise commodity-prices, so now the same effect is achieved by export and import from one country to another. In a country where prices have risen and, owing

---

* Ricardo, *The High Price of Bullion.* "Money would have the *same value* in all countries" (p. 4). Ricardo has qualified this proposition in his *Principles of Political Economy*, but not so as to be of any importance in this context.

** *Op. cit.*, pp. 3-4.

*** *Op. cit.*, p. 4.

to expanded circulation, the value of gold has fallen below its metallic value, gold would be depreciated in relation to other countries, and the prices of commodities would consequently be higher than in other countries. Gold would, therefore, be exported and commodities imported. The opposite movement would take place in the reverse situation. Just as previously the output of gold continued until the proper ratio of values between gold and commodities was re-established, so now the import or export of gold, accompanied by a rise or fall in commodity-prices, would continue until equilibrium of the international currencies had been re-established. Just as in the first example the output of gold expanded or diminished only because gold stood above or below its value, so now the international movement of gold is brought about by the same cause. Just as in the former example the quantity of metal in circulation and thereby prices were affected by every change in gold output, so now they are affected similarly by international import and export of gold. When the relative value of gold and commodities, or the normal quantity of means of circulation, is established, no further production of gold takes place in the former case, and no more export or import of gold in the latter, except to replace worn-out coin and for the use of the luxury industry. It thus follows,

"that the temptation to export money in exchange for goods, or what is termed an unfavourable balance of trade, never arises but from a redundant currency".*

The import or export of gold is invariably brought about by the metal being underrated or overrated owing to an expansion of the currency above its proper level or its contraction below that level.** It follows further: since the output of gold is expanded or diminished in our first case, and gold is imported or exported in our second case, only because its quantity has risen above its proper level or fallen below it, because it is rated above its metallic value or below it, and consequently commodity-prices are too high or too low, every one of these movements acts as its own corrective,*** for, by augmenting or curtailing the

---

* Ricardo, *op. cit.*, pp. 11, 12.
** "The exportation of the coin is caused by its cheapness, and is not the effect, but the cause of an unfavourable balance" (*op. cit.*, p. 14).
*** *Op. cit.*, p. 17.

amount of money in circulation, prices are reduced again to their correct level, which is determined by the value of gold and the value of commodities in the first case, and by the international level of currencies in the second. To put it in other words, money circulates in different countries only because it circulates as coin in each country. Money is simply specie, and the amount of gold present in a country must enter the sphere of circulation; as a token representing itself it can thus rise above or fall below its value. By the circuitous route of these international intricacies we have managed to return to the simple thesis which forms the point of departure.

A few examples will show how arbitrarily actual phenomena are arranged by Ricardo to suit his abstract theory. He asserts, for instance, that in periods of crop failure, which occurred frequently in England between 1800 and 1820, gold is exported, not because corn is needed and gold constitutes money, *i.e.*, it is always an efficacious means of purchase and means of payment on the world market, but because the value of gold has fallen in relation to other commodities and hence the currency of the country suffering from crop failure is depreciated in relation to the other national currencies. That is to say, because the bad harvest reduces the volume of commodities in circulation, the existing quantity of money in circulation exceeds its normal level and all commodity-prices consequently rise.* As opposed to

* Ricardo, *op. cit.*, pp. 74, 75. "England, in consequence of a bad harvest, would come under the case of a country having been deprived of a part of its commodities, and, therefore, requiring a diminished amount of circulating medium. The currency which was before equal to her payments would now become superabundant and relatively cheap, in proportion ... of her diminished production; the exportation of this sum, therefore, would restore the value of her currency to the value of the currencies of other countries." His confusion of money and commodities and of money and specie appears in a quite ridiculous form in the following passage. "If we can suppose that after an unfavourable harvest, when England has occasion for an unusual importation of corn, another nation is possessed of a superabundance of that article, but has no wants for any commodity whatever, it would unquestionably follow that such a nation would not export its corn in exchange for commodities: *but neither would it export corn for money*, as that is a commodity which no nation ever wants absolutely, but relatively" (*l.c.*, p. 75). In his epic poem Pushkin relates that the father of his hero fails to grasp that commodities are money. But that the Russians long ago grasped that money is a commodity is demonstrated not only by the English corn imports from 1838 to 1842, but also by the whole history of their trade.

this paradoxical explanation, statistics show that in the case of crop failures in England from 1793 up to the present, the existing amount of means of circulation was not excessive but on the contrary it was insufficient, and therefore more money than previously circulated and was bound to circulate.*

At the time of Napoleon's Continental System and the English Blockade Decrees, Ricardo likewise asserted that the British exported gold instead of commodities to the Continent, because their money was depreciated in relation to that of continental countries, the prices of their commodities were therefore higher and the export of gold rather than commodities was thus a more profitable commercial transaction. According to him commodities were dear and money cheap on the English market, whereas on the Continent commodities were cheap and money dear.

An English writer states however: "The fact ... I mean the ruinously low prices of our manufactures and of our colonial productions under the operation, against England, of the 'Continental System' during the last six years of the war.... The prices of sugar and coffee, for instance, on the Continent, computed in gold, were four or five times higher than their prices in England, computed in bank-notes. I am speaking ... of the times in which the French chemists discovered sugar in beet-root, and a substitute for coffee in chicory; and when the English grazier tried experiments upon fattening oxen with treacle and molasses—of the times when we took possession of the island of Heligoland, in order to form there a depôt of goods to facilitate, if possible, the smuggling of them into the North of Europe; and when the lighter descriptions of British manufactures found their way into Germany through Turkey.... Almost all the merchandise of the world accumulated in our warehouses, where they became impounded, except when some small quantity was released by a French Licence, for which the merchants at Hamburgh or Amsterdam had, perhaps, given Napoleon such a sum as forty or fifty thousand pounds. They must have been strange merchants ... to have paid so large a sum for liberty to carry a cargo of goods from a dear market to a cheap one. What was the ostensible alternative the merchant had?... Either to buy coffee at 6d. a pound in bank-notes, and send it to a place where it would instantly sell at 3s. or 4s. a pound in gold, or to buy gold with bank-notes at £5 an ounce, and send it to a place where it would be received at £3 17s. 10½d. an ounce.... It is too absurd, of course, to say ... that the gold was remitted instead of the coffee, as a preferable mercantile operation.... There was not a country in the world in which

---

* *Cf.* Thomas Tooke, *History of Prices*, and James Wilson, *Capital, Currency and Banking*. (The latter is a reprint of a series of articles published in the London *Economist* in 1844, 1845 and 1847.)

so large a quantity of desirable goods could be obtained, in return for an ounce of gold, as in England.... Bonaparte ... was constantly examining the English Price Current.... So long as he saw that gold was dear and coffee was cheap in England, he was satisfied that his 'Continental System' worked well."*

In 1810—just at the time when Ricardo first advanced his currency theory, and the Bullion Committee embodied it in its parliamentary report—the prices of all British commodities slumped ruinously in comparison with their level in 1808 and 1809, whereas the relative value of gold rose. Agricultural products were an exception because their import from abroad was impeded and the amount available within the country was greatly reduced by bad harvests.** So completely did Ricardo misunderstand the function that precious metals perform as international means of payment that in his evidence before the Committee of the House of Lords (1819) he could declare:

"that drains for exportation would cease altogether so soon as cash payments should be resumed, and the currency restored to its metallic level".

His death occurred in time before the onset of the crisis of 1825 demonstrated the falsehood of his forecast. The time within which Ricardo's literary activity falls was in general hardly favourable to the study of the function which precious metals perform as world money. Before the imposition of the Continental System Britain had almost continuously a favourable trade balance, and while the System was in force her transactions with the European continent were too insignificant to affect the English rate of exchange. The transfer of money had a predominantly political character, and Ricardo seems to have completely misunderstood the rôle which subsidies played in British gold export.***

Among the contemporaries of Ricardo, *James Mill* was the most important of the adherents of his principles of political economy. He attempted to expound Ricardo's monetary theory on the basis of simple metallic currency, omitting the irrelevant international complications, which conceal the inadequacy of Ricardo's conception, and all con-

---

* James Deacon Hume, *Letters on the Corn Laws*, London, 1834, pp. 29-31.

** Thomas Tooke, *History of Prices*, London, 1848, p. 110.

*** *Cf.* W. Blake, *Observations*, quoted earlier.

troversial references to the operation of the Bank of England. His main propositions are as follows.*

"By value of money, is here to be understood the proportion in which it exchanges for other commodities, or the quantity of it which exchanges for a certain quantity of other things.... It is the total quantity of the money in any country, which determines what portion of that quantity shall exchange for a certain portion of the goods or commodities of that country. If we suppose that all the goods of the country are on one side, all the money on the other, and that they are exchanged at once against one another, ... it is evident that the value of money would depend wholly upon the quantity of it. It will appear that the case is precisely the same in the actual state of the facts. The whole of the goods of a country are not exchanged at once against the whole of the money; the goods are exchanged in portions, often in very small portions, and at different times, during the course of the whole year. The same piece of money which is paid in one exchange to-day, may be paid in another exchange to-morrow. Some of the pieces will be employed in a great many exchanges, some in very few, and some, which happen to be hoarded, in none at all. There will, amid all these varieties, be a certain average number of exchanges, the same which, if all the pieces had performed an equal number, would have been performed by each; that average we may suppose to be any number we please; say, for example, ten. If each of the pieces of the money in the country perform ten purchases, that is exactly the same thing as if all pieces were multiplied by ten, and performed only one purchase each. The value of all the goods in the country is equal to ten times the value of all the money.... If the quantity of money instead of performing ten exchanges in the year, were ten times as great, and performed only one exchange in the year, it is evident that whatever addition were made to the whole quantity, would produce a proportional diminution of value, in each of the minor quantities taken separately. As the quantity of goods, against which the money is all exchanged at once, is supposed to be the same, the value of all the money is no more, after the quantity is augmented, than before it was augmented. If it is supposed to be augmented one-tenth, the value of every part, that of an ounce for example, must be diminished one-tenth.... In whatever degree, therefore, the quantity of money is increased or diminished, other things remaining the same, in that same proportion, the value of the whole, and of every part, is reciprocally diminished or increased. This, it is evident, is a proposition universally true. Whenever the value of money has either risen or fallen (the quantity of goods against which it is exchanged and the rapidity of circulation remaining the same), the change must be owing to a corresponding diminution or increase of the quantity; and can be owing to nothing else. If the quantity of goods diminish, while the quantity of money remains the same, it is the same thing as if the quantity of money had been increased;" and *vice versa*. "Similar changes are produced by any alteration in the rapidity of circulation.... An increase in the number of these purchases has the same effect as an increase in the quantity of money; a

---

* James Mill, *Elements of Political Economy*. [Marx used the French translation by J. T. Parisot published in Paris in 1823.]

180

diminution the reverse.... If there is any portion of the annual produce which is not exchanged at all, as what is consumed by the producer; or which is not exchanged for money; that is not taken into the account, because what is not exchanged for money is in the same state with respect to the money, as if it did not exist.... Whenever the coining of money ... is free, its quantity is regulated by the value of the metal.... Gold and silver are in reality commodities.... It is cost of production ... which determines the value of these, as of other ordinary productions."*

Mill's whole wisdom is reduced to a series of assumptions which are both arbitrary and trite. He wishes to prove that "it is the total quantity of the money in any country" which determines the price of commodities or the value of money. If one *assumes* that the quantity and the exchange-value of the commodities in circulation remain constant, likewise the velocity of circulation and the value of precious metals, which is determined by the cost of production, and if simultaneously one *assumes* that nevertheless the quantity of specie *in circulation* increases or decreases in relation to the volume of money *existing* in a country, then it is indeed "evident" that one has assumed what one has pretended to prove. Mill, moreover, commits the same error as Hume, namely placing not commodities with a determinate exchange-value, but use-values into circulation; his proposition is therefore wrong, even if one accepts all his "assumptions". The velocity of circulation may remain unchanged, similarly the value of precious metals and the *quantity* of commodities in circulation, yet they may nevertheless require sometimes a larger sometimes a smaller amount of money for their circulation as a result of changes in their exchange-value. Mill notices that a part of the money existing in a country circulates while another part stagnates. By means of a very odd rule of averages he *assumes* that all the money present in a country is actually in circulation, although in reality it does not seem to be so. If one assumes that in a given country 10 million silver thalers circulate twice in the course of a year, then, if each thaler were used in only one purchase, 20 million could be in circulation. And if the total quantity of all forms of silver in the country amounted to 100 million, it may be supposed that the 100 million could be in circulation if each coin performed one purchase in five years. One could as well assume that all

---

* James Mill, *op. cit.*, Paris, 1823, pp. 128-36 *passim.* [*Elements of Political Economy*, London, 1821, pp. 95-101 *passim.*]

the money existing in the world circulated in Hampstead, but that each portion of it performed one circuit in 3,000,000 years instead of, say, three circuits in one year. The one assumption is just as relevant as the other to the determination of the relation between the aggregate of commodity-prices and the amount of currency. Mill is aware of the crucial importance of establishing a direct connection between the commodities and the whole stock of money—not just the amount of money in circulation—in a particular country at a given time. He admits that the whole of the goods of a country are "not exchanged at once" against the whole of the money, but says that separate portions of the goods are exchanged for various portions of money at different times throughout the year. In order to remove this incongruity he *assumes* that it does not exist. Incidentally, the whole concept of a direct confrontation between commodities and money and their direct exchange is derived from the movement of simple purchases and sales or from the function performed by money as means of purchase. The simultaneous appearance of commodities and money ceases even when money acts as means of payment.

The commercial crises of the nineteenth century, and in particular the great crises of 1825 and 1836, did not lead to any further development of Ricardo's currency theory, but rather to new practical applications of it. It was no longer a matter of single economic phenomena—such as the depreciation of precious metals in the sixteenth and seventeenth centuries confronting Hume, or the depreciation of paper currency during the eighteenth century and the beginning of the nineteenth confronting Ricardo—but of big storms on the world market, in which the antagonism of all elements in the bourgeois process of production explodes; the origin of these storms and the means of defence against them were sought within the sphere of currency, the most superficial and abstract sphere of this process. The theoretical assumption which actually serves the school of economic weather experts as their point of departure is the dogma that Ricardo had discovered the laws governing purely metallic currency. It was thus left to them to subsume the circulation of credit money or bank-notes under these laws.

The most common and conspicuous phenomenon accompanying commercial crises is a sudden fall in the general level of commodity-prices occurring after a prolonged general rise of prices. A general fall of commodity-prices may be expressed as a rise in the value of money relative to all other commodities, and, on the other hand, a general rise of prices may be defined as a fall in the relative value of money. Either of these statements describes the phenomenon but does not explain it. Whether the task set is to explain the periodic rise in the general level of prices alternating with a general fall, or the same task is said to be to explain the alternating fall and rise in the relative value of money compared with that of commodities—the different terminology has just as little effect on the task itself as a translation of the terms from German into English would have. Ricardo's monetary theory proved to be singularly apposite since it gave to a tautology the semblance of a causal relation. What is the cause of the general fall in commodity-prices which occurs periodically? It is the periodically occurring rise in the relative value of money. What on the other hand is the cause of the recurrent general rise in commodity-prices? It is the recurrent fall in the relative value of money. It would be just as correct to say that the recurrent rise and fall of prices is brought about by their recurrent rise and fall. The proposition advanced presupposes that the intrinsic value of money, *i.e.*, its value as determined by the production costs of the precious metals, remains *unchanged*. If the tautology is meant to be more than a tautology, then it is based on a misapprehension of the most elementary notions. We know that if the exchange-value of A expressed in terms of B falls, it may be due either to a fall in the value of A or to a rise in the value of B; similarly if, on the contrary, the exchange-value of A expressed in terms of B rises. Once the transformation of the tautology into a causal relationship is taken for granted, everything else follows easily. The rise in commodity-prices is due to a fall in the value of money, the fall in the value of money, however, as we know from Ricardo, is due to excessive currency, that is to say, to the fact that the amount of money in circulation rises above the level determined by its own intrinsic value and the intrinsic value of commodities. Similarly in the opposite case, the general fall of commodity-prices is due to the value of money rising above its intrinsic value as a result of an insufficient amount of currency. Prices therefore rise and fall periodically, because periodically there is too much or too little money in circulation. If it is proved, for instance, that the rise of prices coincided with a decreased amount of money in circulation, and the fall of prices with an increased amount, then it is nevertheless possible to assert that, in consequence of some reduction or increase—which can in no way be ascertained statistically—of commodities in circulation, the amount of money in circulation has relatively, though not absolutely, increased or decreased. We have seen that, according to Ricardo, even when a purely metallic currency is employed, these variations in the level of prices must take place, but, because they occur alternately, they neutralise one another. For example, an insufficient amount of currency brings about a fall in commodity-prices, the fall of commodity-prices stimulates an export of commodities to other countries, but this export leads to an influx of money into the country, the influx of money causes again a rise in commodity-prices. When there is an excessive amount of currency the reverse occurs: commodities are imported and money exported. Since notwithstanding these general price movements, which arise from the very nature of Ricardo's metallic currency, their severe and vehement form, the form of crisis, belongs to periods with developed credit systems, it is clear that the issue of bank-notes is not exactly governed by the laws of metallic currency. The remedy applicable to metallic currency is the import and export of precious metals, which are immediately thrown into circulation as coin, their inflow or outflow thus causing commodity-prices to fall or to rise. The banks must now artificially exert the same influence on commodity-prices by imitating the laws of metallic currency. If gold is flowing in from abroad, it is a proof that there is an insufficient amount of currency, that the value of money is too high and commodity-prices too low, and bank-notes must therefore be thrown into circulation in accordance with the newly imported gold. On the other hand, bank-notes must be taken out of circulation in accordance with an outflow of gold from the country. In other words the issue of bank-notes must be regulated according to the import and export of the precious metals or according to the rate of exchange. Ricardo's wrong assumption that gold is simply specie and that consequently the whole of the imported gold is used to augment the money in circulation thus causing prices to rise, and that the whole of the gold exported represents a decrease in the amount of specie and thus causes prices to fall—this theoretical assumption

184

is now turned *into a practical experiment by making the amount of specie in circulation correspond always to the quantity of gold in the country.* Lord *Overstone* (Jones Loyd, the banker), Colonel Torrens, Norman, Clay, Arbuthnot and numerous other writers known in England as the "currency school" have not only preached this doctrine, but have made it the basis of the present English and Scottish banking legislation by means of Sir Robert Peel's Bank Acts of 1844 and 1845. The analysis of the ignominious fiasco they suffered both in theory and practice, after experiments on the largest national scale, can only be made in the section dealing with the theory of credit.* It is obvious however that Ricardo's theory, which regards currency, the fluid form of money, in isolation, ends by attributing to increases and decreases in the amount of precious metals an absolute influence on bourgeois economy such as was never imagined even in the superstitious concepts of the Monetary System. Ricardo, who declared that paper money is the most perfect form of money, was thus to become the prophet of the bullionists.

After Hume's theory, or the abstract opposition to the Monetary System, had been developed to its extreme conclusions, Steuart's concrete interpretation of money was finally restored to its legitimate position by *Thomas Tooke.***

---

* Investigation into the operation of the Bank Acts of 1844 and 1845 was conducted by a Committee of the House of Commons a few months before the onset of the general commercial crisis of 1857. In his evidence to the Committee, Lord Overstone, the theoretical father of these Acts, gave vent to the following piece of boasting: "By strict and prompt adherence to the principles of the Act of 1844, everything has passed off with regularity and ease; the monetary system is safe and unshaken, the prosperity of the country is undisputed, the public confidence in the wisdom of the Act of 1844 is daily gaining strength; and if the Committee wish for further practical illustration of the soundness of the principles on which it rests, or of the beneficial results which it has assured, the true and sufficient answer to the Committee is, look around you; look at the present state of trade of the country, look at the contentment of the people; look at the wealth and prosperity which pervades every class of the community; and then, having done so, the Committee may be fairly called upon to decide whether they will interfere with the continuance of an Act under which these results have been developed." Thus did Overstone blow his own trumpet on July 14, 1857, and on November 12 of the same year the miraculous Act of 1844 had to be suspended by the Cabinet on its own responsibility.

** That Tooke was quite unaware of Steuart's work is apparent from his *History of Prices from 1839 to 1847*, London, 1848, where he summarises the history of theories of money.

Tooke derives his principles not from some theory or other but from a scrupulous analysis of the history of commodity-prices from 1793 to 1856. In the first edition of his *History of Prices*, which was published in 1823, Tooke is still completely engrossed in the Ricardian theory and vainly tries to reconcile the facts with this theory. His pamphlet *On the Currency*, which was published after the crisis of 1825, could even be regarded as the first consistent exposition of the views which Overstone was to set forth later. But continued investigation of the history of prices compelled Tooke to recognise that the direct correlation between prices and the quantity of currency presupposed by this theory is purely imaginary, that increases or decreases in the amount of currency when the value of precious metals remains constant are always the consequence, never the cause, of price variations, that altogether the circulation of money is merely a secondary movement and that, in addition to serving as medium of circulation, money performs various other functions in the real process of production. His detailed research does not belong to the sphere of simple metallic currency and at this stage it is accordingly not yet possible to examine it or the works of *Wilson* and *Fullarton,* who belong to the same school of thought.* None of these writers take a one-sided view of money but deal with its various aspects, though only from a mechanical angle without paying any attention to the organic relation of these aspects either with one another or with the system of economic categories as a whole. Hence, they fall into the error of confusing *money* as distinct from *currency* with *capital* or even with commodities; although on the other hand, they are occasionally constrained to assert that there is a distinction between these two categories and money.** When, for example, gold is sent abroad, then indeed capital is sent abroad, but this is also the case when iron, cotton, corn, in short when any commodity, is exported. Both are capital and the difference

---

* Tooke's principal work—apart from the *History of Prices*, which was published in six volumes by his collaborator Newmarch—is *An Inquiry into the Currency Principle, the Connection of Currency with Prices...* 2nd Ed., London, 1844. Wilson's book has already been quoted. There remains to be mentioned John Fullarton, *On the Regulation of Currencies,* 2nd Ed., London, 1845.

** "We ought to ... distinguish ... between gold considered as merchandise, *i.e.,* as capital, and gold considered as currency..."

between them does not consist therefore in the fact that one is capital, but that one is money and the other commodity. The rôle of gold as international means of exchange is thus due not to the distinctive form it has as capital, but to the specific function it performs as money. Similarly when gold or bank-notes which take its place act as means of payment in domestic trade they are at the same time capital. But it would be impossible to use capital in the shape of commodities instead, as crises very strikingly demonstrate, for instance. It is again the difference between commodities and gold used as money and not its function as capital which turns gold into a means of payment. Even when capital is directly exported as capital, e.g., in order to lend a definite amount on interest abroad, it depends on market conditions whether this is exported in the shape of commodities or of gold; and if it is exported as gold this is done because of the specific function which the precious metals perform as money in contradistinction to commodities. Generally speaking these writers do not first of all examine money in its abstract form in which it develops within the framework of simple commodity circulation and grows out of the relations of commodities in circulation. As a consequence they continually vacillate between the abstract forms which money assumes, as opposed to commodities, and those forms of money which conceal concrete factors, such as capital, revenue, and so forth.*

(Thomas Tooke, *An Inquiry into the Currency Principle*, p. 10). "Gold and silver ... may be counted upon to realise on their arrival nearly the exact sum required to be provided.... Gold and silver possess an infinite advantage over all other description of merchandise ... from the circumstance of ... being universally in use as money.... It is not in tea, coffee, sugar, or indigo that debts, whether foreign or domestic, are usually contracted to be paid, but in coin; and the remittance, therefore, either in the identical coin designated, or in bullion which can be promptly turned into that coin through the Mint or market of the country to which it is sent, must always afford to the remitter the most certain, immediate, and accurate means of effecting this object, without risk of disappointment from the failure of demand or fluctuation of price" (John Fullarton, *op. cit.*, pp. 132, 133). "Any other article" (apart from gold and silver) "might in quantity or kind be beyond the usual demand in the country to which it is sent" (Tooke, *An Inquiry...* [p. 10]).

* The conversion of money into capital will be examined in Chapter Three, which deals with capital and concludes the first section [of this work].

APPENDICES

KARL MARX

INTRODUCTION[27]

I. PRODUCTION, CONSUMPTION, DISTRIBUTION, EXCHANGE (CIRCULATION)

1. PRODUCTION

(a) To begin with, the question under discussion is *material production.*

Individuals producing in a society, and hence the socially determined production of individuals, is of course the point of departure. The solitary and isolated hunter or fisherman, who serves Adam Smith and Ricardo as a starting point, is one of the unimaginative fantasies of eighteenth-century romances *à la* Robinson Crusoe; and despite the assertions of social historians, these by no means signify simply a reaction against over-refinement and reversion to a misconceived natural life. No more is Rousseau's *contrat social*, which by means of a contract establishes a relationship and connection between subjects that are by nature independent, based on this kind of naturalism. This is an illusion and nothing but the aesthetic illusion of the small and big Robinsonades. It is, on the contrary, the anticipation of "bourgeois society", which began to evolve in the sixteenth century and in the eighteenth century made giant strides towards maturity. The individual in this society of free competition seems to be rid of natural ties, etc., which made him an appurtenance of a particular, limited aggregation of human beings in previous historical epochs. The prophets of the eighteenth century, on whose shoulders Adam Smith and Ricardo were still wholly standing, envisaged this 18th-century individual —a product of the dissolution of feudal society on the one hand and of the new productive forces evolved since the sixteenth century on the other—as an ideal whose existence belonged to the past. They saw this individual not as an historical result, but as the starting point of history; not as something evolving in the course of history, but posited by nature, because for them this individual was in conformity with nature, in keeping with their idea of human nature. This delusion has been characteristic of every new epoch hitherto. Steuart, who in some respect was in opposition to the eighteenth century and as an aristocrat tended rather to regard things from an historical standpoint, avoided this naïve view.

The further back we trace the course of history, the more does the individual, and accordingly also the producing individual, appear to be dependent and to belong to a larger whole. At first, the individual in a still quite natural manner is part of the family and of the tribe which evolves from the family; later he is part of a community, of one of the different forms of the community which arise from the conflict and the merging of tribes. It is not until the eighteenth century that in bourgeois society the various forms of the social texture confront the individual as merely means towards his private ends, as external necessity. But the epoch which produces this standpoint, namely that of the solitary individual, is precisely the epoch of the (as yet) most highly developed social (according to this standpoint, general) relations. Man is a ζῶον πολιτιχόν[a] in the most literal sense: he is not only a social animal, but an animal that can be individualised only within society. Production by a solitary individual outside society—a rare event, which might occur when a civilised person who has already absorbed the dynamic social forces is accidentally cast into the wilderness—is just as preposterous as the development of speech without individuals who live *together* and talk to one another. It is unnecessary to dwell upon this point further. It need not have been mentioned at all, if this inanity, which had rhyme and reason in the works of eighteenth-century writers, were not expressly introduced once more into modern political economy by Bastiat, Carey, Proudhon, etc. It is of course very pleasant for Proudhon, for instance, to be able to explain the origin of an economic relationship—whose historical evolution he does not know—in an historico-philosophical manner by means of mythology; alleging that. Adam or Prometheus hit upon the ready-made idea, which was then put into practice, etc. Nothing is more tedious and dull than the fantasies of *locus communis*.

Thus when we speak of production, we always have in mind production at a definite stage of social development,

---

a *Zoon politikon*—social animal. Aristoteles, *De Republica*, Lib. I, Cap. 2.—*Ed*.

production by individuals in a society. It might therefore seem that, in order to speak of production at all, we must either trace the various phases in the historical process of development, or else declare from the very beginning that we are examining *one* particular historical period, as for instance modern bourgeois production, which is indeed our real subject-matter. All periods of production, however, have certain features in common: they have certain common categories. *Production in general* is an abstraction, but a sensible abstraction in so far as it actually emphasises and defines the common aspects and thus avoids repetition. Yet this *general* concept, or the common aspect which has been brought to light by comparison, is itself a multifarious compound comprising divergent categories. Some elements are found in all epochs, others are common to a few epochs. The most modern period and the most ancient period will have [certain] categories in common. Production without them is inconceivable. But although the most highly developed languages have laws and categories in common with the most primitive languages, it is precisely their divergence from these general and common features which constitutes their development. It is necessary to distinguish those definitions which apply to production in general, in order not to overlook the essential differences existing despite the unity that follows from the very fact that the subject, mankind, and the object, nature, are the same. For instance, on failure to perceive this fact depends the entire wisdom of modern economists who prove the eternity and harmony of existing social relations. For example, no production is possible without an instrument of production, even if this instrument is simply the hand. It is not possible without past, accumulated labour, even if this labour is only the skill acquired by repeated practice and concentrated in the hand of a savage. Capital is among other things also an instrument of production, and also past, materialised labour. Consequently capital is a universal and eternal relation given by nature—that is, provided one omits precisely those specific factors which turn the "instrument of production" or "accumulated labour" into capital. The whole history of the relations of production thus appears, for instance in Carey's writings, as a falsification malevolently brought about by the government.

Just as there is no production in general, so also there

is no general production. Production is always a *particular* branch of production—*e.g.*, agriculture, cattle-breeding, manufacture—or it is the *totality* of production. Political economy, however, is not technology. The relation of the general categories of production at a given social stage to the particular forms of production is to be set forth elsewhere (later).

Finally, not only is production particular production, but it is invariably only a definite social corpus, a social subject, that is engaged in a wider or narrower totality of productive spheres. The relation of the academic presentation to the actual process does not belong here either. Production in general. Particular branches of production. Totality of production.

It is fashionable to preface economic works with a general part—and it is just this which appears under the heading "Production", see for instance John Stuart Mill[28]—which deals with the *general conditions* of all production. This general part comprises or purports to comprise:

1. The conditions without which production cannot be carried on. This means in fact only that the essential factors required for any kind of production are indicated. But this amounts actually, as we shall see, to a few very simple definitions, which are further expanded into trivial tautologies.

2. The conditions which promote production to a larger or smaller degree, as in the case of Adam Smith's progressive and stagnant state of society. To give this, which in Smith's work has its value as an *aperçu*, to give it scientific significance, research into the *degree of productivity* at various periods in the development of individual nations would have to be conducted; strictly speaking, such an investigation lies outside the framework of the subject, those aspects which are however relevant to it ought to be mentioned in connection with the development of competition, accumulation, etc. The answer in its general form amounts to the general statement that an industrial nation achieves its highest productivity when it is altogether at the height of its historical development. (In fact, a nation is at the height of its industrial development so long as, not the gain, but gaining remains its principal aim. In this respect the Yankees are superior to the English.) Or else that for example certain races, formations, climates, natural circumstances,

such as maritime position, fertility of the soil, etc., are more conducive to production than others. This again amounts to the tautological statement that the production of wealth grows easier in the measure that its subjective and objective elements become available.

But all this is not really what the economists are concerned about in the general part. It is rather—see for example Mill—that production, as distinct from distribution, etc., is to be presented as governed by eternal natural laws which are independent of history, and at the same time *bourgeois* relations are clandestinely passed off as irrefutable natural laws of society *in abstracto*. This is the more or less conscious purpose of the whole procedure. As regards distribution, however, it is said that men have indeed indulged in a certain amount of free choice. Quite apart from the crude separation of production and distribution and their real interconnection, it should be obvious from the outset that, however dissimilar the mode of distribution at the various stages of society may be, it must be possible, just as in the case of production, to emphasise the common aspects, and it must be likewise possible to confuse and efface all historical differences in laws that are *common to all mankind*. For example, the slave, the serf, the wage-worker, they all receive an amount of food enabling them to exist as a slave, serf or wage-worker. The conqueror who lives on tribute, or the official who lives on taxes, or the landowner who lives on rent, or the monk who lives on alms, or the clergyman who lives on tithes, all receive a portion of the social product which is determined by laws different from those that determine the portion of the slave, and so on. The two principal factors which all economists include in this section are: 1) property and 2) its protection by the judiciary, police, etc. Only a very brief reply is needed:

Regarding 1: production is always appropriation of nature by an individual within and with the help of a definite social organisation. In this context it is tautological to say that property (appropriation) is a condition of production. But it is quite ridiculous to make a leap from this to a distinct form of property, *e.g.*, private property (this is moreover an antithetical form, which similarly presupposes *non-property* as a condition). History has shown, on the contrary, that common property (*e.g.*, among the Indians, Slavs, ancient Celts, etc.) is the original form, and in the shape of communal property it plays a significant rôle for a long time. The question whether wealth develops faster under this or under that form of property is not yet under discussion at this point. It is tautological however to state that where no form of property exists there can be no production and hence no society either. Appropriation which appropriates nothing is a contradiction in terms.

Regarding 2: safeguarding of what has been acquired, etc. If these trivialities are reduced to their real content, they say more than their authors realise, namely that each mode of production produces its specific legal relations, political forms, etc. It is a sign of crudity and lack of comprehension that organically coherent factors are brought into haphazard relation with one another, *i.e.*, into a simple reflex connection. The bourgeois economists have merely in view that production proceeds more smoothly with modern police than, *e.g.*, under club-law. They forget, however, that club-law too is law, and that the law of the stronger, only in a different form, still survives even in their "constitutional State".

While the social conditions appropriate to a particular stage of production are either still in the course of evolution or already in a state of dissolution, disturbances naturally occur in the process of production, although these may be of varying degree and extent.

To recapitulate: there are categories which are common to all stages of production and are established by reasoning as general categories; the so-called *general conditions* of all and any production, however, are nothing but abstract conceptions which do not define any of the actual historical stages of production.

2. THE GENERAL RELATIONS OF PRODUCTION TO DISTRIBUTION, EXCHANGE AND CONSUMPTION

Before starting upon a further analysis of production it is necessary to consider the various sections which economists place alongside it.

The quite obvious conception is this:—In the process of production members of society appropriate (produce, fashion) natural products in accordance with human requirements; distribution determines the share the individual receives of these products; exchange supplies him with the particular products into which he wants to convert the portion accorded to him as a result of distribution; finally, in consumption the products become objects of use, *i.e.* they are appropriated by individuals. Production creates articles corresponding to requirements; distribution allocates them according to social laws; exchange in its turn distributes the goods, which have already been allocated, in conformity with individual needs; finally, in consumption the product leaves this social movement, it becomes the direct object and servant of an individual need, which its use satisfies. Production thus appears as the point of departure, consumption as the goal, distribution and exchange as the middle, which has a dual form since, according to the definition, distribution is actuated by society and exchange is actuated by individuals. In production persons acquire an objective aspect, and in consumption[a] objects acquire a subjective aspect; in distribution it is society which by means of dominant general rules mediates between production and consumption; in exchange this mediation occurs as a result of random decisions of individuals.

Distribution determines the proportion (the quantity) of the products accruing to the individual, exchange determines the products in which the individual claims to make up the share assigned to him by distribution.

Production, distribution, exchange and consumption thus form a proper syllogism; production represents the general, distribution and exchange the particular, and consumption the individual case which sums up the whole. This is indeed a sequence, but a very superficial one. Production is determined by general laws of nature; distribution by random social factors, it may therefore exert a more or less beneficial influence on production; exchange, a formal social movement, lies between these two; and consumption, as the concluding act, which is regarded not only as the final aim but as the ultimate purpose, falls properly outside the sphere of economy, except in so far as it in turn exerts a reciprocal action on the point of departure thus once again initiating the whole process.

The opponents of the economists who accuse the latter of crudely separating interconnected elements, either argue from the same standpoint or even from a lower one, no matter whether these opponents come from within or without

---

[a] In the manuscript: "persons".—*Ed.*

the domain of political economy. Nothing is more common than the reproach that the economists regard production too much as a goal in itself, and that distribution is equally important. This argument is based on the concept of the economists that distribution is a separate and independent sphere alongside production. Another argument is that the different factors are not considered as a single whole; as though this separation had forced its way from the textbook into real life and not, on the contrary, from real life into the textbooks, and as though it were a question of the dialectical reconciliation of concepts and not of the resolution of actually existing conditions.

a. [Production and Consumption]

Production is simultaneously consumption as well. It is consumption in a dual form—subjective and objective consumption. [Firstly,] the individual, who develops his abilities while producing, expends them as well, using them up in the act of production, just as in natural procreation vital energy is consumed. Secondly, it is consumption of the means of production, which are used and used up and in part (as for instance fuel) are broken down into simpler components. It similarly involves consumption of raw material which is absorbed and does not retain its original shape and quality. The act of production itself is thus in all its phases also an act of consumption. The economists concede this. They call *productive consumption* both production that is simultaneously identical with consumption, and consumption which is directly concurrent with production. The identity of production and consumption amounts to Spinoza's proposition: *Determinatio est negatio*.

But this definition of productive consumption is only advanced in order to separate consumption that is identical with production from consumption in the proper sense, which is regarded by contrast as the destructive antithesis of production. Let us therefore consider consumption proper.

Consumption is simultaneously also production, just as in nature the production of a plant involves the consumption of elemental forces and chemical materials. It is obvious that man produces his own body, *e.g.*, through feeding, one form of consumption. But the same applies to any other kind of consumption which in one way or another contributes to the production of some aspect of man. Hence this is consumptive production. Nevertheless, says political economy, this type of production that is identical with consumption is a second phase arising from the destruction of the first product. In the first type of production the producer assumes an objective aspect, in the second type the objects created by him assume a personal aspect. Hence this consuming production—although it represents a direct unity of production and consumption—is essentially different from production proper. The direct unity, in which production is concurrent with consumption and consumption with production, does not affect their simultaneous duality.

Production is thus at the same time consumption, and consumption is at the same time production. Each is simultaneously its opposite. But an intermediary movement takes place between the two at the same time. Production leads to consumption, for which it provides the material; consumption without production would have no object. But consumption also leads to production by providing for its products the subject for whom they are products. The product only attains its final consummation in consumption. A railway on which no one travels, which is therefore not used up, not consumed, is potentially but not actually a railway. Without production there is no consumption, but without consumption there is no production either, since in that case production would be useless. Consumption produces production in two ways.

1. Because a product becomes a real product only through consumption. For example, a dress becomes really a dress only by being worn, a house which is uninhabited is indeed not really a house; in other words a product as distinct from a simple natural object manifests itself as a product, *becomes* a product, only in consumption. It is only consumption which, by destroying the product, gives it the finishing touch, for the product is a product, not because it is materialised activity, but only in so far as it is an object for the active subject.

2. Because consumption creates the need for *new* production, and therefore provides the conceptual, intrinsically actuating reason for production, which is the pre-condition for production. Consumption furnishes the impulse to produce, and also provides the object which acts as the determin-

ing purpose of production. If it is evident that externally production supplies the object of consumption, it is equally evident that consumption *posits* the object of production as a *concept*, an internal image, a need, a motive, a purpose. Consumption furnishes the object of production in a form that is still subjective. There is no production without a need, but consumption re-creates the need.

This is matched on the side of production,

1. by the fact that production supplies the material, the object of consumption. Consumption without an object is no consumption, in this respect, therefore, production creates, produces consumption.

2. But production provides not only the object of consumption, it also gives consumption a distinct form, a character, a finish. Just as consumption puts the finishing touch on the product as a product, so production puts the finishing touch to consumption. *For one thing*, the object is not simply an object in general, but a particular object which must be consumed in a particular way, a way determined by production. Hunger is hunger; but the hunger that is satisfied by cooked meat eaten with knife and fork differs from hunger that devours raw meat with the help of hands, nails and teeth. Production thus produces not only the object of consumption but also the mode of consumption, not only objectively but also subjectively. Production therefore creates the consumer.

3. Production not only provides the material to satisfy a need, but it also provides the need for the material. When consumption emerges from its original primitive crudeness and immediacy—and its remaining in that state would be due to the fact that production was still primitively crude—then it is itself as a desire brought about by the object. The need felt for the object is induced by the perception of the object. An *objet d'art* creates a public that has artistic taste and is able to enjoy beauty—and the same can be said of any other product. Production accordingly produces not only an object for the subject, but also a subject for the object.

Hence production produces consumption: 1) by providing the material of consumption; 2) by determining the mode of consumption; 3) by creating in the consumer a need for the objects which it first presents as products. It therefore produces the object of consumption, the mode of consumption and the urge to consume. Similarly, consumption produces the *predisposition* of the producer by positing him as a purposive requirement.

The identity of consumption and production has three aspects—

1. *Direct identity*: Production is consumption and consumption is production. Consumptive production and productive consumption. Economists call both productive consumption, but they still make a distinction. The former figures in their work as reproduction, the latter as productive consumption. All investigations of the former are concerned with productive and unproductive labour, those of the latter with productive and non-productive consumption.

2. Each appears as a means of the other, as being induced by it; this is called their mutual dependence; they are thus brought into mutual relation and appear to be indispensable to each other, but nevertheless remain extrinsic to each other. Production provides the material which is the external object of consumption, consumption provides the need, *i.e.*, the internal object, the purpose of production. There is no consumption without production, and no production without consumption. This proposition appears in various forms in political economy.

3. Production is not only simultaneously consumption, and consumption simultaneously production; nor is production only a means of consumption and consumption the purpose of production—*i.e.*, each provides the other with its object, production supplying the external object of consumption, and consumption the conceptual object of production—in other words, each of them is not only simultaneously the other, and not merely the cause of the other, but each of them by being carried through creates the other, it creates itself as the other. It is only consumption that consummates the process of production, since consumption completes the product as a product by destroying it, by consuming its independent concrete form. Moreover by its need for repetition consumption leads to the perfection of abilities evolved during the first process of production and converts them into skills. Consumption is therefore the concluding act which turns not only the product into a product, but also the producer into a producer. Production, on the other hand, produces consumption by creating a definite mode of consumption, and by providing an incentive to consumption it thereby creates the capability to consume as a requirement.

The last kind of identity, which is defined in point 3, has been variously interpreted by economists when discussing the relation of demand and supply, of objects and needs, of needs created by society and natural needs.

After this, nothing is simpler for a Hegelian than to assume that production and consumption are identical. And this has been done not only by socialist *belletrists* but also by prosaic economists, such as Say, in declaring that if one considers a nation—or mankind *in abstracto*—then its production is its consumption. Storch[29] has shown that this proposition of Say's is wrong, since a nation, for instance, does not consume its entire product, but must also provide means of production, fixed capital, etc. It is moreover wrong to consider society as a single subject, for this is a speculative approach. With regard to one subject, production and consumption appear as phases of a single operation. Only the most essential point is emphasised here, that production and consumption, if considered as activities of one subject or of single individuals, appear in any case as phases of one process whose actual point of departure is production which is accordingly the decisive factor. Consumption, as a necessity and as a need, is itself an intrinsic aspect of productive activity; the latter however is the point where the realisation begins and thus also the decisive phase, the action epitomising the entire process. An individual produces an object and by consuming it returns again to the point of departure: he returns however as a productive individual and an individual who reproduces himself. Consumption is thus a phase of production.

But in society, the relation of the producer to the product after its completion is extrinsic, and the return of the product to the subject depends on his relations to other individuals. The product does not immediately come into his possession. Its immediate appropriation, moreover, is not his aim, if he produces within society. *Distribution*, which on the basis of social laws determines the individual's share in the world of products, intervenes between the producer and the products, *i.e.*, between production and consumption.

Is distribution, therefore, an independent sector alongside and outside production?

b. [Production and Distribution]

When looking through the ordinary run of economic works, one's attention is attracted forthwith by the fact that everything is mentioned twice, *e.g.*, rent, wages, interest and profit figure under the heading distribution, while under the heading of production land, labour and capital appear as factors of production. As to capital, it is evident from the outset that this is counted twice, first as a factor of production, and secondly as a source of income; *i.e.*, as a determining and determinate form of distribution. Interest and profit appear therefore in production as well, since they are forms in which capital increases and grows, and are thus phases of its production. As forms of distribution, interest and profit presuppose capital as a factor of production. They are forms of distribution whose pre-condition is the existence of capital as a factor of production. They are likewise modes of reproduction of capital.

Wages represent also wage-labour, which is examined in a different section; the particular function that labour performs as a factor of production in the one case appears as a function of distribution in the other. If labour did not have the distinct form of wage-labour, then its share in the product would not appear as wages, as for instance in slavery. Finally rent—if we take the most advanced form of distribution by which landed property obtains a share in the product—presupposes large-scale landed property (strictly speaking, large-scale agriculture) as a factor of production, and not land in general; just as wages do not presuppose labour in general. The relations and modes of distribution are thus merely the reverse aspect of the factors of production. An individual whose participation in production takes the form of wage-labour will receive a share in the product, the result of production, in the form of wages. The structure of distribution is entirely determined by the structure of production. Distribution itself is a product of production, not only with regard to the content, for only the results of production can be distributed, but also with regard to the form, since the particular mode of men's participation in production determines the specific form of distribution, the form in which they share in distribution. It is altogether an illusion to speak of land in the section on production, and of rent in the section on distribution, etc.

Economists like Ricardo who are mainly accused of having paid exclusive attention to production, have accordingly regarded distribution as the exclusive subject of political economy, for they have instinctively treated the forms of distribution as the most precise expression in which factors of production manifest themselves in a given society.

To the single individual distribution naturally appears as a social law, which determines his position within the framework of production, within which he produces; distribution thus being antecedent to production. An individual who has neither capital nor landed property of his own is dependent on wage-labour from his birth as a consequence of social distribution. But this dependence is itself the result of the existence of capital and landed property as independent factors of production.

When one considers whole societies, still another aspect of distribution appears to be antecedent to production and to determine it, as though it were an ante-economic factor. A conquering nation may divide the land among the conquerors and in this way imposes a distinct mode of distribution and form of landed property, thus determining production. Or it may turn the population into slaves, thus making slave-labour the basis of production. Or in the course of a revolution, a nation may divide large estates into plots, thus altering the character of production in consequence of the new distribution. Or legislation may perpetuate land ownership in certain families, or allocate labour as a hereditary privilege, thus consolidating it into a caste system. In all these cases, and they have all occurred in history, it seems that distribution is not regulated and determined by production but, on the contrary, production by distribution.

Distribution according to the most superficial interpretation is distribution of products; it is thus removed further from production and made quasi-independent of it. But before distribution becomes distribution of products, it is (1) distribution of the means of production, and (2) (which is another aspect of the same situation) distribution of the members of society among the various types of production (the subsuming of the individuals under definite relations of production). It is evident that the distribution of products is merely a result of this distribution, which is comprised in the production process and determines the structure of production. To examine production divorced from this distribution which is a constituent part of it, is obviously idle abstraction; whereas conversely the distribution of products is automatically determined by that distribution which is initially a factor of production. Ricardo, the economist of production *par excellence*, whose object was the understanding of the distinct social structure of modern production, for this very reason declares that distribution, *not* production, is the proper subject of contemporary political economy. This is a witness to the banality of those economists who proclaim production as an eternal truth, and confine history to the domain of distribution.

The question as to the relation between that form of distribution that determines production and production itself, belongs obviously to the sphere of production. If it should be said that in this case at least, since production must proceed from a specific distribution of the means of production, distribution is to this extent antecedent to and a prerequisite of production, then the reply would be as follows. Production has indeed its conditions and prerequisites which are constituent elements of it. At the very outset these may have seemed to be naturally evolved. In the course of production, however, they are transformed from naturally evolved factors into historical ones, and although they may appear as natural pre-conditions for any one period, they are the historical result of another period. They are continuously changed by the process of production itself. For example, the employment of machinery led to changes in the distribution of both the means of production and the product. Modern large-scale landed property has been brought about not only by modern trade and modern industry, but also by the application of the latter to agriculture.

The above-mentioned questions can be ultimately resolved into this: what rôle do general historical conditions play in production and how is production related to the historical development as a whole? This question clearly belongs to the analysis and discussion of production.

In the trivial form, however, in which these questions have been raised above, they can be dealt with quite briefly. Conquests may lead to either of three results. The conquering nation may impose its own mode of production upon the conquered people (this was done, for example, by the English in Ireland during this century, and to some extent in India); or it may refrain from interfering in the old mode of production and be content with tribute (*e.g.*, the Turks and Romans); or interaction may take place between the two, giving rise to a new system as a synthesis (this occurred partly in the Germanic conquests). In any case it is the mode of production—whether that of the conquering nation or of the conquered or the new system brought about by a merging of the two—that determines the new mode of distribution employed. Although the latter appears to be a pre-condition of the new period of production, it is in its turn a result of production, a result not simply occasioned by the historical evolution of production in general, but by a specific historical form of production.

The Mongols, for example, who caused devastation in Russia, acted in accordance with their mode of production, cattle-breeding, for which large uninhabited tracts are a fundamental requirement. The Germanic barbarians, whose traditional mode of production was agriculture with the aid of serfs and who lived scattered over the countryside, could the more easily adapt the Roman provinces to their requirements because the concentration of landed property carried out there had already uprooted the older agricultural relations.

It is a long-established view that over certain epochs people lived by plunder. But in order to be able to plunder, there must be something to be plundered, and this implies production. Moreover, the manner of plunder depends itself on the manner of production, *e.g.*, a stock-jobbing nation cannot be robbed in the same way as a nation of cowherds.

The means of production may be robbed directly in the form of slaves. But in that case it is necessary that the structure of production in the country to which the slave is abducted admits of slave-labour, or (as in South America, etc.) a mode of production appropriate to slave-labour has to be evolved.

Laws may perpetuate a particular means of production, *e.g.*, land, in certain families. These laws acquire economic significance only if large-scale landed property is in keeping with the social mode of production, as for instance in Britain. Agriculture was carried on in France on a small scale, despite the existence of large estates, which were therefore parcelled out by the Revolution. But is it possible, *e.g.*, by law, to perpetuate the division of land into small lots? Landed property tends to become concentrated again despite these laws. The influence exercised by laws on the preservation of existing conditions of distribution, and the effect they thereby exert on production has to be examined separately.

c. Lastly, Exchange and Circulation

Circulation is merely a particular phase of exchange or of exchange regarded in its totality.

Since *exchange* is simply an intermediate phase between production and distribution, which is determined by production, and consumption; since consumption is moreover itself an aspect of production, the latter obviously comprises also exchange as one of its aspects.

Firstly, it is evident that exchange of activities and skills, which takes place in production itself, is a direct and essential part of production. Secondly, the same applies to the exchange of products in so far as this exchange is a means to manufacture the finished product intended for immediate consumption. The action of exchange in this respect is comprised in the concept of production. Thirdly, what is known as exchange between dealer and dealer, both with respect to its organisation and as a productive activity, is entirely determined by production. Exchange appears to exist independently alongside production and detached from it only in the last stage, when the product is exchanged for immediate consumption. But (1) no exchange is possible without division of labour, whether this is naturally evolved or is already the result of an historical process; (2) private exchange presupposes private production; (3) the intensity of exchange, its extent and nature, are determined by the development and structure of production: *e.g.*, exchange between town and country, exchange in the countryside, in the town, etc. All aspects of exchange to this extent appear either to be directly comprised in production, or else determined by it.

The conclusion which follows from this is, not that production, distribution, exchange and consumption are identical, but that they are links of a single whole, different aspects of one unit. Production is the decisive phase, both with regard to the contradictory aspects of production and with regard to the other phases. The process always starts afresh with production. That exchange and consumption cannot be the decisive elements, is obvious; and the same applies to distribution in the sense of distribution of products. Distribution of the factors of production, on the other hand, is itself a phase of production. A distinct mode of production thus determines the specific mode of consumption, distribution, exchange and the *specific relations of these different phases to one another*. Production *in the narrow sense*, however, is in its turn also determined by the other aspects. For example, if the market, or the sphere of exchange, expands, then the volume of production grows and tends to become more differentiated. Production also changes in consequence of changes in distribution, *e.g.*, concentration of capital, different distribution of the population in town and countryside, and the like. Production is, finally, determined by the demands of consumption. There is an interaction between the various aspects. Such interaction takes place in any organic entity.

3. THE METHOD OF POLITICAL ECONOMY

When examining a given country from the standpoint of political economy, we begin with its population, the division of the population into classes, town and country, the sea, the different branches of production, export and import, annual production and consumption, prices, etc.

It would seem to be the proper thing to start with the real and concrete elements, with the actual pre-conditions, *e.g.*, to start in the sphere of economy with population, which forms the basis and the subject of the whole social process of production. Closer consideration shows, however, that this is wrong. Population is an abstraction if, for instance, one disregards the classes of which it is composed. These classes in turn remain empty terms if one does not know the factors on which they depend, *e.g.*, wage-labour, capital, and so on. These presuppose exchange, division of labour, prices, etc. For example, capital is nothing without wage-labour, without value, money, price, etc. If one were to take population as the point of departure, it would be a very vague notion of a complex whole and through closer definition one would arrive analytically at increasingly simple concepts; from imaginary concrete terms one would move to more and more tenuous abstractions until one reached the most simple definitions. From there it would be necessary to make the journey again in the opposite direction until one arrived once more at the concept of population, which is this time not a vague notion of a whole, but a totality comprising many determinations and relations. The first course is the historical one taken by political economy at its inception. The seventeenth-century economists, for example, always took as their starting point the living organism, the population, the nation, the State, several States, etc., but analysis led them always in the end to the discovery of a few decisive abstract, general relations, such as division of labour, money, and value. When these separate factors were more or less clearly deduced and established, economic systems were evolved which from simple concepts, such as labour, division of labour, demand, exchange-value, advanced to categories like State, international exchange and world market. The latter is obviously the correct scientific method. The concrete concept is concrete because it is a synthesis of many definitions, thus representing the unity of diverse aspects. It appears therefore in reasoning as a summing-up, a result, and not as the starting point, although it is the real point of origin, and thus also the point of origin of perception and imagination. The first procedure attenuates meaningful images to abstract definitions, the second leads from abstract definitions by way of reasoning to the reproduction of the concrete situation. Hegel accordingly conceived the illusory idea that the real world is the result of thinking which causes its own synthesis, its own deepening and its own movement; whereas the method of advancing from the abstract to the concrete is simply the way in which thinking assimilates the concrete and reproduces it as a concrete mental category. This is, however, by no means the process of evolution of the concrete world itself. For example, the simplest economic category, *e.g.*, exchange-value, presupposes population, a population moreover which produces under definite conditions, as well as a distinct kind of family, or community, or State, etc. Exchange-value cannot exist except as an abstract, *unilateral* relation of an already existing concrete organic whole. But exchange-value as a category leads an antediluvian existence. Thus to consciousness—and this comprises philosophical consciousness—which regards the comprehending mind as the real man, and hence the comprehended world as such as the only real world; to consciousness, therefore, the evolution of categories appears as the actual process of production—which unfortunately is given an impulse from outside—whose result is the world; and this (which is however again a tautological expression) is true in so far as the concrete totality regarded as a conceptual totality, as a mental fact, is indeed a product of thinking, of comprehension; but it is by no means a product of the idea which evolves spontaneously and whose thinking proceeds outside and above perception and imagination, but is the result of the assimilation and transformation of perceptions and images into concepts. The totality as a conceptual entity seen by the intellect is a product of the thinking intellect which assimilates the world in the only way open to it, a way which differs from the artistic, religious and practically intelligent assimilation of this world. The concrete subject remains outside the intellect and independent of it—that is so long as the intellect adopts a purely speculative, purely theoretical attitude. The subject, society, must always be envisaged therefore as the pre-condition of comprehension even when the theoretical method is employed.

But have not these simple categories also an independent historical or natural existence preceding that of the more concrete ones? This depends. Hegel, for example, correctly takes ownership, the simplest legal relation of the subject, as the point of departure of the philosophy of law. No ownership exists, however, before the family or the relations of master and servant are evolved, and these are much more concrete relations. It would, on the other hand, be correct to say that families and entire tribes exist which have as yet only *possessions* and not *property*. The simpler category appears thus as a relation of simple family or tribal communities to property. In societies which have reached a higher stage the category appears as a comparatively simple relation existing in a more advanced community. The concrete substratum underlying the relation of ownership is however always presupposed. One can conceive an individual savage who has possessions; possession in this case, however, is not a legal relation. It is incorrect that in the course of historical development possession gave rise to the family. On the contrary, possession always presupposes this "more concrete legal category". One may, nevertheless, conclude that the simple categories represent relations or conditions which may reflect the immature concrete situation without as yet positing the more complex relation or condition which is conceptually expressed in the more concrete category; on the other hand, the same category may be retained as a subordinate relation in more developed concrete circumstances. Money may exist and has existed in historical time before capital, banks, wage-labour, etc. came into being. In this respect it can be said, therefore, that the simpler category expresses relations predominating in an immature entity or subordinate relations in a more advanced entity; relations which already existed historically before the entity had developed the aspects expressed in a more concrete category. The procedure of abstract reasoning which advances from the simplest to more complex concepts to that extent conforms to actual historical development.

It is true, on the other hand, that there are certain highly developed, but nevertheless historically immature, social formations which employ some of the most advanced economic forms, *e.g.*, co-operation, developed division of labour, etc., without having developed any money at all, for instance Peru. In Slavonic communities too, money—and its pre-condition, exchange—is of little or no importance within the individual community, but is used on the borders, where commerce with other communities takes place; and it is altogether wrong to assume that exchange within the community is an original constituent element. On the contrary, in the beginning exchange tends to arise in the intercourse of different communities with one another, rather than among members of the same community. Moreover, although money begins to play a considerable rôle very early and in diverse ways, it is known to have been a dominant factor in antiquity only among nations developed in a particular direction, *i.e.*, merchant nations. Even among the Greeks and Romans, the most advanced nations of antiquity, money reaches its full development, which is presupposed in modern bourgeois society, only in the period of their disintegration. Thus the full potential of this quite simple category does not emerge historically in the most advanced phases of society, and it certainly does not penetrate into all economic relations. For example, taxes in kind and deliveries in kind remained the basis of the Roman empire even at the height of its development; indeed a completely evolved monetary system existed in Rome only in the army, and it never permeated the whole complex of labour. Although the simpler category, therefore, may have existed historically before the more concrete category, its complete intensive and extensive development can nevertheless occur in a complex social formation, whereas the more concrete category may have been fully evolved in a more primitive social formation.

Labour seems to be a very simple category. The notion of labour in this universal form, as labour in general, is also extremely old. Nevertheless "labour" in this simplicity is economically considered just as modern a category as the relations which give rise to this simple abstraction. The Monetary System, for example, still regards wealth quite objectively as a thing existing independently in the shape of money. Compared with this standpoint, it was a substantial advance when the Manufacturing or Mercantile System transferred the source of wealth from the object to the subjective activity—mercantile or industrial labour—but it still considered that only this circumscribed activity itself produced money. In contrast to this system, the Physiocrats assume that a specific form of labour—agriculture—creates wealth, and they see the object no longer in the guise of money, but as a product in general, as the universal result of labour. In accordance with the still circumscribed activity, the product remains a naturally developed product, an agricultural product, a product of the land *par excellence*.

It was an immense advance when Adam Smith rejected all restrictions with regard to the activity that produces wealth—for him it was labour as such, neither manufacturing, nor commercial, nor agricultural labour, but all types of labour. The abstract universality which creates wealth implies also the universality of the objects defined as wealth: they are products as such, or once more labour as such, but in this case past, materialised labour. How difficult and immense a transition this was is demonstrated by the fact that Adam Smith himself occasionally relapses once more into the Physiocratic system. It might seem that in this way merely an abstract expression was found for the simplest and most ancient relation in which human beings act as producers—irrespective of the type of society they live in. This is true in one respect, but not in another.

The fact that the specific kind of labour is irrelevant presupposes a highly developed complex of actually existing kinds of labour, none of which is any more the all-important one. The most general abstractions arise on the whole only when concrete development is most profuse, so that a specific quality is seen to be common to many phenomena, or common to all. Then it is no longer perceived solely in a particular form. This abstraction of labour is, on the other hand, by no means simply the conceptual resultant of a variety of concrete types of labour. The fact that the particular kind of labour employed is immaterial is appropriate to a form of society in which individuals easily pass from one type of labour to another, the particular type of labour being accidental to them and therefore irrelevant. Labour, not only as a category but in reality, has become a means to create wealth in general, and has ceased to be tied as an attribute to a particular individual. This state of affairs is most pronounced in the United States, the most modern form of bourgeois society. The abstract category "labour", "labour as such", labour *sans phrase*, the point of departure of modern economics, thus becomes a practical fact only there. The simplest abstraction, which plays a decisive rôle in modern political economy, an abstraction which expresses an ancient relation existing in all social formations, nevertheless appears to be actually true in this abstract form only as a category of the most modern society. It might be said that phenomena which are historical products in the United States—*e.g.*, the irrelevance of the particular type of labour—appear to be among the Russians, for instance, naturally developed predispositions. But in the first place, there is an enormous difference between barbarians having a predisposition which makes it possible to employ them in various tasks, and civilised people who apply themselves to various tasks. As regards the Russians, moreover, their indifference to the particular kind of labour performed is in practice matched by their traditional habit of clinging fast to a very definite kind of labour from which they are extricated only by external influences.

The example of labour strikingly demonstrates how even the most abstract categories, despite their validity in all epochs—precisely because they are abstractions—are equally a product of historical conditions even in the specific form of abstractions, and they retain their full validity only for and within the framework of these conditions.

Bourgeois society is the most advanced and complex historical organisation of production. The categories which express its relations, and an understanding of its structure, therefore, provide an insight into the structure and the relations of production of all formerly existing social formations the ruins and component elements of which were used in the creation of bourgeois society. Some of these unassimilated remains are still carried on within bourgeois society, others, however, which previously existed only in rudimentary form, have been further developed and have attained their full significance, etc. The anatomy of man is a key to the anatomy of the ape. On the other hand, rudiments of more advanced forms in the lower species of animals can only be understood when the more advanced forms are already known. Bourgeois economy thus provides a key to the economy of antiquity, etc. But it is quite impossible [to gain this insight] in the manner of those economists who obliterate all historical differences and who see in all social phenomena only bourgeois phenomena. If one knows rent, it is possible to understand tribute, tithe, etc., but they do not have to be treated as identical.

Since bourgeois society is, moreover, only a contradictory form of development, it contains relations of earlier societies often merely in very stunted form or even in the form of travesties, *e.g.*, communal ownership. Thus, although it is true that the categories of bourgeois economy are valid for all other social formations, this has to be taken *cum grano salis*, for they may contain them in an advanced, stunted, caricatured, etc., form, that is always with substantial differences. What is called historical evolution depends in general on the fact that the latest form regards earlier ones as stages in the development of itself and conceives them always in a one-sided manner, since only rarely and under quite special conditions is a society able to adopt a critical attitude towards itself; in this context we are not of course discussing historical periods which themselves believe that they are periods of decline. The Christian religion was able to contribute to an objective understanding of earlier mythologies only when its self-criticism was to a certain extent prepared, as it were potentially. Similarly, only when the self-criticism of bourgeois society had begun, was bourgeois political economy able to understand the feudal, ancient and oriental economies. In so far as bourgeois political economy did not simply identify itself with the past in a mythological manner, its criticism of earlier economies—especially of the feudal system against which it still had to wage a direct struggle—resembled the criticism that Christianity directed against heathenism, or which Protestantism directed against Catholicism.

Just as in general when examining any historical or social science, so also in the case of the development of economic categories is it always necessary to remember that the subject, in this context contemporary bourgeois society, is presupposed both in reality and in the mind, and that therefore categories express forms of existence and conditions of existence—and sometimes merely separate aspects—of this particular society, the subject; thus the category, *even from the scientific standpoint,* by no means begins at the moment when it is discussed *as such.* This has to be remembered because it provides important criteria for the arrangement of the material. For example, nothing seems more natural than to begin with rent, *i.e.,* with landed property, since it is associated with the earth, the source of all production and all life, and with agriculture, the first form of production in all societies that have attained a measure of stability. But nothing would be more erroneous. There is in every social formation a particular branch of production which determines the position and importance of all the others, and the relations obtaining in this branch accordingly determine the relations of all other branches as well. It is as though light of a particular hue were cast upon everything, tingeing all other colours and modifying their specific features; or as if a special ether determined the specific gravity of everything found in it. Let us take as an example pastoral tribes. (Tribes living exclusively on hunting or fishing are beyond the boundary line from which real development begins.) A certain type of agricultural activity occurs among them and this determines land ownership. It is communal ownership and retains this form in a larger or smaller measure, according to the degree to which these people maintain their traditions, *e.g.,* communal ownership among the Slavs. Among settled agricultural people—settled already to a large extent—where agriculture predominates as in the societies of antiquity and the feudal period, even manufacture, its structure and the forms of property corresponding thereto, have, in some measure, specifically agrarian features. Manufacture is either completely dependent on agriculture, as in the earlier Roman period, or as in the Middle

Ages, it copies in the town and in its conditions the organisation of the countryside. In the Middle Ages even capital—unless it was solely money capital—consisted of the traditional tools, etc., and retained a specifically agrarian character. The reverse takes place in bourgeois society. Agriculture to an increasing extent becomes just a branch of industry and is completely dominated by capital. The same applies to rent. In all forms in which landed property is the decisive factor, natural relations still predominate; in the forms in which the decisive factor is capital, social, historically evolved elements predominate. Rent cannot be understood without capital, but capital can be understood without rent. Capital is the economic power that dominates everything in bourgeois society. It must form both the point of departure and the conclusion and it has to be expounded before landed property. After analysing capital and landed property separately, their interconnection must be examined.

It would be inexpedient and wrong therefore to present the economic categories successively in the order in which they have played the dominant rôle in history. On the contrary, their order of succession is determined by their mutual relation in modern bourgeois society and this is quite the reverse of what appears to be natural to them or in accordance with the sequence of historical development. The point at issue is not the rôle that various economic relations have played in the succession of various social formations appearing in the course of history; even less is it their sequence "as concepts" (*Proudhon*) (a nebulous notion of the historical process), but their position within modern bourgeois society.

It is precisely the predominance of agricultural peoples in the ancient world which caused the merchant nations—Phoenicians, Carthaginians—to develop in such purity (abstract precision). For capital in the shape of merchant or money capital appears in that abstract form where capital has not yet become the dominant factor in society. Lombards and Jews occupied the same position with regard to mediaeval agrarian societies.

Another example of the various rôles which the same categories have played at different stages of society are joint-stock companies, one of the most recent features of bourgeois society; but they arise also in its early period in the form of large privileged commercial companies with rights of monopoly.

The concept of national wealth finds its way into the works of the economists of the seventeenth century as the notion that wealth is created for the State, whose power, on the other hand, is proportional to this wealth—a notion which to some extent still survives even among eighteenth-century economists. This is still an unintentionally hypocritical manner in which wealth and the production of wealth are proclaimed to be the goal of the modern State, which is regarded merely as a means for producing wealth.

The disposition of material has evidently to be made in such a way that [section] one comprises general abstract definitions, which therefore appertain in some measure to all social formations, but in the sense set forth earlier. Two, the categories which constitute the internal structure of bourgeois society and on which the principal classes are based. Capital, wage-labour, landed property and their relations to one another. Town and country. The three large social classes; exchange between them. Circulation. The (private) credit system. Three, the State as the epitome of bourgeois society. Analysis of its relations to itself. The "unproductive" classes. Taxes. National debt. Public credit. Population. Colonies. Emigration. Four, international conditions of production. International division of labour. International exchange. Export and import. Rate of exchange. Five, world market and crises.

4. PRODUCTION
Means of Production and Conditions[a] of Production.
Conditions of Production and Communication.
Political Forms and Forms of Cognition in Relation
to the Conditions of Production and Communication.
Legal Relations. Family Relations

Notes regarding points which have to be mentioned in this context and should not be forgotten.

1. *War* develops [certain features] earlier than peace; the way in which as a result of war, and in the armies, etc.,

---

a The German word used by Marx is "Verhältnisse", which can mean both "conditions" and "relations". In this section the word "conditions" has mostly been used to render "Verhältnisse", and it should be borne in mind that "conditions" comprises "relations" as well.—*Tr.*

certain economic conditions, *e.g.*, wage-labour, machinery, etc., were evolved earlier than within civil society. The relations between productive power and conditions of communication are likewise particularly obvious in the army.

2. *The relation of the hitherto existing idealistic historiography to realistic historiography. In particular what is known as history of civilisation*, the old history of religion and states. (The various kinds of historiography hitherto existing could also be discussed in this context; the so-called objective, subjective (moral and others), philosophical [historiography].)

3. *Secondary and tertiary phenomena*, in general *derived* and *transmitted, i.e.*, non-primary, conditions of production. The influence of international relations.

4. *Reproaches about the materialism of this conception; relation to naturalistic materialism.*

5. *Dialectics of the concepts productive power (means of production) and relations of production*, the limits of *this dialectical* connection, which does not abolish the real differences, have to be defined.

6. *The unequal development of material production and, e.g., that of art.* The concept of progress is on the whole not to be understood in the usual abstract form. Modern art, etc. This disproportion is not as important and difficult to grasp as within concrete social relations, *e.g.*, in education. Relations of the United States to Europe. However, the really difficult point to be discussed here is how the relations of production as legal relations take part in this uneven development. For example the relation of Roman civil law (this applies in smaller measure to criminal and constitutional law) to modern production.

7. *This conception appears to be an inevitable development.* But vindication of chance. How? (Freedom, etc., as well.) (Influence of the means of communication. World history did not always exist; history as world history is a result.)

8. *The starting point is of course the naturally determined factors*; both subjective and objective. Tribes, races, etc.

As regards art, it is well known that some of its peaks by no means correspond to the general development of society; nor do they therefore to the material substructure, the skeleton as it were of its organisation. For example the Greeks compared with modern [nations], or else Shakespeare.

It is even acknowledged that certain branches of art, *e.g.*, the *epos*, can no longer be produced in their epoch-making classic form after artistic production as such has begun; in other words that certain important creations within the compass of art are only possible at an early stage in the development of art. If this is the case with regard to different branches of art within the sphere of art itself, it is not so remarkable that this should also be the case with regard to the entire sphere of art and its relation to the general development of society. The difficulty lies only in the general formulation of these contradictions. As soon as they are reduced to specific questions they are already explained.

Let us take, for example, the relation of Greek art, and that of Shakespeare, to the present time. We know that Greek mythology is not only the arsenal of Greek art, but also its basis. Is the conception of nature and of social relations which underlies Greek imagination and therefore Greek [art] possible when there are self-acting mules, railways, locomotives and electric telegraphs? What is a Vulcan compared with Roberts and Co., Jupiter compared with the lightning conductor, and Hermes compared with the *Crédit mobilier*? All mythology subdues, controls and fashions the forces of nature in the imagination and through imagination; it disappears therefore when real control over these forces is established. What becomes of Fama side by side with Printing House Square? Greek art presupposes Greek mythology, in other words that natural and social phenomena are already assimilated in an unintentionally artistic manner by the imagination of the people. This is the material of Greek art, not just any mythology, *i.e.*, not every unconsciously artistic assimilation of nature (here the term comprises all physical phenomena, including society); Egyptian mythology could never become the basis of or give rise to Greek art. But at any rate [it presupposes] a mythology; on no account however a social development which precludes a mythological attitude towards nature, *i.e.*, any attitude to nature which might give rise to myth; a society therefore demanding from the artist an imagination independent of mythology.

Regarded from another aspect: is Achilles possible when powder and shot have been invented? And is the Iliad possible at all when the printing press and even printing machines exist? Is it not inevitable that with the emergence of the press bar the singing and the telling and the muse cease, that is the conditions necessary for epic poetry disappear?

The difficulty we are confronted with is not, however, that of understanding how Greek art and epic poetry are associated with certain forms of social development. The difficulty is that they still give us aesthetic pleasure and are in certain respects regarded as a standard and unattainable ideal.

An adult cannot become a child again, or he becomes childish. But does the naïveté of the child not give him pleasure, and does not he himself endeavour to reproduce the child's veracity on a higher level? Does not the child in every epoch represent the character of the period in its natural veracity? Why should not the historical childhood of humanity, where it attained its most beautiful form, exert an eternal charm because it is a stage that will never recur? There are rude children and precocious children. Many of the ancient peoples belong to this category. The Greeks were normal children. The charm their art has for us does not conflict with the immature stage of the society in which it originated. On the contrary its charm is a consequence of this and is inseparably linked with the fact that the immature social conditions which gave rise, and which alone could give rise, to this art cannot recur.

Written between
the end of August and
the middle of September 1857

FREDERICK ENGELS

KARL MARX, "A CONTRIBUTION TO THE CRITIQUE OF POLITICAL ECONOMY"

PART ONE, FRANZ DUNCKER, BERLIN, 1859

[Review]

I

[*Das Volk*,[30] No. 14, August 6, 1859]

The Germans have long since shown that in all spheres of science they are equal, and in most of them superior, to other civilised nations. Only one branch of science, political economy, had no German name among its foremost scholars. The reason is obvious. Political economy is the theoretical analysis of modern bourgeois society and therefore presupposes developed bourgeois conditions, conditions which for centuries, following the wars in the wake of the Reformation and the peasant wars and especially the Thirty Years' War, could not establish themselves in Germany. The separation of the Netherlands from the Empire[31] removed Germany from the international trade routes and restricted her industrial development from the very beginning to the pettiest scale. While the Germans painfully and slowly recovered from the devastations of the civil wars, while they used up their store of civic energy, which had never been very large, in futile struggle against the customs barriers and absurd commercial regulations which every petty princeling and imperial baron inflicted upon the industry of his subjects, while the imperial cities with their craft-guild practices and patrician spirit went to ruin—Holland, England and France meanwhile conquered the leading positions in international trade, established one colony after another and brought manufactory production to the height of its development, until finally England, with the aid of steam power, which made her coal and iron deposits valuable, headed modern bourgeois development. But political economy could not arise in Germany so long as a struggle had still to be waged against so preposterously antiquated remnants of the Middle Ages as those which hampered the bourgeois development of her material forces until 1830. Only the establishment of the Customs Union[32] enabled the Germans to *comprehend* political economy at all. It was indeed at this time that English and French economic works began to be imported for the benefit of the German middle class. Men of learning and bureaucrats soon got hold of the imported material and treated it in a way which does little credit to the "German intellect". The literary efforts of a hotchpotch of *chevaliers d'industrie*, traders, schoolmasters and bureaucrats produced a bunch of German economic publications which as regards triteness, banality, frivolity, verbosity and plagiarism are equalled only by the German novel. Among people pursuing practical objectives there arose first the protectionist school of the industrialists, whose chief spokesman, List, is still the best that German bourgeois political economy has produced, although his celebrated work is entirely copied from the Frenchman Ferrier, the theoretical creator of the Continental System. In opposition to this trend the free-trade school was formed in the forties by merchants from the Baltic provinces, who fumblingly repeated the arguments of the English Free Traders with childlike, but not disinterested, faith. Finally, among the schoolmasters and bureaucrats who had to handle the theoretical aspects there were uncritical and desiccated collectors of herbaria, like Herr Rau, pseudo-clever speculators who translated foreign propositions into undigested Hegelian language, like Herr Stein, or gleaners with literary pretensions in the field of so-called history of civilisation, like Herr Riehl. The upshot of all this was cameralistics,[33] an eclectic economic sauce covering a hotchpotch of sundry trivialities, of the sort a junior civil servant might find useful to remember during his final examination.

While in this way in Germany the bourgeoisie, the schoolmasters and the bureaucrats were still making great exertions to learn by rote, and in some measure to understand, the first elements of Anglo-French political economy, which they regarded as incontestable dogmas, the German proletarian party appeared on the scene. Its theoretical aspect was wholly based on a study of political economy, and *German political economy* as an independent science dates also from the emergence of this party. The essential foundation of this German political economy is the *materialist conception of history* whose principal features are briefly outlined in the "Preface"[a] to the above-named work. Since the "Preface" has in the main already been published in *Das Volk*, we refer to it. The proposition that "the process of social, political and intellectual life is altogether necessitated by the mode of production of material life"; that all social and political relations, all religious and legal systems, all theoretical conceptions which arise in the course of history can only be understood if the material conditions of life obtaining during the relevant epoch have been understood and the former are traced back to these material conditions, was a revolutionary discovery not only for economics but also for all historical sciences—and all branches of science which are not natural sciences are historical. "It is not the consciousness of men that determines their existence, but their social existence that determines their consciousness." This proposition is so simple that it should be self-evident to anyone not bogged down in idealist humbug. But it leads to highly revolutionary consequences not only in the theoretical sphere but also in the practical sphere. "At a certain stage of development, the material productive forces of society come into conflict with the existing relations of production or—this merely expresses the same thing in legal terms—with the property relations within the framework of which they have operated hitherto. From forms of development of the productive forces these relations turn into their fetters. Then begins an era of *social revolution*. The changes in the economic foundation lead sooner or later to the transformation of the whole immense superstructure.... The bourgeois mode of production is the last antagonistic form of the social process of production—antagonistic not in the sense of individual antagonism but of an antagonism that emanates from the individuals' social conditions of existence —but the productive forces developing within bourgeois society create also the material conditions for a solution of this antagonism." The prospect of a gigantic revolution, the most gigantic revolution that has ever taken place, accordingly presents itself to us as soon as we pursue our materialist thesis further and apply it to the present time.

Closer consideration shows immediately that already the

---

a See this volume, pp. 19-23.—*Ed.*

first consequences of the apparently simple proposition, that the consciousness of men is determined by their existence and not the other way round, spurn all forms of idealism, even the most concealed ones, rejecting all conventional and customary views of historical matters. The entire traditional manner of political reasoning is upset; patriotic magnanimity indignantly objects to such an unprincipled interpretation. It was thus inevitable that the new point of view should shock not only the exponents of the bourgeoisie but also the mass of French socialists who intended to revolutionise the world by virtue of the magic words, *liberté, égalité, fraternité*. But it utterly enraged the vociferous German vulgar democrats. They nevertheless have a partiality for attempting to plagiarise the new ideas in their own interest, although with an exceptional lack of understanding.

The demonstration of the materialist conception even upon a single historical example was a scientific task requiring years of quiet research, for it is evident that mere empty talk can achieve nothing in this context and that only an abundance of critically examined historical material which has been completely mastered can make it possible to solve such a problem. Our party was propelled on to the political stage by the February Revolution and thus prevented from pursuing purely scientific aims. The fundamental conception, nevertheless, runs like an unbroken thread through all literary productions of the party. Every one of them shows that the actions in each particular case were invariably initiated by material causes and not by the accompanying phrases, that on the contrary the political and legal phrases, like the political actions and their results, originated in material causes.

After the defeat of the Revolution of 1848-49, at a time when it became increasingly impossible to exert any influence on Germany from abroad, our party relinquished the field of emigrant squabbles—for that was the only feasible action left—to the vulgar democrats. While these were chasing about to their heart's content, scuffling today, fraternising tomorrow and the day after once more washing their dirty linen in public, while they went begging throughout America and immediately afterwards started another row over the division of the few coins they had collected—our party was glad to find once more some quiet time for research work. It had the great advantage that its theoretical foundation was a new scientific conception the elaboration of which provided adequate work; even for this reason alone it could never become so demoralised as the "great men" of the emigration.

The book under consideration is the first result of these studies.

II

[*Das Volk*, No. 16, August 20, 1859]

The purpose of a work like the one under review cannot simply be desultory criticism of separate sections of political economy or the discussion of one or another economic issue in isolation. On the contrary, it is from the beginning designed to give a systematic *résumé* of the whole complex of political economy and a coherent elaboration of the laws governing bourgeois production and bourgeois exchange. This elaboration is at the same time a comprehensive critique of economic literature, for economists are nothing but interpreters of and apologists for these laws.

Hardly any attempt has been made since Hegel's death to set forth any branch of science in its specific inner coherence. The official Hegelian school had assimilated only the most simple devices of the master's dialectics and applied them to everything and anything, often moreover with ridiculous incompetence. Hegel's whole heritage was, so far as they were concerned, confined exclusively to a template, by means of which any subject could be knocked into shape, and a set of words and phrases whose only remaining purpose was to turn up conveniently whenever they experienced a lack of ideas and of concrete knowledge. Thus it happened, as a professor at Bonn has said, that these Hegelians knew nothing but could write about everything. The results were, of course, accordingly. For all their conceit these gentlemen were, however, sufficiently conscious of their failings to avoid major problems as far as possible. The superannuated fossilised type of learning held its ground because of its superior factual knowledge, and after Feuerbach's renunciation of the speculative method, Hegelianism gradually died away, and it seemed that science was once more dominated by antiquated metaphysics with its rigid categories.

For this there were quite natural reasons. The rule of the Hegelian Diadochi, which ended in empty phrases, was naturally followed by a period in which the concrete content of science predominated once more over the formal aspect. Moreover, Germany at the same time applied itself with quite extraordinary energy to the natural sciences, in accordance with the immense bourgeois development setting in after 1848; with the coming into fashion of these sciences, in which the speculative trend had never achieved any real importance, the old metaphysical mode of thinking, even down to the extreme triviality of Wolff, gained ground rapidly. Hegel was forgotten and a new materialism arose in the natural sciences; it differed in principle very little from the materialism of the eighteenth century and its main advantage was merely a greater stock of data relating to the natural sciences, especially chemistry and physiology. The narrow-minded mode of thinking of the pre-Kantian period in its most banal form is reproduced by Büchner and Vogt, and even Moleschott, who swears by Feuerbach, frequently flounders in a highly diverting manner through the most simple categories. The jaded cart-horse of the commonplace bourgeois mind falters of course in confusion in front of the ditch separating substance from appearance, and cause from effect; but one should not ride cart-horses if one intends to go coursing over the very rough ground of abstract reasoning.

In this context, therefore, a question had to be solved which was not connected with political economy as such. Which scientific method should be used? There was, on the one hand, the Hegelian dialectics in the quite abstract "speculative" form in which Hegel had left it, and on the other hand the ordinary, mainly Wolffian, metaphysical method, which had come again into vogue, and which was also employed by the bourgeois economists to write their bulky rambling volumes. The second method had been theoretically demolished by Kant and particularly by Hegel so that its continued use in practice could only be rendered possible by inertia and the absence of an alternative *simple* method. The Hegelian method, on the other hand, was in its *existing* form quite inapplicable. It was essentially idealist and the main point in this case was the elaboration of a world outlook that was more materialist than any previous one. Hegel's method took as its point of departure pure thought, whereas here the starting point was to be inexorable facts. A method which, according to its own avowal, "came from nothing through nothing to nothing" was in this shape by no means suitable. It was, nevertheless, the only element in the entire available logical material which could at least serve as a point of origin. It had not been subjected to criticism, not been overthrown; none of the opponents of the great dialectician had been able to make a breach in the proud edifice. It had been forgotten because the Hegelian school did not know how to apply it. Hence, it was first of all essential to carry through a thorough critique of the Hegelian method.

It was the exceptional historical sense underlying Hegel's manner of reasoning which distinguished it from that of all other philosophers. However abstract and idealist the form employed, yet his evolution of ideas runs always parallel with the evolution of universal history, and the latter was indeed supposed to be only the proof of the former. Although this reversed the actual relation and stood it on its head, yet the real content was invariably incorporated in his philosophy, especially since Hegel—unlike his followers—did not rely on ignorance, but was one of the most erudite thinkers of all time. He was the first to try to demonstrate that there is an evolution, an intrinsic coherence in history, and however strange some things in his philosophy of history may seem to us now, the grandeur of the basic conception is still admirable today, compared both with his predecessors and with those who following him ventured to advance general historical observations. This monumental conception of history pervades the *Phänomenologie, Ästhetik* and *Geschichte der Philosophie*, and the material is everywhere set forth historically, in a definite historical context, even if in an abstract distorted manner.

This epoch-making conception of history was a direct theoretical pre-condition of the new materialist outlook, and already this constituted a connecting link with the logical method as well. Since, even from the standpoint of "pure reasoning", this forgotten dialectics had led to such results, and had moreover with the greatest ease coped with the whole of the former logic and metaphysics, it must at all events comprise more than sophistry and hairsplitting. But the critique of this method, which the entire official philosophy had evaded and still evades, was no small matter.

Marx was and is the only one who could undertake the work of extracting from the Hegelian logic the nucleus containing Hegel's real discoveries in this field, and of establishing the dialectical method, divested of its idealist wrappings, in the simple form in which it becomes the only correct mode of conceptual evolution. The working out of the method which underlies Marx's critique of political economy is, we think, a result hardly less significant than the basic materialist conception.

Even after the determination of the method, the critique of economics could still be arranged in two ways—historically or logically. Since in the course of history, as in its literary reflection, the evolution proceeds by and large from the simplest to the more complex relations, the historical development of political economy constituted a natural clue, which the critique could take as a point of departure, and then the economic categories would appear on the whole in the same order as in the logical exposition. This form seems to have the advantage of greater lucidity, for it traces the *actual* development, but in fact it would thus become, at most, more popular. History moves often in leaps and bounds and in a zigzag line, and as this would have to be followed throughout, it would mean not only that a considerable amount of material of slight importance would have to be included, but also that the train of thought would frequently have to be interrupted; it would, moreover, be impossible to write the history of economy without that of bourgeois society, and the task would thus become immense, because of the absence of all preliminary studies. The logical method of approach was therefore the only suitable one. This, however, is indeed nothing but the historical method, only stripped of the historical form and diverting chance occurrences. The point where this history begins must also be the starting point of the train of thought, and its further progress will be simply the reflection, in abstract and theoretically consistent form, of the historical course. Though the reflection is corrected, it is corrected in accordance with laws provided by the actual historical course, since each factor can be examined at the stage of development where it reaches its full maturity, its classical form.

With this method we begin with the first and simplest relation which is historically, actually available, thus in this context with the first economic relation to be found. We analyse this relation. The fact that it is a *relation* already implies that it has two aspects which are *related to each other*. Each of these aspects is examined separately; this reveals the nature of their mutual behaviour, their reciprocal action. Contradictions will emerge demanding a solution. But since we are not examining an abstract mental process that takes place solely in our mind, but an actual event which really took place at some time or other, or which is still taking place, these contradictions will have arisen in practice and have probably been solved. We shall trace the mode of this solution and find that it has been effected by establishing a new relation, whose two contradictory aspects we shall then have to set forth, and so on.

Political economy begins with *commodities*, with the moment when products are exchanged, either by individuals or by primitive communities. The product being exchanged is a commodity. But it is a commodity merely by virtue of the *thing*, the product being linked with a *relation* between two persons or communities, the relation between producer and consumer, who at this stage are no longer united in the same person. Here is at once an example of a peculiar fact, which pervades the whole economy and has produced serious confusion in the minds of bourgeois economists—economics is not concerned with things but with relations between persons, and in the final analysis between classes; these relations however are always *bound to things* and *appear as things*. Although a few economists had an inkling of this connection in isolated instances, Marx was the first to reveal its significance for the entire economy thus making the most difficult problems so simple and clear that even bourgeois economists will now be able to grasp them.

If we examine the various aspects of the commodity, that is of the fully evolved commodity and not as it at first slowly emerges in the spontaneous barter of two primitive communities, it presents itself to us from two angles, that of use-value and of exchange-value, and thus we come immediately to the province of economic debate. Anyone wishing to find a striking instance of the fact that the German dialectic method at its present stage of development is at least as superior to the old superficially glib metaphysical method as railways are to the mediaeval means of transport, should look up Adam Smith or any other authoritative economist of repute to see how much distress exchange-value and use-value caused these gentlemen, the difficulty they had in distinguishing the two properly and in expressing the determinate form peculiar to each, and then compare the clear, simple exposition given by Marx.

After use-value and exchange-value have been expounded, the commodity as a direct unity of the two is described as it enters the *exchange process*. The contradictions arising here may be found on pp. 20 and 21.[a] We merely note that these contradictions are not only of interest for theoretical, abstract reasons, but that they also reflect the difficulties originating from the nature of direct interchange, *i.e.*, simple barter, and the impossibilities inevitably confronting this first crude form of exchange. The solution of these impossibilities is achieved by investing a specific commodity—*money*—with the attribute of representing the exchange-value of all other commodities. Money or simple circulation is then analysed in the second chapter, namely (1) money as a *measure of value*, and, at the same time, value measured in terms of money, *i.e., price*, is more closely defined; (2) money as *means of circulation* and (3) the unity of the two aspects, *real money* which represents bourgeois material wealth as a whole. This concludes the first part, the conversion of money into capital is left for the second part.

One can see that with this method, the logical exposition need by no means be confined to the purely abstract sphere. On the contrary, it requires historical illustration and continuous contact with reality. A great variety of such evidence is therefore inserted, comprising references both to different stages in the actual historical course of social development and to economic works, in which the working out of lucid definitions of economic relations is traced from the outset. The critique of particular, more or less one-sided or confused interpretations is thus substantially given already in the logical exposition and can be kept quite short.

The economic content of the book will be discussed in a third article.[34]

Written between
August 3 and 15, 1859

---

[a] See this volume, pp. 43-44.—*Ed.*

NOTES

[1] Marx's *Zur Kritik der politischen Ökonomie*, which marks an important stage in the elaboration of Marxian political economy, was written between August 1858 and January 1859. According to Marx's original plan, the entire work was to consist of six books, and in the first of these he intended to give an analysis of capital.

In the course of his work on book one Marx composed a number of bulky manuscripts, some of which were first published under the title *Grundrisse der Kritik der politischen Ökonomie (Rohentwurf)* in Moscow in 1939 and 1941. They fill two large volumes of over 1,000 pages.

Although the first edition of the *Critique*, which came out in Berlin in 1859, was marked "Part One", no further parts were published, and subsequently Marx abandoned his initial design and planned to write a work on capital in four volumes.   p. 19

[2] See this volume, pp. 188-217.   p. 19

[3] *Rheinische Zeitung für Politik, Handel und Gewerbe*—a daily newspaper published in Cologne from January 1, 1842, to March 31, 1843. It was founded by members of the bourgeoisie in the Rhine Province who were opposed to Prussian absolutism. Marx began to contribute articles to the paper in April 1842 and became an editor of it the following October. The revolutionary and democratic character of the paper became more pronounced while Marx was editor. The government established a specially strict censorship and subsequently closed down the paper.   p. 19

[4] *Allgemeine Zeitung*—a reactionary daily paper; it was founded in 1798 and from 1810 to 1882 was published in Augsburg.   p. 20

[5] *Deutsch-Französische Jahrbücher*—an annual which was edited by Karl Marx and Arnold Ruge and published in German. Only one issue, a double number, came out in February 1844. In addition to Marx's *Zur Kritik der Hegelschen Rechtsphilosophie. Einleitung (A Contribution to a Critique of Hegel's Philosophy of Law. Introduction)*, the issue also contained other essays by Marx and Engels, which indicate that the authors definitely adopted a materialist and communist standpoint.   p. 20

[6] Marx refers to *Umrisse zu einer Kritik der Nationalökonomie*. (It was published under the title *Outlines of a Critique of Political*

Economy by Frederick Engels, in the Appendix to Marx, *Economic and Philosophical Manuscripts of 1844*, Moscow, 1959.) p. 22

[7] An allusion to *Die deutsche Ideologie*. (See Karl Marx and Frederick Engels, *The German Ideology*, Moscow, 1964.) p. 22

[8] Marx is referring to *Lohnarbeit und Kapital* published in English under the title *Wage-Labour and Capital*. p. 22

[9] The Association was founded by Marx and Engels towards the end of August 1847. Its aim was political education of German workers living in Belgium and propagation of the ideas of scientific communism. p. 22

[10] *Neue Rheinische Zeitung. Organ der Demokratie*—a daily paper, the militant organ of the proletarian wing of democracy, published in Cologne from June 1, 1848, to May 19, 1849. Its editor-in-chief was Marx; Marx and Engels wrote leading articles which determined the attitude of the paper to the principal questions of the revolution in Germany and Europe. After the defeat of the German revolution the paper ceased publication. p. 22

[11] *New York Daily Tribune*—an American newspaper published from 1841 to 1924. Marx was a contributor to the paper from 1851 to 1862. Many of the articles were, at Marx's request, written by Engels. p. 23

[12] Marx quotes from *A Treatise of Taxes and Contributions*, London, 1667, which was published anonymously. p. 35

[13] *The Spectator*—an English literary magazine published in London from 1711 to 1714. p. 52

[14] The "parallelograms of Mr. Owen" are mentioned in Ricardo's *On Protection to Agriculture*, London, 1822, p. 21.
   In his utopian plans for social reform Owen sought to prove that settlements designed in the shape of a parallelogram or square were most appropriate from the point of view of both the economy and the home. p. 60

[15] "Theory of Exchange" is the title of the fourth chapter of *The Elements of Political Economy* by H. D. Macleod. p. 61

[16] That is before the Act of Union of 1707 as a result of which the Scottish parliament ceased to exist and all economic boundaries between England and Scotland were abolished. p. 72

[17] *Leges barbarorum* (laws of the barbarians)—Records of the customary or common law of various Germanic tribes, compiled between the fifth and ninth centuries. p. 74

[18] *Société générale de crédit mobilier*—a large French joint-stock company set up by the brothers Péreire in 1852. Its main purpose was to act as intermediary in credit operations and to further the establishment of industrial limited companies. The major part of the company's income was derived from speculative transactions on the stock exchange. *Crédit mobilier* went bankrupt in 1867 and was liquidated in 1871. The rise of this new type of financial enterprise in the 1850s was symptomatic of this period of reaction which was marked by unbridled speculation in stocks. p. 95

[19] Peter Schlemihl, the hero of Chamisso's story *Peter Schlemihts wundersame Geschichte,* sells his shadow for a magic purse.   p. 115

[20] Marx is referring to the wars of independence waged by the Spanish colonies in America from 1810 to 1826, in the course of which most countries of Latin America freed themselves from Spanish domination.   p. 135

[21] Shylock's words in Shakespeare's *Merchant of Venice,* Act 4, Scene 1.   p. 140

[22] An allusion to the Treaty of Kyakhta, which Russia and China signed on October 21, 1727. As a result of it barter between the two countries expanded considerably.   p. 150

[23] The so-called second Opium War waged by Britain and France against China. It ended with the defeat of China and the conclusion of the predatory Tientsin agreement.   p. 150

[24] Peter Martyr's passage is quoted by Marx from William Hickling Prescott, *History of the Conquest of Mexico...,* Vol. I, London, 1850, p. 123, footnote.   p. 154

[25] This is a reference to the reactionary trend in history and law which arose in Germany at the close of the eighteenth century.   p. 167

[26] John Law, the Scottish financier and economist, attempted to put into practice his absurd notion that the State could increase the wealth of the country by issuing bank-notes without any cover. In 1716 he founded a bank in France, which was converted into a national bank towards the end of 1718. The bank issued paper notes in unlimited quantities and at the same time withdrew specie from circulation. An unprecedented spate of speculation on the stock exchange followed, until in 1720 the bank went bankrupt and with it Law's system.   p. 169

[27] The "Introduction" is an unfinished rough draft, which was found among Marx's papers after his death. It was first published in the magazine *Die Neue Zeit* in 1903 and constitutes the first of the set of manuscripts published under the title *Grundrisse der Kritik der politischen Ökonomie (Rohentwurf),* Moscow, 1939 (reprinted in Berlin in 1953).   p. 188

[28] See John Stuart Mill, *Principles of Political Economy,* Vol. I, London, 1848, Book I, *Production.*   p. 191

[29] *Cf.* H. Storch, *Considérations sur la nature du revenu national,* Paris, 1824.   p. 199

[30] *Das Volk*—a German weekly published in London from May 7 to August 20, 1859. Marx, Engels, Freiligrath, W. Wolff, Heise were contributors to the paper.   p. 218

[31] The Netherlands, which formed part of the Holy Roman Empire from 1477 to 1555, passed to Spain when the Empire was divided in October 1555. It subsequently freed itself from Spanish rule and became an independent republic.

    In consequence of the separation of the Netherlands, Germany was deprived of direct access to the principal maritime routes and had to depend on the Dutch carrying trade; this hampered the economic development of the country. p. 218

[32] The Customs Union was formed under Prussian hegemony in 1834, and comprised most German states apart from Austria. By abolishing internal customs barriers it created a common German market. p. 219

[33] *Cameralistics*—a mixture of administration, finance and economics taught at the universities of various European countries in the Middle Ages and also later. p. 219

[34] The third part of the review did not appear and the manuscript has not been found. p. 227

NAME INDEX

A

Arbuthnot, George (1802-1865)—185

Aretino, Pietro (1492-1556)—168

Aristotle (384-322 B.C.)—27, 42, 50, 68, 117, 137, 155

Arrivabene, Jean (Giovanni), comte de (1787-1881)—133

Athenaeus of Naucratis (end of the second to the beginning of the third century A.D.)—73

Attwood, Thomas (1783-1856)—82

Aurangzeb (1618-1707)—130

B

Bailey, Samuel (1791-1870)—72, 143

Barbon, Nicholas (1640-1698)—78

Bastiat, Frédéric (1801-1850)—37, 189

Bekker, Immanuel (1785-1871)—27, 68

Berkeley, George (1685-1753)—35, 78, 79, 118

Bernier, François (1625-1688)—130

Blake, William (first half of the nineteenth century)—104, 179

Blanc, Jean Joseph Louis (1811-1882)—167

Boisguillebert, Pierre Le Pesant, sieur de (1646-1714)—52, 54, 55, 61, 96, 103, 124, 125, 126, 146, 147

Bosanquet, Charles (1769-1850)—170, 174

Bosanquet, James Whatman (1804-1877)—98

Bray, John Francis (1809-1895)—86

Brougham, Henry Peter (Lord Brougham and Vaux) (1778-1868)—61

Buchanan, David (1779-1848)—113

Büchner, Ludwig (1824-1899)—223

Burleigh, William Cecil, Lord (1520-1598)—144

Büsch, Johann Georg (1728-1800)—167

C

Carey, Henry Charles (1793-1879)—189, 190

Carli, Giovanni Rinaldo, conte (1720-1795)—151

Castlereagh, Robert Stewart (1769-1822), became Viscount Castlereagh in 1796 and Marquis of Londonderry in 1821—81

Cato, Marcus Porcius (The Elder) (234-149 B.C.)—128

Charles II (1630-1685)—54

Chevalier, Michel (1806-1879)—117, 157

Clay, Sir William (1791-1869)—185

Cobbett, William (1762-1835)—97

Columbus, Christopher (1451-1506)—157

Constancio, Francisco Solano (1772-1846)—61

INDEX OF AUTHORITIES

AUTHORS

A

Aristoteles: *Ethica Nicomachea*, L. 5, C. 8, ed. Bekkeri, Oxonii, 1837 (Aristotle, *Ethica Nicomachea*, Book V, Chapter 8, translation by W. D. Ross, Oxford, 1925).—68, 117
—*De Republica*: L. I, C. 9, ed. Bekkeri, Oxonii, 1837 (Aristotle, *Politica*, by Benjamin Jowett, revised edition, Oxford, 1966).—27, 42, 50, 117, 137
Athenaeus: *Deipnosophistai*, L. IV, 49, v. II, ed. Johannes Schweighäuser, t. 2, Argentorati, 1802.—73
Attwood, T., Wright, T. B., Harlow, J.: *The Currency Question, the Gemini Letters*, London, 1844.—82

B

Bailey, Samuel: *Money and Its Vicissitudes in Value; as They Affect National Industry and Pecuniary Contracts: with a Postscript on Joint-Stock Banks*, London, 1837.—72, 143
Barbon, Nicholas: *A Discourse Concerning Coining the New Money Lighter, in Answer to Mr. Locke's Considerations about Raising the Value of Money*, London, 1696.—78
Bastiat, Frédéric: *Harmonies économiques*, 2e éd., Paris, 1851.—37

Berkeley, George: *The Querist, Containing Several Queries, Proposed to the Consideration of the Public*, London, 1750.—35, 79, 118
Bernier, François: *Voyages Contenant la description des états du Grand Mogol, de l'Indoustan, du Royaume de Cachemire etc.*, t. 1, Paris, 1830.—130
Blake, William: *Observations on the Effects Produced by the Expenditure of Government during the Restriction of Cash Payments*, London, 1823.—104, 179
Blanc, Louis: *Histoire de la révolution française*, t. 1-2, Paris, 1847.—167
Boisguillebert, Pierre Le Pesant: *Le détail de la France*. In: *Economistes financiers du XVIIIᵉ siècle*. Par Eugène Daire, Paris, 1843.—55, 96, 103 126, 146
—*Dissertation sur la nature de la richesse, de l'argent et des tributs où l'on découvre la fausse idée qui règne dans le monde à l'égard de ces trois articles*. In: *Economistes financiers du XVIIIᵉ siècle*. Par Eugène Daire, Paris, 1843.—55, 125
Bosanquet, J. W.: *Metallic, Paper and Credit Currency, and the Means of Regulating their Quantity and Value*, London, 1842.—98

Bray, John Francis: *Labour's Wrongs and Labour's Remedy; or, the Age of Might and the Age of Right*, Leeds, 1839.—86

Buchanan, David: *Observations on the Subjects Treated of in Doctor Smith's Inquiry into the Nature and Causes of the Wealth of Nations*, Edinburgh, 1814.—113

Büsch, Johann Georg: *Abhandlung von dem Geldumlauf in anhaltender Rücksicht auf die Staatswirtschaft und Handlung*, Th. 1-2, 2. verm. und verb. Aufl., Hamburg und Kiel, 1800. —167

C

Cato, the Elder: *De agricultura*.—128

Chevalier, Michel: *Cours d'économie politique* fait au Collége de France. La monnaie, Bruxelles, 1850.—117, 157

Cobbett, William: *Political Register*. From July to December, 1807, Vol. 12, London, 1807.—97

Cooper, Thomas: *Lectures on the Elements of Political Economy*, London, 1831.—35

Corbet, Thomas: *An Inquiry into the Causes and Modes of the Wealth of Individuals; or the Principles of Trade and Speculation Explained*, in 2 parts, London, 1841.—97

The Currency Theory Reviewed in a Letter to the Scottish People on the Menaced Interference by Government with the Existing System of Banking in Scotland. By a banker in England. Edinburgh, 1845.—109

Custodi, Pietro: *Scrittori classici italiani di economia politica*. Parte antica, t. 1-7, Milano, 1803-1804. Parte moderna, t. 1-50, Milano, 1803-1816.—110

D

Dante Alighieri: *Divina Commedia (The Divine Comedy*, Illustrated Modern Library, Inc., 1944).—23

Darimon, Alfred: *De la réforme des banques*, avec une instruction par Émile de Girardin, Paris, 1956.—86

Debates in the House of Commons on Sir R. Peel's Bank Bills of 1844 and 1845. Reprinted verbatim from *Hansard's Parliamentary Debates*, London, 1875.—82

Dodd, George: *The Curiosities of Industry and the Applied Sciences*, London, 1854.—109

E

Engels, Friedrich: *Die Lage der arbeitenden Klasse in England*. Nach eigner Anschauung und authentischen Quellen, Leipzig, 1845 (Frederick Engels, "The Condition of the Working Class in England", *On Britain*, Moscow, 1962).—22

—*Umrisse zu einer Kritik der Nationalökonomie*. In: *Deutsche-Französische Jahrbücher*, Paris, 1844 (*Economic and Philosophic Manuscripts of 1844*, Moscow, 1961).—22

F

Franklin, Benjamin: *A Modest Inquiry into the Nature and Necessity of a Paper Currency*. In: *The Works of Benjamin Franklin*, ed. by Jared Sparks, Vol. II, Boston, 1836.—56, 57

—*Remarks and Facts Relative to the American Paper Money*. In: *The Works of Benjamin Franklin*, ed. by Jared Sparks, Vol. II, Boston, 1836.—56-57, 118

Fullarton, John: *On the Regulation of Currencies; Being an Examination of the Principles*,

PERIODICALS

A

phosis of the commodity—138
—consumption as the antithesis of production—195

Appropriation
—appropriation as a condition of production—192

Army
—monetary system in the Roman Army—208
—certain economic features were evolved earlier in the army than within civil society —215

Art—197, 215-16

Asia
—communal property—34
—formation of hoards—125-28, 134-35
—hoarding of silver—150
—ratio of gold to silver in ancient Asia—156
—demand of Asian countries for silver—157

Asiatic mode of production. See Mode of production

Assignats—81, 169

Australia
—discovery of gold in Australia —107
—use of Australian gold—135

B

Bank Acts of Sir Robert Peel— 62, 74, 185

Bank-notes—81, 169
—bank-notes in Amsterdam—80
—convertibility of bank-notes— 83
—circulation of bank-notes—102
—circulation of bank-notes and investigations of monetary matters in the nineteenth century—169

Barter
—barter evolves on the borders of primitive communities—50
—barter and formation of money —50-51
—barter between Siberia and China—74
—barter and circulation of commodities—90, 91

—Mill reduces the process of circulation to direct barter—97

Bimetallism—75-77

Bourgeois mode of production. See Mode of production

Bourgeois society
—bourgeois society as the last antagonistic form—21
—London is a convenient vantage point for the observation of bourgeois society—22-23
—bourgeois society and the law of value—60
—bourgeois mode of production and "labour money"—85-86
—buyer and seller, bourgeois economic types—94-95
—antagonistic nature of bourgeois production—95
—Monetary System and the rudimentary stage of bourgeois production—158-60
—development of bourgeois society since the sixteenth century—188
—United States as the most modern form of bourgeois society—210
—bourgeois society as the most advanced historical organisation of production—210
—bourgeois society as a contradictory form of development— 211
—bourgeois society and agriculture—213

C

California
—discovery of gold in California —107

Capital
—capital within the system of bourgeois economy—19, 34
—confusion of money and capital by bourgeois economists—159, 187
—export of capital—187
—commodity, money and capital —186
—capital is an eternal phenomenon according to bourgeois economists—190

—division of labour comprises all aspects of social labour—51
—Petty's idea of division of labour—52
—division of labour and individual exchange—60
—commodity circulation presupposes an advanced division of labour—92
—no exchange is possible without division of labour—204
—developed division of labour may exist in historically immature social formations—207-08
—international division of labour—214

E

Economic law—120, 147, 192
—law of value and bourgeois society—59
—law of exchange-value asserts itself in its antithesis—62
—law determining the amount of money in circulation—106
—laws governing the circulation of gold and of paper money—121-22
—laws of capitalist production are presented by bourgeois economists as the eternal natural laws—192
—distribution is based on social laws—199
Egypt—127, 161
England
—classical political economy—52
—contrast between English and French political economy—52, 54
—in Petty's time—52
—fractions of an ounce of gold as units of measurement of money—68
—diminishing weight of the pound—72
—units of weight and units of money—73
—money of account—74
—history of the monetary system—74-75
—commercial crisis of 1857—76

—depreciation of money—76
—suspension of cash payments by the Bank of England—81, 169
—grain shortage and the amount of money in circulation—104
—political economy after Ricardo—105
—monetary laws—111
—silver and copper coins—112-14
—gold and silver articles—134-36
—variations in the value of money—143
—crop failures between 1800 and 1820—177
—trade between England and the Continent—179
—conquests of Ireland and India—202
—big landed property—203
Equilibrium
—Mill's metaphysical equilibrium of purchases and sales—97
—usual equilibrium in the interchange of products between nations—150
—disturbances in the international equilibrium of currencies—174-75
Equivalent
—equivalence of commodities is independent of their physical divisibility—41
—commodities are exchangeable only as equivalents—43
—circuit M—C—M presupposes exchange of non-equivalents—123
Europe
—wearing away of coins—108-09
—decrease in the amount of circulating coin—135
—gold and silver stocks—135-36
—revolution caused by the fall in the value of precious metals—148
—commodity exchange between Europe and Asia—150
—Europe and discovery of gold mines in America—157
—price increases in the sixteenth and seventeenth centuries—163
Exchange—40, 50, 127, 128

quires a fictitious value in the process of circulation in which it represents commodities—164
See also *Silver*

Greece
—creation of State hoards—127
—money reaches its full development only in the period of disintegration of ancient society—208
—art—215-17

H

Hegelianism—199
History—189, 211, 215
—historical development and production—201-02
—sequence of historical development and economic categories—213
—history of civilisation—215
Hoarding—125-37
—gold and silver as hoards—127, 134-35
—hoarding in ancient times—127
—conditions of hoarding—128
—avarice as a motive power of hoarding—128
—burying of hoards—131
—the hoarder is a Protestant by religion and still more a Puritan—130
—formation of hoards has no intrinsic limits in itself—132
—passion for enrichment—132
—formation of hoards and accumulation—133
—the less advanced is the production of commodities the more important is hoarding—134
—hoards act as channels for the supply or withdrawal of circulating money—136
—hoards must not be confused with reserve funds of coin—136
—formation of hoards decreases when the bourgeois mode of production reaches an advanced stage—151
Holland
—the predominant trading nation in the seventeenth century—53
—gold currency replaced by silver-currency—107, 123-24

I

Idealism
—idealism of Berkeley—79
Identity
—identity of consumption and production—191, 197
India
—communal property—33
—demand for silver—75
—trade between Europe and India—129-31
—formation of hoards—134-35
—buying opium from India—140
—English conquest of India—202
Individual
—individual and society—188
—rôle played by the individual in the process of distribution and exchange—194
—to the single individual distribution appears as a social law—201
Industry—202
Interaction
—interaction takes place in any organic entity—205
—interaction between production and other aspects—205
Interest
—interest and capital—200
Ireland—53, 202
Italy
—two schools of political economy: one at Naples and the other at Milan—55
—a number of economists come close to a correct analysis of the commodity—57
—economists and debased coins—110

J

Japan—156
Joint-stock companies
—one of the most recent features of bourgeois society, though

253

they arise also in its early period—214

K

Kyakhta
—barter—150

L

Labour—29, 30, 34, 98, 209, 210
—labour that creates exchange-value—28, 34
—materialised labour—28
—homogeneous, simple labour—29, 30
—abstract general labour—29
—labour as the substance of exchange-value—29
—social labour—30
—labour as the source of use-values and exchange-values—29
—labour-time as an inherent measure of labour—30
—labour reduced to simple labour—30
—human labour in general as productive expenditure of human muscles, nerves, brains—31
—average labour—31
—simple (unskilled) labour and complicated (skilled) labour—31
—social labour in a specific type of society creates exchange-value—31-32
—communal labour—33
—labour as the only source of exchange-value—29, 35
—abstract and concrete labour—35
—labour is not the only source of material wealth, i.e., of use-value—36
—labour as a natural condition of human existence—36
—productivity of labour and exchange-value—37
—productivity of labour and natural conditions—37
—individual labour and universal

social labour—45
—universal social labour is not a ready-made prerequisite but an emerging result—45
—division of labour comprises the totality of the physical aspects of social labour—51
—two forms of labour—52
—labour in bourgeois economy—54
—Franklin's analysis of labour—55, 56, 57
—labour as the source of bourgeois wealth according to the Physiocrats—57
—Steuart's analysis of labour—58
—labour as the sole source of material wealth according to Adam Smith—59
—bourgeois form of labour as the eternal natural form of labour according to Ricardo—60-61
—labour becomes social labour only as a result of the universal alienation of individual kinds of labour on the basis of commodity production—84-85
—accumulated labour—190
—productive and unproductive labour—198
Labour money—86
Labour-time
—labour-time as the quantitative aspect and inherent measure of labour—29-30
—congealed labour-time—30
—determination of exchange-value by labour-time—30, 32-33
—necessary labour-time—31, 33
—universal labour-time—32
—commodity as materialised labour-time—43
—universal labour-time as an abstraction—45
—social labour-time exists in commodities in a latent state—45
—labour-time of individuals and universal labour-time—45
—determination of value by labour-time according to Ricardo—60

—socially necessary labour-time and transformation of exchange-value into price—69
—labour-time as the substance and the inherent measure of value—83
—Gray's theory that labour-time is the direct measure of money —83

Landed property
—landed property and conquests —201-03
—landed property and revolution —201, 203
—landed property in pastoral tribes and among settled agricultural people—212

Language—189

Law
—legal relations and the material conditions of life—20
—mode of production and legal relations—193
—club-law—193
—legal relations—214
—legal relations and relations of production—215

M

Machinery
—employment of machinery and changes in the process of distribution—202

Materialism—215

Means of circulation. See *Medium of circulation*

Means of payment—143, 145
—money as universal means of payment—141
—difference between means of purchase and means of payment and crises—141
—distinction between means of purchase and means of payment according to Luther—141
—the evolution of the credit system causes money to function increasingly as means of payment—143
—money as means of pay-

ment becomes the universal commodity of contracts—143
—volume of money in circulation as means of payment—144
—velocity with which the same coin acts repeatedly as means of payment—144
—payments may offset one another—145
—reserve funds—147-50
—circulation of means of payment modifies the law governing the quantity of money in circulation—147
—means of payment and variations in the value of precious metals—148
—means of payment on the world market—150
—the function which world money fulfils as means of payment develops with the development of international commodity exchange—150

Means (instruments) of production—190
—consumption of means of production in the process of production—195
—distribution of means of production—201

Measure
—measure of labour—29
—labour-time as the measure of value—29
—labour-time as the inherent (intrinsic) measure of value—82, 84

Measure of value—64, 75, 149
—gold as the measure of value—65
—measure of value and hard money—70
—measure of value and the standard of price—70
—Berkeley confuses the measure of value with the standard of price and with means of circulation—78
—labour-time as the substance and the inherent measure of value—82, 84
—standard of value and medium of circulation—120-21

—totality of relations of production constitutes the economic structure of society—20
—relations of production assume the shape of things—34
—relations of production and means of production—214
—dialectics of the concepts productive power and relations of production—215

Religion—130, 211

Rent

—rent and large-scale landed property—200
—rent, tribute, tithe—211
—nothing seems more natural than to begin with rent when analysing production—212
—rent cannot be understood without capital, but capital can be understood without rent—213

Reproduction

—profit and interest as modes of reproduction of capital—200

Revolution

—social revolution—21
—revolution and abolition of large estates—201, 203

Rome

—communal property—33
—private property—33
—copper coins—114
—hoarding—127
—ratio of gold to silver—156
—rising prices as a result of conquests—161
—Romans were content with tribute in their conquests—202-03
—Roman provinces conquered by Germanic barbarians—203
—taxes in kind and money—208

Rural patriarchal system of production—33

—in the Middle Ages—33

Russia

—communal property—33
—tokens of value—116
—purchase of agricultural goods by foreign merchants—140

—trade with China—74, 150
—devastation caused by Mongols—203

S

Sale—88, 139, 140, 141

—to sell in order to purchase—87
—separation and independence of the acts of sale and purchase—92
—purchase is simultaneously a sale—92
—antithetical rôles of buyer and seller—95
—unity and separation of sale and purchase—93-94, 96, 125, 126
—Mill's metaphysical equilibrium of purchases and sales—96-97
—first condition of hoarding is to sell as much as possible and to buy as little as possible—128

Scotland—53, 58, 74, 114

Siberia—74

Silver

—as a standard of price—74
—value-ratio of silver and gold—75, 156
—gold currency replaced by silver currency in Holland—106
—silver coins as a symbol of gold—113. See also *Gold*

Slavery

—as a result of conquest—201
—slave-labour—203

Slavs

—communal property—33, 193

Socialism

—French socialism—55, 61, 86, 221
—English socialists and Ricardo—61, 86

Social relations

—social relations of individuals as social relations between things—34